Immigrants, Unions, and the New U.S. Labor Market

To comrade Staughton

Immigrants, Unions,
and the
New U.S.
Labor Market

Immanuel Ness

Temple University Press
PHILADELPHIA

Immanuel Ness is Professor of Political Science at Brooklyn College—City University of New York. He is editor of the journal *WorkingUSA*. His books include *Trade Unions and the Betrayal of the Unemployed: Labor Conflict in the 1990s* and *Organizing for Justice in Our Communities: Central Labor Councils and the Revival of American Unionism*.

Temple University Press
1601 North Broad Street
Philadelphia PA 19122
www.temple.edu/tempress

⊗ The paper used in this publication meets the requirements of the American National Standard for Information Sciences—Permanence of Paper for Printed Library Materials, ANSI Z39.48-1992

Library of Congress Cataloging-in-Publication Data

Ness, Immanuel.
    Immigrants, unions, and the U.S. labor market / Immanuel Ness.
      p.   cm.
    Includes bibliographical references and index.
    ISBN 1-59213-040-2 (alk. paper)—ISBN 1-59213-041-0 (pbk. : alk. paper)
    1. Alien labor—New York (State)—New York.   2. Working class—New York (State)—New York.   3. Labor movement—New York (State)—New York.
    4. Alien labor—Labor unions—Organizing—New York (State)—New York.
    5. Immigrants—New York (State)—New York.   I. Title.

HD8085.N53N47 2005
331.6'2'097471—dc22   2004062559

2 4 6 8 9 7 5 3 1

Contents

Preface

I began fieldwork for this book in the spring of 1995, propelled by the stark recognition of a new reality in New York City—a dramatic, decade-long increase in new, low-wage immigrant workers employed at firms of all sizes throughout the urban region. The new immigrants arriving in the city were substantially different from previous waves of migrants to the metropolis. Most newcomers were found working in positions that just twenty years ago were decent-paying jobs with good wages and working conditions. In contrast to previous waves of immigrant and native-born workers, new transnationals were often employed in the underground economy, an economy in which employers failed to honor government labor regulations concerning wages and working conditions.

This book examines three case studies of immigrant worker organizing drives: greengrocery employees, delivery workers, and black-car drivers. The information is based on fieldwork utilizing ethnographic research methods rather than on statistical surveys of workers or on government data. To understand the lives of workers, qualitative methodology better captures the highly diverse histories and experiences of new immigrants in New York City. This book refrains from structured survey instruments, instead replacing abstract and sometimes irrelevant questions with workers' oral histories and their own interpretations of the motivations that led them to mobilize to achieve dignity on the job.

From April 1998 through October 2003, eighty-three workers working in three industries were interviewed to better understand the parameters of each organizing drive. Forty-eight interviews were held with greengrocery workers, seventeen with supermarket delivery workers, and fourteen with black-car drivers. About half the interviews were set up in advance; the other half were carried out without notice at places of employment and at organizing meetings. Additionally, three group interviews with workers involved in mobilization were conducted as a means of capturing the differences between individual and collective interpretations and explanations for social mobilization. These "focus groups" revealed ways in which individuals are transformed into organized actors pursuing collective demands. In addition, this book draws upon observations of workplaces, organizing meetings, and immigrant worker demonstrations.

My research began with participation in the Lower East Side Community Labor Coalition, a labor-rights group in Lower Manhattan seeking to call attention to and improve the poor conditions of immigrant workers in restaurants, laundries, bars, greengroceries, and supermarkets performing services at exceedingly low wages. Beyond the important objective of responding to the abject exploitation of workers, I sought to understand how immigrant workers themselves seek to improve their conditions through organizing and mobilizing against their employers. While there is a growing body of literature documenting poor wages and working conditions among new immigrant workers (Cordero-Guzmán, Smith, and Grosfoguel 2001; Hondagneu-Sotelo 2001; Kwong 1997; Sassen 1991; Stoller 2003), studies of how these workers organize and protest their conditions are only now beginning to emerge (Bronfenbrenner et al. 1998; Delgado 1993; Fink 2003; Milkman 2000; Milkman and Wong 2000; Ness 1998). Typically, new arrivals have been seen as passively consigned to their conditions of exploitation and too frightened and powerless to challenge their oppressors.

This counterintuitive propensity for new immigrants to challenge their employers is rooted in their active social networks on the job and the absence of countervailing networks that could possibly develop through greater exposure to mass society. Indeed, it is this very exclusion from mainstream organizations that causes immigrants to depend to a greater extent on narrower social networks developed on the job through interaction with fellow workers of the same ethnicity. In contrast, native-born workers are less likely to organize among themselves on the job precisely because they are atomized in the mass culture of the United States, and therefore often lack the close relationships and mutually supportive networks that new immigrants must rely upon for their survival.

Acknowledgments

I am grateful to the many individuals who have helped make this book a success. In particular, this work is the culmination of the struggles of immigrant workers—mostly neglected by unions— fighting for dignity, justice, and respect against rapacious bosses.

I am forever indebted to all the workers who took the time to share their experiences and struggles. The workers who demonstrated solidarity through sharing their experiences have helped build enduring relationships that will stay strong with or without organizational support. It is this sharing of experience that marks the silent struggles of oppressed immigrant workers. Through this book, I recognize the solidarity of the workers that has enabled their struggles to come to life. In particular, I want to thank Gerardo Dominguez, Jorge Marín, Mamadou Camara, and Syed Al-Armughan, for their unending support through thick and thin. Each brought their keen knowledge and insight, and permitted me access to meetings, marches, and protests.

I genuinely thank academics and colleagues at the City University of New York and readers throughout the United States and beyond who incisively commented on the book as it took shape. Each helped in invaluable ways. I am grateful to many people who helped out by sharing expertise, knowledge, resources, and ideas, offering suggestions, and reading all or part of this manuscript. I would like to thank Stuart Acuff, John Amman, Ted Auerbach, Stanley Frances Benson, Stanley Aronowitz, Elaine Bernard, Annette Bernhardt, Richard Block, Valerie Boiarintseva, Heather Boushey, Jeremy Brecher, Aaron Brenner, Kate Bronfenbrenner, Paul Buhle, Héctor Cordero-Guzmán, Dan Cornfield, Ellen Dannin, Benjamin Day, James DeFilippis, Bhairavi Desai, Michael Donovan, Steve Early, Jeffrey Eichler, Frank Emspak, Ken Estey, Michael Farrin, Bill Fletcher, Amy Foerster, Harris Freeman, Sheldon Friedman, Fernando Gapasin, Robert Ginsburg, Michael Goldfield, George Gonos, Lawrence Goodwyn, Juan Gonzalez, Jennifer Gordon, Margaret Gray, Chester Hartman, Rick Hurd, Saru Jayaraman, Tom Juravich, Stephen Jenkins, Michelle Kaminski, Pawel Kedzior, Christine Kelly, Thomas Kriger, Gordon Lafer, Jane Latour, Stephen Leberstein, Anela Radoncic, Margaret Levi,

Staughton Lynd, Jack Metzger, Pamala Miller, Lorraine Minnite, Vernon Mogensen, Joseph Ness, Bruce Nissen, Steven Pitts, Frances Fox Piven, Pat Purcell, Anela Radoncic, Peter Ranis, David Reynolds, Damone Richardson, Joel Rogers, Saskia Sassen, Kim Scipes, Louise Simmons, Susan Stetzer, Sean Sweeney, Nik Theodore, Louis Uchitelle, Nick Unger, Monica Varsani, Thomas Wheatley, Joseph Wilson, Jeanette Zelhof, Ronald Zullo, and Michael Zweig. Thanks to Joanne Bowser and Lesa Shearer for seeing this manuscript through the production process. Finally, I would like to thank all my informants who provided valuable information on each of the struggles.

Of course, I take responsibility for any errors, omissions, and oversights.

I thank all those who have helped me over the last five years of work on this project. I thank Peter Wissoker of Temple University Press for his foresight of the importance of telling the real stories of immigrant workers taking risks beyond expectations.

As we mark the hundredth anniversary of the founding of the Industrial Workers of the World, I pay tribute to the history of solidarity and worker self-organizing that is an enduring feature of the labor movement. I hope this book will provide inspiration to others as they face new challenges in the future.

1 Why New Immigrants Organize

East Natural, a greengrocery on the corner of Fifth Avenue and 13th Street in Lower Manhattan, was a haven for harried office workers, college students, and nearby residents foraging for salads, sandwiches, and gourmet food. One of the largest all-purpose, around-the-clock markets in the area, East Natural suddenly went dark in May 2001; newspapers draped the store windows to prevent passersby from looking in. The shuttered doors resulted from a year-long labor struggle that ended in a stalemate when management chose to close the market rather than improve their workers' wages and working conditions. In the end, thirty-five workers—mostly newcomers from Mexico—lost their jobs, jobs that had paid well below minimum wage for years. Just one month earlier the same owners, refusing to recognize workers' petitions to form a union, shuttered another greengrocery three blocks north. The labor conflict was not limited to the two stores. It had spread like wildfire through Manhattan in the spring of 2001, as thousands of Mexican workers laboring in what became popularly known as "green sweatshops" organized a series of strikes to raise wages, gain respect, and improve working conditions.

Most jobs in the greengrocery industry are offered to young men who have recently arrived in New York City from Mexico, pushed from their homes by declining living standards and pulled to the metropolis by the scarcity of resident workers willing to work for the low wages greengrocers offer. These Mexican peasants and workers are not unique. Immigrants of distinct social and ethnic origins staff many jobs in New York City's low-wage service industries. They are part of a new, transnational labor force in service industries and an important component of the dramatically reconstituted labor markets seen in New York City and other major

1

urban centers (Michael Peter Smith 2001, 1–20). These workers are also organizing themselves in ways not seen in New York for many years.

This book sheds light on their distinctive forms of organizing. It challenges the view held by many employers—and indeed some scholars—that immigrants are complacent and disinclined to fight for improved wages and working conditions (Briggs 2001). Based on conversations about and observations of immigrant organizing, it documents that the opposite is true: Today's newcomers are *more* likely to organize and protest than are their native-born counterparts. In doing so it demonstrates that these low-wage workers have an improbable willingness to take inordinate risks to build worker power, raise wages, and improve conditions in disparate workplaces.

The improbable formation of a distinct immigrant class consciousness has encouraged workers to contest power within the workplace, the community, and the state. This class-based organization of transnational workers in New York has appeared on ethnic ascriptive identity and identity imposed by objective working conditions and shared experiences on the job that are the basis for why and how immigrant workers have successfully mobilized. In the hurly-burly New York City labor market, transnational workers—without easy access to conventional paths of struggle—make use of cultural interpretations and meanings to challenge predatory employers, labor contractors, and, frequently, indifferent state actors.

The constraints faced by these transnational workers derive from employers' need for flexibility in the increasingly oppressive neoliberal economy of New York City and other international financial centers. *Neoliberalism* refers to an ideology that advocates expanding global free trade and competition and withdrawing the state from regulating economic activity; the result is the degradation of basic living standards among the poor and working class.[1] The growth of neoliberal global economic policies has created significant uncertainties for workers and the poor around the world, many of whom are forced to migrate to survive. In New York City, the neoliberal economy has created a growing demand for cheap labor, and firms have been able to take advantage of the increase in low-wage migration from the Southern Hemisphere that was spurred on by neoliberal policies there.

Immigrants and U.S. Labor

What broader constraints do transnational workers face when they seek to organize in the United States? They are viewed as essential to the profitability of U.S. business and yet reviled as "illegals" who pose a danger to the nation. Supporters consider new immigrants indispensable to the vitality of the economy because they willingly work in critical occupations that no longer attract native-born workers. And because new immigrants are paid less and work harder than their predecessors, wage costs and labor standards have been significantly lowered, with employers reaping the benefits (Castles 2002; Sassen 1991; Waldinger 1996; Waldinger and Lichter 2003).

Conversely, unions and anti-immigrant critics view the recent expansion of transnational migration as harmful to established norms regarding wages and working conditions that arose during the New Deal Era (Briggs 2001; Buchanan 2001). In the aftermath of September 11, 2001, immigrants who perform business and personal services jobs have come to be seen as potential sources of terrorism and violence (Schlosser 2003). Employers wittingly or unwittingly benefit from public xenophobia against immigrants, playing on native resentment to restrain transnational workers' efforts to mobilize and organize into unions.

These contradictory positions do not offset each other, but rather each in its own way further complicates immigrant workers' efforts to improve their conditions. The paradox facing new immigrants is manifested in the perfunctory enforcement of federal labor law covering wages and working conditions. All workers in the United States, regardless of immigration status, are entitled to protection under federal wage and hour laws first created in 1938 with the passage of the Fair Labor Standards Act (FLSA). These laws were designed to protect workers from rapacious employers preying on destitute and impoverished workers during the Depression Era. But most new immigrant workers are unfamiliar with existing wage and hour laws, and fear that if they complain, they will lose their jobs or be reported to immigration authorities. Further, federal and state labor enforcement agencies rarely prosecute wage and hour violations against employers and individuals. In the mid-1990s, even as hundreds of thousands of new immigrants were working below the minimum wage and under poor working conditions, the State of New York City assigned only four lawyers to investigate and prosecute employer violations (interview, M. Patricia Smith, Office of New York State Attorney General Eliot Spitzer, May 6, 2003). When immigrants organize to improve their conditions, employers and contractors retaliate much as they do against organizing campaigns by native-born workers. In the wake of a March 2002 U.S. Supreme Court ruling that prohibits undocumented workers fired for union activities from pursuing back pay, the bar has been raised even further (*Hoffman Plastic Compounds v. NLRB*).[2]

It is remarkable that despite these seemingly insurmountable obstacles, transnational workers in New York City are engaged in substantial organizing efforts that connect their sense of exploitation on the job to their status as members of an immigrant underclass. In every case presented in this book, the research demonstrates that workers themselves—not unions—have originated organizing drives. Once the organizing is already underway, however, established unions almost always see such efforts as an opportunity, though sometimes they also consider them a threat as will become clear in the analysis of greengrocer organizing in Chapter 4. Viewing immigrants' organizing efforts as a way to increase their membership, unions have sometimes expended resources with the ultimate goal of strengthening their own organizing campaigns. But the three case studies presented here show that unions do not always succeed in recruiting transnational workers as new members in the conventional sense, even though these organizing efforts usually significantly improve working conditions. In these cases, and indeed in all questions of union organizing, the success of these efforts should be measured by improvements in working conditions and the degree to which workers are organized into stronger social networks capable of challenging employer and state power rather than being measured solely by membership gains or greater union density.

The organized labor movement only began to focus substantial attention on immigrants in the late 1990s. Understanding *why* immigrant workers tend to organize among themselves outside of the union context, and why and when they are responsive to union-organizing efforts is vital to a complete understanding of the formal labor movement. The unions' standard explanation is that new immigrants are amenable to recruitment efforts because they tend to fill the low-wage jobs that have traditionally formed the bedrock of organized labor (Bronfenbrenner et al. 1998; Foner 2001; Milkman 2000; Waldinger 1996). But evidence from immigrant and native-born organizing efforts reveals that low wages and poor conditions alone are not enough to rouse workers to action.

If local and national unions want to cultivate a stronger labor movement and help consolidate this surprising collective action among immigrant workers, they must provide resources and support while respecting the independence and autonomy of emerging worker organizations. A labor movement cannot establish power exclusively through disparate local organizing or through organizing directed by remote bureaucratic union leaders who do not respect the autonomy of worker self-organization. A stronger labor movement can only grow through rank-and-file campaigns supported by the power and resources of unions.

Transnational Workers in a Neoliberal Union City

This study of transnational labor struggles in New York City takes place thirty years after a global process of corporate restructuring transformed the labor market from one dominated by manufacturing firms to one dominated by services. Since the 1970s, the expanding service sector has come to rely increasingly on new immigrant labor employed in nonstandard jobs that, by and large, replaced workers employed in the old manufacturing workforce with its standardized wages and working conditions.

Thus, during the past fifteen years, New Yorkers have become increasingly dependent on immigrants to perform business tasks, personal services, and even household chores. Yet throughout the city, most people seem oblivious to their reliance on new immigrants to perform menial service jobs such as setting and clearing tables, cooking, washing dishes, delivering meals, cleaning and folding clothing, cutting and preparing ready-to-eat fruit and vegetables, delivering groceries, housecleaning, and caring for children and the elderly. The ready availability of low-wage immigrant service workers has enabled more New Yorkers to forego routine domestic work—tasks that traditionally have been performed by women. Today, immigrant women and men are increasingly providing these workaday services for New York City households and businesses in exchange for low wages.

Within this context of rapid economic change and shifts in the labor market, we begin to understand the recent social history of new immigration to New York City and the development of its postindustrial economy. During the past several decades, perhaps the most well-known form of worker abuse in New York City could be found in the apparel industry, in which new immigrants regularly worked twelve hours a day, six days a week, for piece rates that rarely exceeded $2 an hour. In today's garment factories in the Manhattan Fashion District and in Sunset Park, Brooklyn, nearly every worker in the industry is a recent immigrant. The majority of immigrant workers in the city's apparel industry is subject to discrimination and faces safety and health hazards on a daily basis. Moreover, more than 40 percent of these workers complain that their employers have withheld money from them or that they currently are owed back wages. Research shows that more immigrants in the city today are transient workers who intend to return to their home countries or are sending remittances back to families in their home countries. Thus, unlike previous generations, new immigrants make up part of what is now being called a *transnational division of labor,* as the global market replaces the nation-state as the dominant organizing force in the lives of migrant workers (Basch, Glick Schiller, and Szanton Blanc 1993).

This book documents changes in the global and local economy that have increased the demand for low-wage immigrant workers. The root of these changes is the restructuring of corporations through subcontracting and outsourcing, with the effect of undermining established geographic labor market standards.

Chapter 2 examines national and local factors that advance or hinder the immigrant-worker organization in New York City. What are the characteristics of organized labor that reduce worker participation and stymie immigrant union organizing? How does the long legacy of unions in New York City crowd out possibilities for the creation of new labor organizations representing immigrant workers? How does the city's inter-union competition advance or hinder the interests of immigrant workers? How can unions forge a supportive relationship with immigrant (and native-born) rank-and-file workers, and what is the potential for building alliances that benefit both? Critical considerations include unions' positions on defending and advancing immigrant rights, and how unions have responded to attacks against immigrants in the post–September 11 era.

To understand the political forces beyond economics that motivate worker organizing, this book examines three main themes: (1) the new transnational character of immigrant workers in New York City, (2) the formation of independent labor organizations outside of traditional unions that help workers to contest power on the job, and (3) the response of unions to immigrant-worker action and the potential for national unions to assist this rank-and-file organizing to build a stronger labor movement. The book examines several important questions:

- How have unions responded to the changing economy and work-force?
- How and why is immigrant-worker organizing different from the native-born–worker?
- What are the primary social networks immigrants use to improve their conditions?
- How have less-formalized, independent workers' organizations contributed to immigrant-worker mobilization?

- What lessons can the labor movement draw from transnational workers' organizing efforts inside and outside unions?
- What lessons can unions draw from the camaraderie and risk-taking new immigrants share when they go into battle with more than just their jobs on the line?
- Bearing in mind the substantial barriers they face, why do immigrant workers have such a propensity to challenge employer domination? What distinguishes immigrant workers from native-born workers—besides their low wages—and why are immigrant workers more likely to organize?

To answer these questions, Chapter 3 examines the crucial factors that create solidarity among transnational workers in the informal economy, particularly the class relations that emerge in the restructured workplace in advanced urban centers. The term *informal economy* refers to the exchange of goods and services in the black market not regulated or taxed by state authorities, typically found in the private transportation, domestic, and food service industries. In the informal economy, minimum wage and workplace standards are obviously not enforced by the state. The status of transnational workers in New York City today and the demographic forces that encourage class solidarity among them are explored.

Three case studies of union-organizing drives are presented in Chapters 4, 5, and 6, each resulting in a different outcome for workers. These case studies primarily focus on the unexplored territory of new, low-wage immigrant-workers' independent organizing efforts in New York City. The case studies provide details about the activities of three groups of workers—Mexican, West African, and South Asian. This diversity allows for more accurate theorizing about the many aspects of transnational workers' lives and organizing activities, including the roles of immigrant social structures, changing labor markets, new industries, economic restructuring, legal developments, and union policy. The case studies provide new insights into how organized labor responds to economic change, an increasingly multinational workforce, and the overall decline of union power. These case studies also shed light on the present day phenomenon of independent worker organizing outside traditional union boundaries—and how unions are adapting to, encouraging, or retarding such activity. Each case has a different outcome related to the nature of the industry, the labor market, and the support (or lack thereof) of established unions in the sector.

Chapter 4 examines how the growth of an informal labor market in New York City has lowered wages and workplace standards. The chapter chronicles and analyzes the struggle for unionization among greengrocery workers in New York City from 1997 to 2003. Most workers in this industry are undocumented Mexican immigrants who entered the local labor market during the previous ten years. In this case, a union rapidly losing members to globalization decided to reach out to Mexican workers employed at greengroceries and delis owned mostly by Koreans. In the preceding decade, this union—UNITE Local 169—had lost thousands of members once employed in the metropolitan region's men's garment industry. By 1998, the union's membership had dropped to less than one thousand. During a period of three years, the union expended considerable resources on the effort, which was condemned by the United Food and Commercial Workers (UFCW) as an encroachment on its jurisdiction, even though the UFCW had not initiated an organizing campaign in the local food industry for more than thirty years.

Chapter 5 recounts the self-organization of New York City supermarket deliverymen[3] hired by labor contractors in 1998 and 1999—a sector in which a union already represented workers and had negotiated collective bargaining agreements. The deliverymen, who were nearly all recent immigrants from Francophone West Africa, were not covered by unionization; they had been outsourced to independent labor contractors as self-employed businessmen earning less than $100 per week. A critical element in this organizing drive was the racial and class solidarity created through the development of distinct social networks in the labor market— their shared African heritage certainly influenced their shared sense of exploitation.

Chapter 6 discusses the organization of workers in the for-hire car industry, a segment of the service economy that emerged twenty years ago after a new local labor law redefined drivers as independent contractors. These workers, primarily from South Asia, suffered particularly onerous working conditions. Though service standards were largely unchanged, new labor policies contributed to deunionization of the industry, leading to a downward spiral of wages and working standards. A segment of these workers—black-car drivers—beginning in 1995 and continuing today, successfully organized to improve conditions, thereby forcing industry operators to change their status from independent contractors to employees. This new identity allowed drivers to join a union and improve their wages, working conditions, and due process rights on the job through direct actions and a political campaign.

The three different outcomes in the three case studies of immigrant-worker self-organizing show how unions exert negative and positive influences on campaigns. Chapters 4 and 5 (covering the greengrocer and delivery campaigns) demonstrate that unions both assist and interfere with organizing. In the case of greengrocer organizing, the first union to support workers was undermined by its national after the death of the local's president, leading to the fatal weakening of the campaign. The deliveryman campaign reveals a bureaucratic union's failure to represent important groups in the shops where they have an organized presence. The campaign also shows that many immigrants will act in solidarity without unions to overcome oppressive conditions in spite of the obvious obstacles and risks. Each of the two organizing drives discussed in Chapters 4 and 5 ended with mixed results. Workers organized to improve conditions but bureaucratic unions intervened to squash the autonomous voices of workers.

The black-car campaign examined in Chapter 6 demonstrates the best of all worlds. The Machinists union gave the drivers an independent immigrant union and financial and logistical support to mobilize workers seeking improved wages and conditions. The campaign succeeded in changing the law so that drivers could exercise their rights as workers rather than as independent contractors.

Chapter 7 explores the ramifications of the September 11 terrorist attacks on all three immigrant-organizing campaigns. Each campaign suffered setbacks resulting from the deepening recession and the federal government's crackdown on undocumented immigrants. In particular, the USA PATRIOT Act program of surveillance, detention, and deportation has targeted South Asians, Arabs, and other Muslims who are predominant in the black-car and taxi industries.

Chapter 8 assesses the soundness of this book's arguments in light of the three case studies of immigrant-worker organizing. After nearly half a century of dormancy, American unions have again taken up the organizing banner, attempting to build a larger and stronger labor movement through mobilizing disparate workers struggling to improve their conditions. Achieving this goal, however, requires organizing efforts appropriate to a workforce very different from the workers organized in the heyday of the U.S. labor movement some sixty-five years ago. Today's workforce is significantly more diverse than it was in the 1930s and 1940s when white male workers in manufacturing dominated the employment landscape. Thus, there is a need for strategies that adapt to a changing, corporate-led global economy.

Each case study in the book supports the claim that immigrant-worker organizing emerges directly from the newly reconstituted workplace of neoliberal capitalism. A key factor in understanding worker struggles in New York City is the development of an informal economy through the creation of substandard jobs filled by recent transnational workers. The three case studies demonstrate that isolation and limited social networks are critical factors advancing immigrant solidarity. The fact that transnational workers often spend virtually all their waking hours at work tends to create a convergence at the workplace and enhances the development of class consciousness and mobilization. Moreover, the fact that labor markets are typically structured on the basis of color, gender, language, religion, and nationality creates a strong basis for the expression of worker militancy.

To advance the labor movement today, unions must understand the characteristics and conditions of immigrants in their workplaces and in their communities. The emergence and growth of a large class of transnational workers in New York City and other cities in the past two decades should compel unions to respond both by protecting old jobs that have not yet been restructured and by improving conditions for immigrant workers in the new informal economy.

2 The Political Economy of Transnational Labor in New York City: The Context for Immigrant Worker Militancy

After years of working in obscurity in the unregulated economy, transnational workers in New York City catapulted themselves to the forefront of labor activism in November and December 1999 through three separate organizing drives among low-wage workers. Immigrants initiated all three drives: Mexican immigrants organized and struck for improved wages and working conditions at greengroceries; Francophone African delivery workers struck for unpaid wages and respect from labor contractors for leading supermarket chains; and South Asians organized for improved conditions and a union in the for-hire car service industry.

This chapter argues that the militancy of immigrant workers arises from their distinct position within the political economy of New York City. Immigrant workers occupy specific economic and social niches characterized by exploitation and isolation that nurture class consciousness and militancy. These niches are the result of local and international economic processes and policies. Delineating the parameters of immigrant life on the job and in the community clarifies why seemingly invisible workers rise up to contest power in their workplaces and why immigrant workers are currently more prone to self-organization and unionization than are native-born workers.

Transnational Migration and New York City's
Industrial Restructuring

During the decades on either side of the turn of the twentieth
century, New York City's ethnic composition changed dramatically
with the influx of Southern and Eastern European immigrants. They
came to work in the city's burgeoning apparel, fur, printing, construction, and transportation industries. Many of these immigrants
formed the backbone of the city's labor movement. By building the
International Ladies Garment Workers Union, the Furriers Union,
the International Brotherhood of Teamsters, and other unions, they
made New York City a leading union center even before the passage
of major federal labor legislation in the 1930s (Tichenor 2002).

Immigration to the United States and New York City declined
dramatically with World War I and the passage of the Quota Act
of 1921. The Immigration Act of 1924 (Johnson–Read Act) virtually shut the door to immigrants, especially from outside Northern
Europe. As a result, it was the children of those earlier immigrants
who launched the wave of industrial unionism in the 1930s. After
World War II, most immigrants were Europeans displaced by war
and Mexican agricultural workers.

Passage of the Hart–Celler Act in 1965 transformed immigration by eliminating country-of-origin quotas that had restricted
immigration from non-European countries. The new legislation
contributed to the expansion of immigration from Latin America,
Asia, Africa, and the Caribbean, creating what sociologist Roger
Waldinger (1996) calls "the new immigrants" (44–47). However,
U.S. immigration policy since the 1980s has been incongruent with
economic reality. On the whole, migration to the United States is
growing with the demand for low-wage labor in manufacturing,
services, and agriculture. The Immigration Reform and Control Act
(IRCA) of 1986 intended to restrict unauthorized immigration but
did almost nothing to stem the tide, as migration grew even faster.
Ten years later, the Immigration Reform and Immigrant Responsibility Act of 1996, passed by the right-wing Republican majority
in Congress, placed harsh restrictions on undocumented immigration. It, too, failed to halt the flow of immigrants. The failure of
recent immigration restriction has been intentional, as economic

priorities trumped political preference. In effect, there are two national immigration policies: the official policy of restricting immigration passed to satisfy anti-immigrant political constituencies and the actual policy of allowing a steady flow of immigration to satisfy the demands of corporate constituencies in search of cheap labor. This creates the best of both worlds for employers. On the one hand, low-wage immigrant labor is readily available. On the other, immigrant workers' illegal status increases employers' leverage in all aspects of the employment relationship.

As it did a century ago, the influx of immigrants at the turn of the twenty-first century has once again rearranged the ethnic mix of New York City. Many of the descendents of European immigrants have left the city for the suburbs, and their places have been taken by immigrants from Asia, Latin America, the Caribbean, Africa, and a new wave from former Communist countries in Eastern Europe. In the 1990s, New York State's officially documented foreign-born population—the vast majority of whom live in New York City—grew by nearly one million (Camarota and McArdle 2003, 10). The city's 2.9 million foreign-born residents make up 35.9 percent of the population. More than half the city's immigrants are from Latin America. A quarter is from Asia, a fifth from Europe, and 3.2 percent from Africa (United States Census Bureau 2000). Table 2.1 provides statistics on the country-of-origin breakdown of New York City immigrants.

Unlike their counterparts a century ago, many newcomers to New York City are now here illegally. Immigration restrictions have led to the creation of an underground population of transnational immigrants (See Basch Glick Schiller, and Szanton Blanc. 1993). Workers from Latin America typically migrate illegally without proper documentation; those from Africa, Asia, and Europe commonly arrive with business, worker, student, or tourist visas, which they overstay. In the wake of the events of September 11, 2001, the U.S. Bureau of Citizenship and Immigration Services (BCIS), a component of the new Department of Homeland Security, replaced the Immigration and Naturalization Service (INS) and cracked down on immigrants who overstay their visas by arresting and deporting many of them. BCIS has singled out southern and southwestern Asians for deportation because they tend to be on the Department

Table 2.1 Legally Admitted Immigrants: Top 20 Source Countries to New York City Primary Metropolitan Statistical Areas, Fiscal Years 1992–2002

	Total Number Counted		New Arrivals 1992–2002		Adjustments*	
1	Dominican Rep.	179,596	Dominican Rep.	156,922	Former USSR	121,705
2	Former USSR	140,016	China	71,043	China	31,261
3	China	102,304	Jamaica	51,000	Dominican Rep.	22,674
4	Jamaica	68,070	Guyana	45,283	Jamaica	17,070
5	Guyana	54,488	Haiti	29,693	Trinidad & Tobago	14,992
6	India	39,382	Bangladesh	29,122	Philippines	14,099
7	Haiti	38,885	India	28,663	India	10,719
8	Ecuador	38,064	Ecuador	28,627	Korea	9,640
9	Poland	32,981	Poland	24,786	Ecuador	9,437
10	Bangladesh	32,828	Pakistan	23,106	Colombia	9,260
11	Trinidad & Tobago	32,173	Colombia	18,497	Guyana	9,205
12	Philippines	29,047	Trinidad & Tobago	17,181	Haiti	9,192
13	Pakistan	27,849	Former USSR	18,311	Poland	8,195
14	Colombia	27,757	Philippines	14,943	Mexico	8,342
15	Korea	16,606	Ireland	13,875	Former Yugoslavia	6,820
16	Ireland	14,897	Peru	11,307	United Kingdom	5,360
17	Peru	15,509	Ghana	9,185	Pakistan	4,743
18	Mexico	15,570	El Salvador	8,246	Israel	4,442
19	El Salvador	13,431	Honduras	8,112	El Salvador	5,185
20	Ghana	12,519	Mexico	7,228	Peru	4,202
	Total:	931,972		615,130		326,543

Source: Minnite, Lorraine. 2004. "Legally Admitted Immigrants: Top 20 Source Countries to New York City Primary Metropolitan Statistical Areas, Fiscal Years 1992–2002." Tabulation. New York.

*Adjustments represent immigrants overlooked in original enumeration.

of Homeland Security émigré watch list. Undocumented workers from the West Indies, Latin America, Eastern Europe, and East Asia—though frequently harassed—are less likely to be deported.

Whether they are in New York City legally or not, most recent immigrants work. In some cases, they do virtually the same work immigrants did a century ago. For example, just as Russian and Italian women sewed garments in sweatshops on the Lower East Side in the early twentieth century, today women from China and Latin America do the same thing in sweatshops in Chinatown and Sunset Park. Other new immigrants work in new or vastly altered industries, such as greengrocery, transportation, health care, domestic service, communications, delivery, and construction. Between 1990 and 2000, the percentage of immigrants in New York City increased from 28.4 percent to 35.9 percent. The 2000 Census reported that immigrants comprised nearly 2.9 million of the city's total population of just over eight million. Due to a high labor force participation rate, immigrants comprise 47 percent of the city's workforce. According to data compiled by the Fiscal Policy Institute based on the 2000 Census and 2003 Current Population Survey, immigrants represent 62 percent of the low-wage workforce earning between $5.15 and $7.10 an hour (Parrot 2004). Officially, workers from Latin America and the Caribbean (Dominican Republic, Haiti, and Trinidad and Tobago) comprise a large share of low-wage immigrants (see Table 2.2).

From 1970 to the present, the primary occupational trend in New York City's workforce has been the shift away from manufacturing to service industries. As the garment and printing trades have shrunk, retailing, personal services, and business services sectors of the economy have expanded. On the whole, native-born whites have gravitated to high-paying professional service jobs, African Americans and native-born Latinos have occupied jobs that rely on public sector funding. Meanwhile, over the past thirty years, immigrants tend to fill many of the low-wage jobs created in the new sectors of the economy. Low-end jobs in the service sector pay low wages and provide few, if any, benefits. These new jobs include private transportation, hotel and restaurant, delivery, security, building maintenance, and other low-wage services (Harris 1995; Kazis and Miller 2001).

Table 2.2   New York City's Low-Wage Immigrant Workforce by Place of Birth*

Country of Birth	Share of low-wage immigrants	Approximate number of low-wage immigrants	Share of foreign-born population, Census 2000
Dominican Republic	17.9%	90,000	12.9%
Mexico	13.7%	68,500	4.3%
China	6.0%	30,000	7.2%
Jamaica	5.7%	28,600	6.2%
Ecuador	5.4%	26,900	4.0%
Guyana	4.7%	23,700	4.6%
Haiti	3.5%	17,400	3.3%
Trinidad and Tobago	3.0%	15,000	3.1%
Russia	3.0%	15,000	2.8%
Colombia	2.5%	12,500	2.9%
Korea	2.2%	11,000	2.5%
India	2.0%	10,200	2.4%
El Salvador	2.0%	9,900	0.9%
Bangladesh	1.9%	9,600	1.5%
Poland	1.8%	8,900	2.3%
Total, 15 Countries	75.2%	377,200	60.9%

Source: Fiscal Policy Institute analysis of Current Population Survey Outgoing Rotation Group files provided by the Economic Policy Institute; Census 2000.
*Low-wage workforce defined as those earning less than $10/hour in inflation-adjusted 2003 dollars. The immigrant low-wage workforce numbered approximately 500,000 for the four-year period 2000 to 2003.

The recent influx of immigrant workers is the result of industrial restructuring and capital mobility that has eroded traditional industries and remade New York City's political economy in the last thirty years (Bronfenbrenner 2000). One very general aspect of this restructuring is the decline of manufacturing. Through the first three quarters of the twentieth century New York City was a center for small-scale, flexible manufacturing that employed skilled and semi-skilled workers who made a myriad of goods, including garments, printed matter, electrical equipment and supplies, non-electrical machinery, furniture, chemicals and allied products, leather and leather products, and food and beverage products. Today, with a few important exceptions such as apparel making and food service, most of these industries are either completely gone or marginal to the city's economy.

The loss of manufacturing jobs in New York City, like that elsewhere in the United States, has two basic sources: relocation and technological obsolescence. Neither process is particularly new, though they work at different paces in different periods. Manufacturing jobs have relocated out of New York City for many reasons, including the high cost of real estate, the difficulty and expense of transportation, and the relatively high rate of unionization. Rampant industrial closings have cut the city's manufacturing base from one million workers in 1950 to fewer than 200,000 today (Bureau of Labor Statistics 2002). In a typical recent example of job loss resulting from labor costs, the Swingline Stapler factory closed its doors in Long Island City in 2000, moving 450 manufacturing jobs to Nogales, Mexico, where workers earn a fraction of the wage earned in New York City. Often jobs can be moved because productivity has improved to the point where unskilled workers can replace skilled workers or jobs are rendered wholly redundant through advances in computerization (Levy and Murnane 2004, 31–54). In the middle of the twentieth century, as electrical equipment manufacturing grew more standardized production began to move from the city to New Jersey and Pennsylvania, and eventually to Mexico and China. Throughout the twentieth century, thousands of employers in chemicals, furniture, leather, and other industries made similar moves. Technological innovation eliminated many of the city's high-paying manufacturing jobs altogether. The most notable example of this is the printing and publishing industry, formerly home to one of the city's largest concentrations of unionized workers, where electronic publishing and computerized printing eliminated thousands of typesetters and pressmen. As standard jobs have been replaced by contingent work, a larger share of the labor market is falling into the informal sectors (Bailey and Waldinger 1991). Those industries in New York City that employ

Table 2.3   Informal Occupations—California

Occupational Category	Percent Informal
Private household services	42.82
Construction laborers	29.64
Cleaning and building	27.50
Food service	24.75
Construction trades	15.95
Motor-vehicle operators	13.68
Health technologists and technicians	5.18
Secretaries, stenographers, and typists	3.00
Teachers, elementary and secondary	1.91
Engineers	0.85
Police and fire fighting	0.71
Architects, mathematicians, and scientists	0.70

Source: Data derived from Marcelli, Pastor, and Joassart 1999, 586.

the greatest share of immigrants parallel the informalization of the industry in other large U.S. cities, as reflected in the Los Angeles data, where a large informal economy has grown in the low-wage service sector (see Table 2.3).

The decline of manufacturing has had manifold implications for the city's workforce. Most importantly, it has eliminated numerous possibilities for stable, well-paid employment and undermined some of the city's most powerful unions. The unemployment created by the shrinking, relocation, and closing of manufacturing establishments has put downward pressure on wages and working conditions in the rest of the city's economy. It has also freed up workers for employment in a whole new set of service industries. In these industries, specific strategies for corporate restructuring have led to the influx of immigrants from around the world.

None of the service industries that have risen to prominence in New York City's economy over the past half-century is particularly new. Finance, insurance, real estate, media, retail, and even

technology have had long histories in the city. But these industries did not just get larger. They altered the way they did business. Most importantly, through subcontracting and outsourcing
they have stimulated the development of highly competitive markets for various business and consumer services. Firms have broken
down their work into smaller parts and farmed these parts out to
weaker, marginal firms who compete on the basis of cheap labor.
In the garment industry, one of the few remaining manufacturing
industries, this age-old practice has seen a revival in recent decades
as a network of small nonunion subcontractors employing immigrant workers in sweatshop conditions have popped up to undersell
unionized apparel makers. The same phenomenon has occurred in
construction and in the service sector. Chapter 5 describes how
New York City supermarkets contract out their delivery services
to labor contractors who hire West African immigrants at below
minimum wage. In an extreme form of this practice, firms do not
actually hire their workers. Instead, they treat them as independent contractors, responsible for all the supplies and equipment
needed to do their jobs. This was the case for South Asian black
car drivers, discussed in Chapter 6, before they unionized, and it
is the case for immigrant and native-born telemarketing agents for
banks, telephone companies, and retailers.

The decline of manufacturing and the rise of services altered the
social geography of work in New York City. Service jobs tend to be
dispersed in small firms throughout the city. Previous generations
of immigrants who worked in small garment or printing shops benefited from the concentration of industries in specific areas of the
city. As labor historian Joshua Freeman observes, mid-twentieth
century New York City had a garment district, a printing district,
a fur district, and a meatpacking district. The industrial geography of New York City, divided as it was into specialized economic
zones, imparted a particular character to the city's economic life,
labor relations, and even its culture. Areas like the garment district were swarming with local restaurants, cafeterias, bars, clubs,
employment agencies, and union halls where employers and workers exchanged information, sought work or workers, socialized,
organized, and developed shared ideas about life, work, and politics (Freeman 2000, 13–14). The immigrant social networks of the

past established through these interchanges stimulated a class consciousness among employees at different companies that spurred the organizing of unions in various trades, crossing barriers of ethnicity.

That industrial topography is now extinct. This loss of manufacturing jobs has undermined the solidarity among workers that created strong unions. Since the 1970s, once-thriving industrial zones have been displaced by commercial and residential gentrification, which has made it almost impossible for small and medium-sized firms to remain. In the absence of commercial rent stabilization laws, rising real estate costs have uprooted entire trades from their old neighborhoods and dispersed them throughout the city and beyond. Only vestiges of the original industries remain. For example, between 1980 and 2000, Lower Manhattan's printing industry was displaced by commercial offices and residential housing. At the same time, technological advances enabled the publishing industry to outsource large segments of the production process to low-cost operators in the region. Service companies do not cluster, either. A growing number of low-wage services—domestic and janitorial work, for-hire vehicle services, restaurants, supermarkets, and retail stores—do not concentrate in a particular industrial zone, but are spread all over the city to meet customer needs.

The proliferation of geographically dispersed subcontractors who compete on the basis of low wages encourages a process of *informalization*—a term referring to a redistribution of work from regulated sectors of the economy to new unregulated sectors of the underground or informal economy. The result is a reduction of wages and a decline of working conditions below government-established norms. Although informalization is typically associated with underground economies in the developing world, there is growing recognition of the link between the regulated and unregulated sectors in advanced industrial regions. The regulated sector increasingly depends on unregulated economic activity through subcontracting and outsourcing of production to firms employing low-wage immigrant labor (Portes 1995; Portes and Castells 1991; Sassen 1991; 1999). Major corporations employ or subcontract to businesses employing transnational workers in what were once established sectors of the economy with decent wages and working conditions. Now the reliable jobs in the established labor market have been replaced by low wage jobs with substandard conditions commonly found underground. Thus, informalization does not represent industrial decline but horizontal restructuring, often done to maintain and increase flexibility and competitiveness in regional, national, and international markets.

Informalization requires government regulatory agencies to look the other way. For decades federal and New York State regulatory bodies have ignored violations of laws governing wages, hours, and workplace safety, leading to illegally low wages and declining workplace health and safety practices. The process of informalization is furthered by reduction and elimination of government wage protections such as disability insurance, Social Security, health care coverage, unemployment insurance, and workers compensation. Without these protections, workers—especially immigrant workers—are more dependent on their employers and more desperate for work.

The decline of union power and the process of informalization in New York City have been mutually reinforcing. On the one hand, the failure of unions to organize the newly established subcontractors in grocery, transportation, garment, construction, and other industries has allowed the subcontractors to flourish. On the other hand, the appearance of nonunion subcontractors has undermined the power of unions to win decent wages and working conditions from organized employers. In the regulated sector, between 1989 and 1999, jobs paying less than $25,000 per year increased by 81 percent; jobs paying $25,000 to $50,000 declined by 66.3 percent (Levitan 2000).

Creating a Pool of Low-Wage Workers

The informal sector is not limited to immigrant workers but also has grown to include a larger share of native-born workers employed in domestic services, personal services, and garment production. The size of the informal sector varies by occupation. For example, in 1999, the informal occupations in Los Angeles ranged from a low of 0.7 percent among architects, mathematicians, and scientists to 42.82 percent among domestic workers. Although no equivalent data breakdown of the informal economy is available for New York

Table 2.4   New York City Industries Employing the Greatest Numbers of Immigrant Workers

Industry	Approximate number of immigrant workers	Immigrant share of industry's employment (%)	Median hourly wage of industry's immigrant workforce (2003 dollars)
Eating and drinking places	125,470	73	8.55
Construction	100,270	62	13.30
Hospitals	79,900	45	16.36
Health services	71,670	64	8.69
Apparel and accessories manufacturing	54,160	89	8.39
Elementary and secondary schools	45,840	26	15.34
Real estate	39,670	47	14.15
Grocery stores	38,670	64	8.01
Private households	38,360	85	7.96
Bus service and urban transit	33,680	46	14.69

Source: FPI analysis of CPS ORG files provided by EPI; Census 2000.

City, but because both cities have high numbers of new immigrants, one can extrapolate that the city's informal economy is equally large and growing at a rapid rate (see Table 2.4).

In essence, the growth of unregulated labor has dragged down wages in the regulated sector—in precisely the jobs where unions had been strongest. Some labor markets that had been under union control as late as the 1980s are now dominated by transnational workers. As a result, unions face something of a catch-22: They need to organize to increase their leverage against employers, but they need to demonstrate their ability to beat employers if they are to organize.

Still, unions are not helpless. While no labor market sector has been immune to informalization, worker organizing can sometimes reverse the trend, and labor markets can shift back and forth between standard and substandard. For example, in the building and construction industry a growing number of jobs formerly controlled by unions are now subcontracted to nonunion firms that perform an increasing proportion of construction work and hire marginal workers. Interior demolition and asbestos removal—the most strenuous, grimy, and dangerous construction work—is performed largely by Latin American and Eastern European immigrants. The nonunion firms have evaded state regulation, wages have fallen significantly below industry standards, and state and federal authorities have frequently ignored poor safety and health conditions. Even worse is that construction unions have been implicated in the mistreatment of transnational workers. In 1994, the New York City Mason and Tenders District Council of Greater New York of the Laborers' International Union of North America (LIUNA), which was dominated by organized crime in the 1980s and 1990s, was placed into trusteeship by the federal government after it collected evidence that the union allowed firms to hire nonunion immigrant workers at a small fraction of normal union wages. However, only two years later, the union facilitated the organization of some 2,000 new members into LIUNA Local 78, a new local. Through the organization of immigrant workers within their communities and direct action at workplaces, the union again became a viable force in the building and construction industry (Kieffer and Ness 1999).

By the 1990s, substandard jobs employing transnational workers had become crucial to key sectors of the economy of New York City. Today, immigrants have gained a major presence as bricklayers, demolition workers, and hazardous waste workers on construction and building rehabilitation sites; as cooks, dishwashers, and busboys in restaurants; and as taxi drivers, domestic workers, and delivery people. Employers frequently treat these workers as self-employed. They have no union protection and little or no job security. With government enforcement shrinking, they lack the protection of minimum-wage laws and they have been excluded from Social Security and unemployment insurance. They are increasingly victimized by employers who force them to accept nineteenth-century working conditions and wages below the federally mandated minimum of $5.15 per hour.

Despite and because of industrial restructuring, New York City has become a nexus of international labor migration, with a constantly churning labor market. As long as there is a demand for cheap labor, immigrants will continue to enter the United States in large numbers. Stephen Castles (2002), an authority on immigration, challenges the conventional and parochial position that migration is caused solely by economic deprivation in the undeveloped world of the global South:

> Migration does not present an economic or social crisis for the North. . . . [T]he main reason for the presence of economic migrants is that they are needed to fill jobs in industry and services. Undocumented entry of unskilled workers is seen as a problem, but is actually a result of Northern economic structures and immigration policies. Since there is a high demand for such workers in construction, manufacturing and services, the result is a burgeoning of undocumented workers in the informal sector. (188)

While many transnational workers migrate illegally and are treated inhospitably by employers and the general populace in their new countries, they have become crucial to corporate strategies that demand fluidity of capital, production, and labor (Michael Peter Smith 2001; Stalker 2001).

Although the *demand* for low-wage labor induces immigration from the global South, the *availability* of an immigrant work force enables employers in the urban centers of the global North such as New York City to pursue business strategies that rely on low-wage labor. New immigrants from the global South are crucial to the expansion of New York City's labor market and are the basis for the three case studies examined in chapters 4, 5, and 6 of this book. The reserve army of immigrant worker labor provides an enormous incentive for larger corporations to create and use subcontracting firms. Without this workforce, employers in the regulated economy would have more incentive to invest in labor-saving technology, increase the capital–labor ratio, and seek accommodation with unions. As Guerin-Gonzalez and Strikwerda (1993) assert: "The international migration of workers is . . . one element in a struggle for control over labor power and the conditions of work between industrial capitalists and workers (16)."[1]

Employers in restructured labor markets neglect native-born workers and recruit from among foreign immigrant workers in a process explained in the following chapters. In most cases, immigrants do not directly displace native-born workers. Instead, employers undermine established wage and working standards through industrial restructuring. This can take the form of union busting, relocation, outsourcing, the establishment of subsidiaries, or through the entrance of new capital and the creation of new firms. In each case, new jobs are created but at much lower wages and with worse working conditions precisely because the firms seek their competitive advantage through the use of low-wage labor. To meet this goal, they seek out workers who are willing to work for lower wages. New unauthorized immigrants residing and working in the U.S. are ideal: Their undocumented legal status makes them more tractable since they constantly fear deportation as 'illegals.' Undocumented immigrants understand less than do native-born workers about established labor standards, and even low U.S. wages represent an improvement over earnings in their home countries. The result of this interaction between supply and demand is a labor market segmented by race, nationality, and gender. For example, gender plays an important role among domestic workers in the Los Angeles labor market. The mostly female labor force has replaced some professional women in the household by performing domestic work, caring for children and the elderly, doing laundry, and running errands (Hondagneu-Sotelo 2001; Stafford 1985).[2]

The perception that new immigrants undermine the norms of the regulated labor market and threaten native-born workers by undercutting prevailing wage and work standards cannot be entirely dismissed. Immigrants in the underground economy reduce the labor market leverage of native-born workers and weaken government labor protections won by workers in the past century. But it is corporations—not immigrant workers—who benefit from this state of affairs. Rather than attributing the decline in working conditions to businesses that exploit immigrant labor and profit from lowered labor standards, some analysts blame immigration for the decline in native-born wages and working conditions (Briggs 2001; Buchanan 2001).

In the 1990s postindustrial era, the reduction of trade restrictions is driving consumer demand for low-wage goods and services. A large sector of this new growth is driven by expanding corporate and consumer dependence on informal goods and services. The postindustrial economic restructuring from goods production to services in the North and the growing impoverishment in the South is the impetus for growing migration. Notably, the informal economy is not isolated from the formal sector, but becomes integrated into the broader economy. Low-wage and low-skill service jobs are not isolated but vital to the formal sector as the need for domestic workers, delivery, retail, food services, transportation, hospitality, and other tasks becomes essential to the mainstream economy. While the informal sector is not regulated by the government, the formal sector remains dependent on workers for low-skill work.

The results of neoliberal policy and the legacy of colonization have undermined rural society and created unemployment and underemployment in many source countries. Without this process, most people would not leave those countries and would not provide the workforce necessary for the informalization process. Thus, undocumented migration is caused, on the one hand, by growing poverty conditions produced by neoliberal market reforms that eliminate social protection in the global South, and on the other hand, by demand for low-skill, low-wage labor in the global North creating the need for a pool of low-wage workers. Informal work is created through economic restructuring on a global and local level that fuels interdependency between formal and informal sectors.

Neoliberal policies have encouraged economic restructuring in the South that is the basis for the migration to the North. The availability of a large pool of low-wage migrant workers increases business reliance on low-wage and low-skill jobs in both formal and informal sectors. Indeed, foreign remittances from undocumented workers in the U.S. are an important source of revenue for countries of the global South. Deregulation of economic activity has displaced workers and rural peasants in Central America and the Caribbean through the creation of free-trade zones and the removal of government-sponsored social services for the poor.

Long-established government subsidies provided by countries of the South that had sustained rural peasants and the urban working classes have been cut back significantly, precipitating the decline in food price supports, publicly subsidized housing, health care, and universal education. International migration is thus facilitated by the failure of governments of the South to support those with the fewest independent resources.

Forging Immigrant Solidarity

As a result of deliberate corporate and government policies that have transformed the New York City economy, myriad immigrant workers now occupy a range of employment niches at the bottom of the city's job hierarchy. They work under harsh conditions in unconventional work relationships. Because of restructured labor markets, outsourcing, nonenforcement of labor laws governing wages and working conditions, and the decline of union power, New York City businesses are engaging in exploitative labor practices not seen in nearly a century. As the case studies in Chapters 4, 5, and 6 show, employers have frequently redefined immigrant workers as independent contractors, or even as entrepreneurs, while they actually resemble indentured servants. New low-wage transnational workers endure greater exploitation than did the workers who preceded them in similar occupations.

How then do new immigrants with tenuous ties to the organized labor movement and the state assert their interests? The answer lies in the character of immigrant work and social life. Both on the job and off, immigrants are concentrated by ethnicity, color, gender, language, religion, and nationality. As a consequence, they can draw on shared experiences and identities to create solidarity at work and in their communities.

New immigrants typically find jobs through social networks that are established in their home countries and reinforced in New York City. These networks usually point them to jobs in ethnic niches, creating what Foner refers to as the "ethnic division of labor" (2001, 1–31). But this division of labor actually includes a broader range of identities that goes beyond ethnicity. The "ethnic niche" hypothesis put forward by Waldinger suggests that employer–worker social networks create segmented immigrant labor markets. However, by focusing only upon country of origin, Waldinger misses the larger range of identities that funnels immigrants into certain industries. "Ethnic niches" can be expanded to include a broader range of distinctions—color, gender, language, religion, and nationality—that can collectively be called "identity niches." These niches are often reproduced outside the job in identity-defined communities.

Transnational workers bring social identities from their home countries, while new identities are shaped through socialization and work in this country. In New York City, the segmentation of immigrant workers from specific countries reinforces ethnic, national, and religious identities and helps to form other identities that may stimulate solidarity. For example, before arriving in the United States, Mexican immigrant workers often see themselves as peasants but not as "people of color," while Francophone Africans see themselves as Malian or Senegalese ethnics but not necessarily "black." Life and work in New York can encourage immigrants to adopt these new identities.

Isolated in their jobs and communities, immigrant workers have few social ties to unions, community groups, and public officials, and few resources to call upon to assist them in transforming their workplaces. Because new immigrants have few social networks outside the workplace, the ties they develop on the job are especially solid and meaningful—and are nurtured every day. The workers' very isolation and status as outsiders, and their concentration into industrial niches by employers who hire on the basis of identity, tend to strengthen old social ties, build new ones, and deepen class solidarity. Having few ties to well-established social organizations, immigrants' common bonds become stronger and more important (Foner, Rumbaut, and Gold 2000).

It is through these thick relationships developed on the job and frequently in the community that mutual resentment of the employer evolves into class consciousness and class solidarity. Typically, few workplace hierarchies exist among immigrant workers, since hardly any employees rise to supervisory positions. As a result, immigrant workers suffer poor treatment equally at the hands of employers. The interviews in this book show a gathering sense of collective exploitation that usually transforms individualistic activities into shared action. In the rare cases where there are immigrant foremen and crew leaders, recognizing this solidarity, many side with the workers, not with management. One former manager employed for a fast-food sandwich chain in New York City said: "We are hired only to divide the workers but I was really trying to help the workers get better pay and shorter hours" (interview, anonymous Mexican worker, October 2, 2003).

The timing of immigrant worker militancy is difficult to calculate, but it is usually based on a simultaneous process of workers realizing that they are treated in a disrespectful and worthless fashion, are paid unfair wages, and cannot make ends meet. Personal forms of abuse and discrimination are practiced every day in transnational immigrant work environments. But there is usually a trigger that sets workers off—nonpayment of wages or management verbal and physical abuse. Another important factor is the organizing that goes from workplace to workplace like wildfire. When workers realize that they *can* fight and prevail, it creates a sense of invincibility that stimulates militant action that would otherwise be avoided at all costs. This demonstration effect is vitally important, as was the case in past strikes among garment workers and coal miners.

Immigrant social networks established through ascriptive ties derived from heritage and through labor market niches provide the basis for worker militancy by solidifying and intensifying solidarities at the workplace. The concentration of immigrant networks at one job or labor market creates shared experiences on the basis of common exploitation that translate into more intense levels of resistance against employers and labor contractors. For example, over the last decade, concentration of Ecuadorian laborers in menial jobs as busboys and dishwashers in New York City's restaurant industry has consolidated labor solidarity on the basis of national origin. Because recent immigrant workers work all day and go home to neighborhoods, buildings, and even apartments in racially segregated communities, labor exploitation on the job is often the primary conversation on the street corner, soccer field, or at the dinner table. The fact that new immigrants work at subminimum wages under harsh conditions sets in motion labor resistance and worker militancy on the job.

Long days and nights spent working and living together give immigrant workers the opportunity to form ties that are thicker and more resilient than those of native-born workers who work shorter and fewer days and live separately. The typical immigrant in the informal sector can expect to work twelve-hour days, seven days a week. When arriving home, immigrant workers frequently share the same apartments, buildings, and neighborhoods. These employment ghettos typify immigrant communities in Harlem and Washington Heights, Manhattan; South Bronx; Woodside and Elmhurst, Queens; and Sunset Park and Brighton Beach, Brooklyn. Workers cook for one another, share stories about their oppressively long and hard days, commiserate about their ill treatment at work, and then go to sleep only to start the same day anew.

Immigrant social networks contribute to workplace militancy. Conversely, activism at work can stimulate new social networks that can expand workers' power. Evidence of the social interaction that is crystallized in the workplace and in the community is found in the formation of informal organizations, employee meetings to respond to employer abuse, and action on the shop floor in defiance of employer abuse. These social networks, for example among workers in the for-hire transportation industry, do not only emerge from the identity backgrounds of workers, but are shaped by their common struggles on the job.

In cases where workers are treated as a generic bloc, as with West Africans, they tend to switch identity from Senegalese, to French West Africans, to Africans. Despite the threat of job loss and deportation, on-the-job and community organizing leads to improved working conditions, respect, and dignity on the job. Organizing among transnational workers gains the attention of labor unions, which then see a chance to recruit new members and may provide resources to help immigrant workers mobilize at work and join the union.

The identities that already exist among workers through ethnicity, nationality, language, and religion are reinforced here in the States by the class identity immigrants are made to assume on the job. The ethnographic case studies of transnational immigrants that make up the heart of this book demonstrate that social identities are reinforced on a class basis in the restructured workplace.

Employers' segmentation of transnational workers strengthens existing social networks and prevents the formation of new networks extending into the broader labor market. That is, immigrants cleave to traditional bonds based on ethnicity, nationality, language, and religion, and are not assimilated into the dominant society.

Religious Identity

A growing body of research demonstrates that immigrants retain and reinforce their religious faith upon arrival in the United States—even becoming more observant. For example, in a study of new immigrants, Ebaugh and Chafetz (2000) found that Buddhist, Greek Orthodox, and Zoroastrian faiths, transplanted through the founding of new institutions, have profoundly changed the character of Houston neighborhoods. An ethnographic study of religion in New York City's Chinatown by Guest (2003) shows that the dramatic growth in immigration from Fuzhou Province in China since the 1980s has reinforced Buddhist, Daoist, Protestant, and Catholic religious identities. Religion is an important means of gaining access to labor markets, solidifying labor enclaves, and establishing class bonds through friendships formed in churches and mosques.

The case studies in Chapters 4, 5, and 6 further demonstrate that religion is an important part of identity and can strengthen class solidarity. Just as color and ethnicity are used to drive immigrants into certain labor niches, religion delineates boundaries between native-born and foreign workers. Immigrants—whether observant or not—frequently find it advantageous to refer to their religious faith to gain friends, find work, and form bonds on the job.

New immigrants from Mexico often go to churches to socialize, find job openings, and protest working conditions. Mexican churches in New York City neighborhoods are among the few forums for discussion about workplace conditions and the local labor market. At Our Lady of Guadeloupe, a Roman Catholic Church in Lower Manhattan, recent Mexican immigrants congregate for weekly services, religious, and national holidays. Workers use connections they make through fellow congregants to find leads to jobs in industries that often hire Mexicans. They join the church's Mexican immigrant organization, Tepeyac, for help during disputes with employers, and they frequently participate in demonstrations calling for a general amnesty for immigrants and for Mexican immigrant workers' rights. Brother Joel Magallan, pastor of the church, is a long-time advocate of those rights. In 2002, Our Lady of Guadeloupe sponsored the formation of the Mexican Workers Union (MWU) to help greengrocery workers organize and to advocate on behalf of fellow nationals in labor disputes with employers.

New immigrants from Islamic countries typically find jobs in the same industries as Muslims who preceded them. The personal transportation industry, comprised of taxicabs, limousines, and other for-hire vehicles, is a magnet for immigrants from the Muslim world, and most drivers are adherents of Islam. Interviews with for-hire vehicle drivers[3] demonstrate that Islamic faith overrides all other forms of identity, including language, nationality, and ethnicity. These ties lead to the formation of prayer groups held in workers' homes, workplaces, and the growing number of New York City mosques that become gatherings for discussion and debate about labor conditions.

Gender and the Division of Immigrant Labor

Patterns of gender stratification found in the general labor market are even more apparent among undocumented workers. Rarely do migrant workers of the same sex work in the same labor market. The gender differentiation is frequently reinforced by religion. Also, given the prohibition of male and female communication within civil society, even those women who work in the labor market tend to work in domestic work, garment factories, and other jobs in the lowest rungs of the economy segmented on the basis of gender. The transnational workers in this book's case studies are almost all male. The preponderance of men in the greengrocery, delivery, and for-hire driving industries stems from migration patterns and employers' reliance on gender stereotypes. The men in a family, rather than the women, typically make the first trips to the United States. Most female relatives commonly stay in their countries of origin to care for the families of transnational workers, although younger women frequently make the trek to New York City to work in the garment industry.

Some jobs in the nonunion economy, such as construction and driving, are stereotypically considered "men's work." Although food preparation is stereotypically "women's work," Latinos have had a history of working in the food service industry since the early twentieth century when they were recruited to work on American farms as contract laborers. However, women predominate in the apparel industry, make up the majority of domestic and childcare workers, and are increasingly found washing clothes in laundries. Like their male counterparts, female transnational workers usually arrive in the United States alone, without their families, precluding or greatly impeding permanent settlement and the establishment of immigrant communities.

Conclusion

The distinctiveness of migrant worker militancy in low-wage jobs above expectations and against the odds is critical to understanding native-born worker militancy as well. This unanticipated militancy is a product of the corporate restructuring that has created sub-minimum wage, dead-end, jobs below the poverty line. A major finding of this book is that immigrants tend to engage in collective action at least as much as native-born workers. However, at the same time this book finds that immigrants do not possess any inherently greater militancy or passivity than native workers. Cultures of militancy and passivity among all workers are structured by social relations producing ripe conditions for organizing. That is, immigrants do not have a cultural propensity to organize and native workers are not out-and-out hostile to organizing.

Three workplace conditions seem to produce greater militancy on the job among immigrant workers than native-born workers: first, collective social isolation that engenders stronger ties among immigrants than native-born workers in low-skill and low-wage jobs where organizing is frequently seen as the only way to improve conditions. Because immigrants work in jobs that tend to be more amenable to organizing, they are highly represented among newly unionized workers. The occurrence of strong social ties to the work-place drives immigrants to form their own embryonic organizations and to rely on unorthodox repertoires of struggle against their employers. The new social organizations formed by immigrants are ripe for union representation.

Second, employers play a major role in immigrant workers being more likely to organize than are native-born workers. Firms employing native-born workers tend to be larger and are often much harder to organize than the small businesses where immigrants in New York City work. The Merriam-Webster dictionary, published in June 2003, includes the new word *McJob,* defined as "a low-paying job that requires little skill and provides little opportunity for advancement." The reference reflects the relentless thirty-year economic restructuring that has created low-end jobs in the retail sector that pay low wages, provide few benefits, lack job security, and have poor working conditions. Corporate restructuring has downgraded both wages and working conditions among both native and immigrant workers. In another example, the retail giant Wal-Mart epitomizes the proliferation of postindustrial jobs in the retail industry that fail to pay enough to cover workers' basic needs.

Organizing against McDonalds or Wal-Mart is completely different from organizing against smaller employers who have fewer resources. Wal-Mart uses many of the same tactics against workers that immigrants contend with: failure to pay overtime, stealing time (intentionally paying workers for less hours than actually worked), no health care, part-time work, high turnover, and gender division of labor. The difference is that Wal-Mart has far more resources to oppose unionization than do the smaller employers who are frequently subcontractors to larger firms.

The redefinition of labor in the underground immigrant economy that this book examines is substantially different from low-wage nonunion work proliferating through the growth of chain stores and restaurants like Wal-Mart and McDonalds. Why do workers appear complacent in giant retail and restaurant chain stores while new immigrants frequently employed in smaller firms are so militant?

Under current labor law, both unorganized immigrant workers and native-born workers are hired and fired without due process at the behest of employers. As labor law has eroded, employers are emboldened to exploit workers to gain greater profits. There are no job protections, except those against discrimination—and these protections are weakly enforced. But, because native-born workers tend to be socially isolated and atomized in McJobs, they do not have the same opportunities immigrants have to resist through organizing and collective action. Employers may be aware that undocumented immigrants are legally vulnerable, but are unaware of the solidarity that is built up through collective social isolation.

Finally, the fact that native-born workers have an exit strategy and transnational workers do not is a significant and important difference. The notion of *exit* draws on Albert Hirschman's (1990) study, *Exit, Voice, and Loyalty: Responses to Decline in Firms, Organizations, and States*, which argues that the public and consumers have two different ways of demonstrating dissatisfaction with the quality of services. In this case, native-born workers have the option to exit from their jobs whereas immigrant workers are more prone to use voice to change the situation because they have far fewer options. By exercising voice, immigrant workers can push firms to improve their wages and working conditions. Workers employed at large firms like Wal-Mart and its ilk are unable to use voice, since they have little power and will be summarily fired for any form of dissent.

Labor–management conflict in the sprawling nonunion service sector is regulated by the state and business codes of conduct, which demarcate the boundaries of struggle. If you violate the terms of Wal-Mart's or McDonalds' employee manual by, say, arriving late, and then are summarily fired—due to social isolation on the job produced by constant employee turnover—no one is there to fend for you as is usually the case among undocumented workers employed in a small business.[4]

The expanding non-immigrant low-end service sector tends to produce unskilled part-time jobs that do not train workers in skills that keep them in the same labor market. Because jobs at the low end of the economy require little training, workers frequently move from one industry to the next. One day a native-born worker may work as a sales clerk for Target and the next day work for as a waiter at Olive Garden. Because they are not stuck in identity-defined niches, native-born immigrants can more easily exit a job they do not like, giving them less reason to organize and unionize.

Exit is, however, not the option of choice for most immigrant workers. Frequently, migrant workers engage in direct action against their employers to obtain higher wages and respect on the job. Employers firing new immigrant workers may risk a demonstration, picket line, or even a strike. Native-born workers employed by large and small employers protest through quitting and finding a new job elsewhere; they do not develop the same dense connections as do new immigrants driven into labor market niches who forge solidarity through working together.

Immigrant workers are pushed into low-wage labor market niches as day laborers, food handlers, delivery workers, and nannies; these niches are difficult if not impossible to escape. Consequently, with the exception of day laborers, immigrants tend to be employed for longer time spans in the same industry and with the same employer than are native-born workers. This longevity fosters greater solidarity for immigrants compared with native workers who may work in a litany of industries. As Chapters 4, 5, and 6 demonstrate, immigrant workers who are relegated to dead-end jobs in the lowest echelons of the labor market in food, delivery, and car service work show a greater eagerness to fight it out to improve their wages and conditions than do native workers who can move on to another dead-end job.

The perilous state of low-wage labor in New York City resembles the precarious conditions of the early twentieth century. In his account of immigrant organizing during the Progressive Era, Dubofsky notes that, from 1900 to 1910, the vast majority of low-wage workers in the city's industries were nonunionized Jewish and Italian immigrants. Throughout the following decade, labor unrest and strikes by these immigrant industrial workers remade the New York City labor movement. Union membership in the apparel industry increased from 30,000 garment workers in 1909 to 250,000 in 1913, primarily through the organization of female immigrants (Dubofsky 1969, 4).[5]

Early twentieth-century immigrant workers were more militant than the native-born because they had greater expectations for a better life in America. Dubofsky contends that, unlike native-born workers, they had not anticipated low wages and exceptionally arduous working conditions before they arrived in the United States. The occurrence of militancy and activism among immigrant workers, a key question this book seeks to answer, is partly addressed in this phenomenon of unmet expectations. Nearly ninety years later, low-wage immigrant workers labor under abusive conditions not unlike those of a century ago. Jarred by the harsh reality of working in New York City's unregulated sectors, recent immigrants regularly recount sorrowful stories of their unmet expectations in America.

Labor militancy among today's immigrants is no new, unique phenomenon. It is a response to the degradation of wages and working conditions over the past thirty years, after organized labor greatly improved working conditions from the 1940s to the 1970s. Those decades of labor power were a departure from the corporate domination, labor suppression, and class conflict that preceded and followed them. The breaking of the employer–employee compact, which had been established under the New Deal, by businesses in the 1970s, severely compromised the power of organized labor, leaving many workers with no recourse but renewed struggle within the workplace. Militancy among immigrants inside and outside of unions today is a response to business' thirty-year assault against American workers, largely without government penalties or substantial labor unrest. Economic restructuring and union concessions have given rise to a new workplace, where dissent is not filtered through union agents but is expressed by workers themselves.[6] That immigrant workers are at the vanguard of new organizing is startling, considering their paucity of resources and allies in organized labor. But the organizing is predictable, given workers' deep social ties built on the job and the absence of legal or employer regulations governing the workplace.

3 Unions and Immigrant Worker Organizing: New Models for New Workers

In recent years, leaders of the AFL-CIO have provided at least rhetorical support for transnational workers. Yet debates continue to simmer within the labor movement about how unions should relate to immigrant workers. To understand the relationship between unions and transnational workers, both nationally and in New York City, this chapter examines the evolution of AFL-CIO policies on immigration restrictions, amnesty, employer sanctions, and the current crackdown on immigrants (Bacon 2000a; Chishti 2000). It then examines the state of the labor movement in New York City, with particular attention to union strategies for organizing workers in general and immigrant workers in particular. Because these strategies have so far largely failed, the chapter concludes by offering some steps the labor movement can take to become more relevant and more welcoming to transnational workers, as it must in order to revitalize union power in New York City and the United States as a whole.

Labor's Changing Immigration Policies

Most labor unions in the United States have historically viewed immigrants, especially those from Mexico, China, the Caribbean, and Africa, as competitors for jobs and threats to better wages and working conditions. Unions have repeatedly supported immigration restriction, even as the country opened its doors more widely to entrants from developing regions. In 1986, the AFL-CIO supported the employer sanction provision of the Immigration Reform and Control Act (IRCA). The provision requires employers to keep records—I-9 Forms—of workers' immigration status and punishes those who hire undocumented workers. In effect, the act's consequences have been the opposite of its intentions. The government rarely enforces I-9 sanctions against employers. In 2002, it collected only $2.6 million in fines from 320 employers who hired undocumented immigrants. The lack of enforcement of I-9 sanctions provides employers with a powerful weapon to fight the organization of immigrant workers. Facing unionization, employers call in the government to verify the I-9 forms, leading to firings, deportations, and through the replacement of workers, the decimation of workers' fledgling organizations. As a result, the act has encouraged employers to hire even more undocumented workers, thereby increasing the ranks of a vulnerable workforce and undermining the possibilities for unionization. It is no coincidence that many of the industries with high proportions of undocumented workers, including meatpacking, poultry processing, and garment manufacture, were once heavily unionized but are now almost union-free.

Several unions, including the Service Employees International Union (SEIU), the Union of Needletrades, Textile, and Industrial Employees (UNITE), and the United Farm Workers (UFW), understood IRCA's implications at the time of its passage and several more quickly came to see the anachronism of labor's anti-immigration stance.[1] However, the familiar pro-union rationale for exclusion lives on in the work of Vernon Briggs, a labor economist who decries the "extensive presence of illegal immigrants" in recent decades (Briggs 2001, 4). Briggs and his supporters believe that, because undocumented immigrants are vulnerable to deportation, they are more submissive to employers than native-born workers, and therefore more difficult to organize. He argues that unenforced immigration has allowed employers to dominate union and nonunion workplaces alike, thereby contributing to growing disparities in income within the U.S. population. He suggests that unions and U.S. workers should support restrictions on immigration as a means of defending union jobs (1–8).

When this pervasive argument is applied to New York City and other major U.S. cities, it fails to account for significant changes in the economy in the past fifty years. New immigrants have always been a foundation of the New York City labor market and have been essential to the city's economic growth (Department of Planning 1992). As the case studies of labor struggles presented in the following chapters demonstrate, the city's immigrant workers are often *more* militant than its native-born workers. Immigrants in New York's unregulated sector frequently engage in walkouts and sit-down strikes for higher wages and union recognition in the apparel, food service, private transportation, and delivery industries. Contrary to Briggs, immigrant status is not a barrier to unionization. Rather than fight an inhumane battle against immigration, unions should fight for immigrants' rights as workers and unionize them.

Despite these realities, anti-immigration sentiment remains widespread in organized labor. Why did the AFL-CIO reverse course in 2000 by opposing I-9 restrictions on undocumented immigrants and then begin to champion the legal and human rights of immigrant workers as a central part of its national program? The majority of labor leaders finally recognized in hindsight that the draconian policies toward undocumented laborers established by IRCA in 1986 hamstrung those workers' efforts to organize. The labor movement's original support of the I-9 restrictions had been a grievous error.

The labor movement's about-face reflects two important factors—pragmatism by union leaders and pressures from workers and activists. First, the AFL-CIO's shift in position can be seen as a sensible response to its inability to influence federal trade policy, a weakness that was starkly obvious in President Clinton's support for NAFTA (North American Free Trade Agreement) in 1993. The expansion of regional and global free trade sent tremors throughout the labor movement and highlighted the increasing threats to labor's survival in an era of globalization and rising immigration. These threats, combined with the long-term slide in union density, led the AFL-CIO to elect John Sweeney of SEIU as AFL-CIO president in October 1995. His New Voice slate espoused removal of the I-9 sanctions and pledged resources and logistical support to organize immigrant workers.

Still, despite much prodding, it took some four years after Sweeney's election for the AFL-CIO to change course. At its national convention in Los Angeles in October 1999, delegates voted for repeal of the I-9 sanctions (AFL-CIO Executive Council Actions 2000; Greer 2000; Haus 2002). In February 2000, the AFL-CIO went further, calling for comprehensive amnesty for the approximately six million undocumented immigrants currently working and living in the United States. Amnesty would greatly ease the organization and unionization of immigrants (Greenhouse 2000; Greer 2000).

To inaugurate its new policy, the AFL-CIO used the slogan "Recognizing Our Common Bonds," obliquely promoting a new unity between native-born and immigrant workers. The federation alluded to a "joint destiny" to reflect the collective interests of working people and, more importantly, to uphold the importance of labor unions in organizing the newly arrived low-wage workers.

Three years later, to symbolize the importance of immigrant organizing, the AFL-CIO and its affiliates championed the Immigrant Workers Freedom Ride in the fall of 2003. The Freedom Ride of 2003 evoked the Freedom Rides in the South during the early 1960s, which galvanized support for the civil rights movement by challenging racial segregation in public transportation.[2] The objectives of the 2003 rides were not limited to workplace issues and the right to organize, but also included amnesty for undocumented immigrants and an end to discrimination and racial profiling. The coast-to-coast demonstration garnered broad support among immigrants for organized labor—evidenced by the tens of thousands attending public rallies—at a time when the government had been bearing down on them in the wake of the September 11, 2001 terrorist attacks.

The Freedom Ride of 2003 was important in shaping public opinion, energizing immigrants to organize, and countering opponents' efforts to characterize undocumented immigrants as a dangerous social burden. The event demonstrated to the public that immigrants work hard at low wages, stimulate the economy, and pay taxes. The absence of a clear, fair government policy on undocumented immigrant workers adds to their uneasiness and insecurity, which helps companies to exploit them. Precisely because the U.S. Bureau of Citizenship and Immigration Services (BCIS) continues to threaten deportation, immigrants can be intimidated into working at low wages under intolerable conditions without complaining publicly. Because some immigrants can be arbitrarily deemed security risks to federal authorities due to their ethnic background, they are also wary of reporting poor working conditions to public authorities.

The second factor in the AFL-CIO's reversal of its immigration policy was pressure from workers and activists in the labor movement (Haus 2002; Watts 2002). As union leaders came to recognize that organized labor lacked the power to halt immigration, immigrant workers and their supporters began to push labor leaders toward a new stance on government restrictions. More and more employers were penalizing these workers for complaining about working conditions, mobilizing protest, and trying to organize into labor unions (Greenhouse 2000; Swoboda 2000). Recognition of the importance of immigrants to union-organizing campaigns in the 1990s helped to change organized labor's position to support repeal of the 1986 IRCA law penalizing undocumented workers. Employers facing immigrant-organizing drives regularly called in the INS and the Social Security Administration as a means to break worker unionization campaigns. When employees of Bear Creek Production Company of Bakersfield, California—the world's largest rose grower—tried to organize a union, the company turned more than one thousand personnel records in to the INS, and three hundred immigrants found to be undocumented were terminated by the company. In Northern California, the Labor Immigrant Organizers Network, a coalition of immigrant rights activists, protested the Social Security Administration's frequent audits of immigrant records. Indeed, growing militancy and pressure among undocumented workers was helpful in pushing the AFL-CIO—as several national leaders in the federation finally recognized that the 1986 IRCA law was not protecting worker rights—to support repeal of the employer sanctions provision of the law.

The growing number of undocumented immigrants in traditionally unionized industries has obliged many unions to reassess their long-standing practices of excluding foreign-born workers and has compelled a growing number of unions to develop organizing strategies directed at these workers. In September 1999, even before the AFL-CIO adopted its new policy to encourage immigrant organizing and oppose government penalties and restrictions on undocumented workers, the New York City Central Labor Council (NYC-CLC) and affiliated unions identified immigrants as a primary target for new organizing. As noted in Chapter 1, unions in New York City have had to welcome new immigrants. Recognizing that transnational workers may help to rebuild the labor movement in metropolitan New York City, the NYC-CLC made immigrant rights a vital part of its program. On October 4, 2003, the labor council sponsored a rally of tens of thousands of people at the last stop of the coast-to-coast Immigrant Workers Freedom Ride in Flushing Meadows Park in the borough of Queens, home to the largest new immigrant population in the city (Greenhouse 2003).

But while New York City unions have enthusiastically raised the banner of organizing new immigrants, up until now, few have successfully organized transnational workers into their ranks. For example, the SEIU has accelerated its campaigns to organize building maintenance and health care workers, the Hotel Employees and Restaurant Employees (HERE) have initiated campaigns to incorporate low-wage immigrant workers in the hospitality industry into their international union. In the late 1990s, UNITE recruited immigrant laundry workers through several high-profile organizing campaigns throughout the country and by capturing control of workers in the independent Textile Processors Union. In July of 2004, UNITE and HERE merged to form a single more powerful international union—UNITE HERE—that as a combined entity would have greater resources and clout to wage successful organizing drives.

These industry-based campaign victories may be considered only a drop in the bucket, but they are important in demonstrating the renewed interest in immigrants and the renewed will of the unions to organize immigrants. Still, only a minority of national unions have devoted significant resources to recruitment and organizing campaigns. Organizing failures among immigrant workers have occurred for three reasons: (1) the absence of will, evident in the limited resources and staff that unions have dedicated to organizing, (2) a minimal understanding of the restructured immigrant labor markets that have displaced traditional ones, and (3) the legal barriers to organizing workers in general and immigrants in particular.[3] In part due to organized labor's inadequate efforts, immigrants are organizing among themselves—with or without unions—inside and outside labor law—into various types of labor organizations to defend their rights on the job. Immigrants, to a great extent, are pushing organized labor to take action.

The New York City Labor Movement and Transnational Workers

Despite recognizing that organizing transnational workers is essential, most New York City unions have exhibited an ambivalent reaction to recent new immigrants. Only a few unions have attempted to organize. The reasons for this lie in the particular contexts of the New York City labor movement that is comprised of three dominant sectors: construction and building trades, private sector production and services, and public sector and nonprofits.

Since the late nineteenth century, leadership over organized labor in New York City was dominated by craft-oriented construction and building trade unions that survived through restricting membership to ethnic and racial cohorts as a means of controlling wages and labor standards. Construction unions have maintained a hold on high-wage large-scale projects in the central business districts and public construction projects as immigrant workers from Eastern Europe and Latin America concentrate in lower-wage small projects, rehabilitation, demolition, and hazardous waste removal (Kieffer and Ness 1998).

Since the 1970s, private sector manufacturing in New York City, once dominated by the garment and printing unions, has been in freefall decline as garment production has moved offshore and new technology has displaced workers in the printing industry. Since garment production is based on piecework, membership in the garment unions has further declined due to the marginal wage differentials between union and nonunion sectors. Despite much ballyhooed anti-sweatshop campaigns, most remaining union and nonunion garment producers continue to employ new East Asian and Mexican immigrants on a piecework basis that fails to lift wages above the minimum.

While manufacturing has largely disappeared since the 1970s, services have grown sharply and have created a demand for low-skill, low-wage workers (Feránandez-Kelly and Sassen 1991). Unions have maintained a presence in building maintenance, supermarkets, and narrow segments of the service industry, but their density in the industries has eroded. In other traditional private service sectors—taxi drivers, retail trade, and hospitality industries, traditional union membership has all but vanished. In the last thirty years, private-sector services have become integral to the New York City postindustrial economy.

Economic restructuring has fostered informal jobs where people work off-the-books, under-the-table, are paid in cash, and are not taxed. Features of the informal service sector include self-employment, casual labor, and lack of regulation. In the last three decades there has been a new growing reliance of primary services on informal sector workers in domestic services and child care, security, taxis, private transportation, delivery, food preparation, vending, and other nonunion consumer service jobs. As a rule, the new "low road" service sectors forms part of the informal economy.

Two contradictory characteristics come together in New York City. It is an international financial center and also a union town with a long history of labor activism (Freeman 2000). On one hand, as a center of global finance, the city epitomizes the predatory nature of capital, which has instituted economic policies that are displacing traditional workplace norms and standards in the United States. On the other hand, many consider New York a working-class city, based on its past history of labor activism and high union membership. In 2003, 24.5 percent of workers in New York City were union members, nearly twice the national rate of 13 percent (Hirsch and Macpherson 2004).

This relatively high union density in New York City is largely a product of past labor conflict, from apparel industry organizing in the early twentieth century to public sector organizing in the 1950s and 1960s. However, since the 1970s, union membership has not grown, except in the health care industry. Today's unions are mere vestiges of the city's illustrious labor-organizing past. While

New York has more unions and higher density than most large U.S. cities, union membership is falling precipitously as the economy shifts from manufacturing to services and immigrants replace native-born workers. Union membership has dropped sharply, from about two million in 1975 to about one million today. Despite the decline, the total number of unions in the city has remained roughly the same. The city now has about four hundred union locals in the public and private sectors, representing workers in both declining and growing labor markets. Though unions may lose members, merge, and consolidate, they rarely shut their doors.

To a great extent, the maze of unions in New York City mirrors the decentralized and fragmentary nature of industries that have emerged, expanded, and faded away. Unlike Akron, Detroit, Houston, Pittsburgh, Seattle, and other cities, New York has never had a single industry dominating its economy. Instead, the city's industrial labor markets have developed piecemeal, as small and medium-sized shops have grown up in distinct industrial areas. As a result, unions have commonly had to focus on trades and labor markets, rather than on single firms.

Labor-market organizing is significantly harder than factory-based organizing, however, because it necessitates reaching out to workers at many firms with many owners. As noted in Chapter 2, specialized industrial areas ameliorated some of the obstacles created by the dispersion of workers among many small firms (Dubofsky 1968; Freeman 2000). But since the 1970s, this pattern of industrial organization has begun to unravel as manufacturing has moved abroad and local businesses have moved to new locations in the New York metropolitan area to escape high real estate costs.

Today, the largest unions in New York City are those in the public and private sectors whose members depend directly or indirectly on local and state government funding for their jobs. These include uniformed service workers (police, fire, and sanitation), non-uniformed service employees (municipal employees of all types, and health care and public hospital workers), transit workers, and teachers. Even unions that represent healthcare workers in private hospitals rely on state funding. New York is beginning to reflect the rest of the nation: Private-sector unionism is declining rapidly and public-sector unions are the mainstay of organized labor.[4] This decline in private-sector unionism largely reflects the restructuring of industry and the emergence of nonunion, nonstandard jobs that are often filled by immigrants.

New York still has a range of private-sector unions, both in the declining manufacturing industries and in the emerging service businesses. The oldest unions in the city are remnants of craft unions in the building and construction trades, printing, and arts and entertainment. Although most unions in the private sector originated in New York City itself, in the 1990s several national unions began recruiting workers in the growing sectors of the city's economy—health care, hospitality industries, and industrial laundries. In cities dominated by several large firms, national unions command labor-management relations; in New York, local unions tend to have more control, negotiating directly with the small and medium-sized firms that comprise the lion's share of industry.

Unlike most national unions that represent workers in specific industrial sectors, New York's unions tend to include members from a wide range of industries. Unions tend to compete in the service sector by reaching into new labor markets that no union has organized or that have been organized by unions in other occupational jurisdictions. For example, in New York, the United Auto Workers (UAW) represents office workers at public institutions, public service lawyers, writers, publishing employees, and it competes with the American Federation of Teachers (AFT) in organizing graduate student employees and adjunct professors. The International Longshoreman's Association (ILA) represents Domino sugar processing workers and grocery workers. Locals of the International Brotherhood of Teamsters (IBT) represent workers at the Red Cross, United Parcel Service, New School University, and small manufacturing companies. The International Association of Machinists (IAM) represents car drivers as well as airline workers. Locals of the United Food and Commercial Workers (UFCW) represent employees at supermarkets, greengroceries, restaurants, food processors, discount retail stores, and drugstore chains.

The ethnic and racial composition of unions in New York City is changing significantly as new members enter union jobs and others are organized. As a rule, workers entering low-skill and low-wage jobs tend to be new immigrants of color while those in high-wage professional jobs remain largely white. The shift from white workers to immigrants of color is happening in the majority of unions, but predominantly among unskilled workers. The membership of the UFCW and HERE is increasingly comprised of new immigrants as older workers retire. Even the construction industry—long dominated by Irish and Italian Americans—is changing as immigrants from Latin America and Eastern Europe enter the industry.

New York City affiliates of the national unions with sustained organizing campaigns tend to focus on labor markets in which immigrant workers are increasing rapidly. National unions that have expanded membership in some local unions are HERE, the Laborers' International Union of North America (LIUNA) in construction, the SEIU in building maintenance and health care, and UNITE in industrial laundries. However, because most new immigrants typically work in small shops, unions tend to ignore them, preferring firms with larger numbers of employees. UNITE has neither the resources nor the will to organize new Mexican immigrants washing and folding clothes in a small corner laundry. While immigrants tend to be employed in larger laundries too, the vast majority of workers are dispersed throughout the city in small shops. To meet the needs of new immigrants, unions must tangibly support organizing efforts at small shops as well as at larger establishments.

Some locals have ignored workers they might logically have sought. For decades, SEIU Local 32B-32J took no notice of immigrant service workers in buildings it had not organized, until the international union put the local into trusteeship in the mid-1990s. Local 100 of HERE also overlooked restaurant workers until put into trusteeship. Some locals have been stained by corruption and put into trusteeship by the government or their national unions. LIUNA locals connected to organized crime have traded union hazardous-waste jobs for money (Keiffer and Ness 1998).

The sheer number and diversity of New York unions formed over the past century produces fierce inter-union rivalries that present potential obstacles to organizing new members and make it hard for new unions to take root. Arrays of unions who are struggling to stay viable compete for immigrant workers outside the declining manufacturing sector. Given this competition, one can question whether unions help or hinder efforts to improve conditions for immigrants. This question is not new. In the early twentieth century, unions shunned new immigrants from Eastern Europe, Southern Europe, and East Asia on the basis of ethnic chauvinism, while craft unions fought to block the establishment of unions in basic industry, where most immigrant workers found themselves.

Competition among New York unions with long histories limits the possibilities for new unions, to represent new groups of employees in emerging industries, because unions protect their jurisdictions, even if they don't organize them. If one union with little or no history in one industrial sector organizes workers in another, it is frequently considered an act of aggression, as was the case when UNITE organized beer distribution truck drivers in the late 1990s. Organizing drives initiated by workers tend to be channeled into the Byzantine web of unions that has developed over the past hundred years. For example, it is difficult for independent organizing efforts to develop when a supermarket union guards its turf. Existing unions will frequently seek to gain the goodwill of workers by appropriating the independent organizing efforts by others.

Moreover, unions that no longer organize new members often stymie workers' organizing efforts in their jurisdictions for fear that the new workers may gain sway over their organizations. The rapidly growing undocumented immigrant population in New York City exerts a significant influence on unions' primary labor markets and on decisions to organize in these markets. Organizing recent immigrants is such a new endeavor, and the legal environment so volatile, that union organizers have little experience upon which to draw. Still, because many undocumented immigrants work in industries that are targeted by unions—building services, industrial laundries, health care, and delivery services—union leaders serious about increasing membership consider it crucial to work with immigrant activists.

Support for immigration among unions and in the general population is more resilient, broad-based, and bipartisan in New York City than at the federal level. Elected officials, even the conservative former Mayor Rudolph Giuliani, have regularly backed new immigrants and favored continued migration to the city. In January 1997, Giuliani, a Republican, convened an Immigration Coalition—a business and community group—to oppose Republican-sponsored federal legislation that discriminated against legal immigrants by denying them disability benefits, food stamps, welfare, and other federal benefits (Giuliani 1997).

To protect the rights of transnational workers, New York City has a long-standing policy, begun under Democratic mayor Edward I. Koch in 1989, that prohibits city employees from sharing information on immigration status with federal agencies, including the United States Bureau of Citizenship and Immigration Services, except in criminal cases. That policy, which was continued under another Democratic mayor, David Dinkins, and his Republican successors, Rudolph Giuliani and Michael Bloomberg, was ostensibly invalidated by the 1996 Immigration Reform Law, which increased penalties on illegal immigrants. Hoping to avoid compliance with the 1996 law, the city unsuccessfully sued the U.S. government.

Nationwide public opinion regarding immigration grew more favorable for a time and buoyed optimism among immigrant workers hoping to gain amnesty. However, in the aftermath of September 11, 2001, the U.S. government significantly slowed its efforts to create a coherent policy that would give amnesty to immigrants and create a guest worker program. The failure to establish a coherent national policy has fueled resentment in immigrant communities. Officially, New York City maintains a generally hospitable policy toward immigrants, despite the rise in individual hate crimes after September 11 (see Chapter 7 for a discussion of the effect of 9/11 on new immigrants).

Notwithstanding their ideological components, these shifting attitudes and policies do not eliminate the self-interest that drives most leaders. Politicians want to win elections, employers want a steady supply of cheap labor, and unions want more members and greater influence.

Local unions in New York City have responded, both conceptually and in practice, to the challenges posed by unrestrained immigration. For unions, the key factor in mobilizing immigrants is defending workers through reducing worker competition in labor markets and shielding workers from exploitation. The severe exploitation of transnational workers, many of whom perform jobs that were once unionized, exerts a widespread pernicious effect, lowering the living standards of native-born workers, depressing overall wages, undermining workplace safety, and hindering union organizing. Yet these workers are now an integral part of the U.S. economy (Sassen 1991).

In recent decades, labor leaders have increasingly recognized the connection between the growth of low-wage, nonunion jobs and the rising number of undocumented immigrants. For unions, undocumented transnational workers present a paradox: They depress wages, yet they are ripe for organizing. Over the past twenty years the labor movement, perhaps shortsightedly, has emphasized the former (Delgado 1994). Today, however, unions in California, Florida, New York State, and Texas are beginning to see immigrants as potential members (Milkman 2000; Milkman and Wong 2000).

On the whole, New York unions recognize that immigrants account for a large and growing proportion of workers in the primary labor markets in which they represent workers. Between 1985 and 2000, Latino immigrants increased from 22 percent to 32 percent of primary union labor markets; Asian immigrants grew from 7 to 12 percent; West Indian and African immigrants increased from 7 to 11 percent. During the same fifteen years, the ranks of recent Eastern European immigrants remained at 11 percent. Surprisingly, union leaders do not seem to notice the disparity between the current ethnic makeup of New York City and the ethnic composition of most unions, which reflects the city's workforce of a generation ago more than it does its current composition. More and more, union leaders reflect the composition of members of two or three generations ago. Most New York labor leaders recognize transnational workers' importance to their unions' survival and growth, but few have launched sustained campaigns to organize them.

With varying degrees of success, HERE, LIUNA, SEIU and UNITE are converging on organizing immigrants. Each of these national unions is concentrating on firms and labor markets with many workers. Unions typically prefer to devote their resources to large establishments, where recognition agreements would bring in many new members, rather than organize a few small businesses. No national union has yet expended the considerable resources needed to organize the overwhelming majority of service workers at the small and medium-sized firms that are the hallmark of the city's economy.

Revitalizing the Union Movement

How can labor respond to the corporate restructuring that has severely eroded U.S. wage and workplace standards? Unions have increasingly lost power. In the process, they have lost credibility with workers by making concessions in bargaining with management and by referring workers' grievances to regional and national officers instead of challenging employers directly in the workplace. Unions are reluctant to take militant actions such as strikes, fearing they are too weak to win and that defeat may threaten their survival. Labor leaders take the easy road instead. Wedded to predictable, conservative practices geared to workplace stability, union officials defuse the power of the rank and file, promoting cynicism among workers about the prospects of organizing to improve their conditions. Workers know that such attempts to organize will be scotched by both the management and the union.

In New York City, organized labor cannot revitalize itself unless it is willing to risk diminishing its power and embark on a sustained social protest movement that encompasses the broader working class—which includes immigrant workers employed in the new economy. Devoid of a membership that actually reflects the dramatically changing nature of the working class, organized labor in New York will lose its relevance to most workers, weakening its already-diminished influence in shaping state and local labor policies and state spending crucial to those workers' survival. To sustain and perhaps rebuild the local labor movement, far-sighted leaders inside and outside of organized labor must challenge the existing system. Such a movement must contend with labor leaders who seem at times to fear their own members—and potential new immigrant members—more than they fear management. Many unions have rhetorically adopted the progressive AFL-CIO platform embracing immigrants. But few are willing to put it into practice by devoting adequate resources to organizing transnational workers, fighting employers' abuses of them, and engaging immigrant workers in direct action, both in the workplace and in the political sphere. Some unions may even take action, but they do so without consulting the workers who have the most to risk.

To resuscitate the union movement, labor must adopt an organizing model that fosters workers' participation in problem solving and collective action, not just during bargaining. To avoid becoming relics, traditional unions will have to promote autonomous organizing among workers in their labor markets and encourage them to form their own, parallel, rank-and-file organizations. Unions have much to teach and learn from workers—members and nonmembers, immigrant and native-born alike—about how to engage in collective action to advance the political and economic power of working people.

To encourage participation, labor organizations of all kinds must educate workers about their rights and limitations within the capitalist system that has become even more exploitative in the last thirty years. They must help develop workers' skills and nurture new leadership by sharing information and communicating openly. To promote immigrant involvement, unions must decentralize their structures and encourage the creation of novel organizations that can represent new workplaces in ways that old structures cannot. Unions must be independent of management and must listen to, and learn from, workers' dissent and militancy, rather than ignoring or resisting it. While the labor movement is constrained by a political and economic climate that is hostile to workers' rights, conventional bureaucratic unions have themselves become an impediment to autonomous labor organizing.

Because employers are using immigrants to undermine labor standards, not just in the Third World, but also in the United States, unions need to develop the will and the capacity to support the struggles of transnational workers. While immigrant workers in New York are geographically dispersed, they have a strategic advantage because they typically work in labor markets that are shaped by employer and worker social networks. Clustered together in the same labor niches, with limited connections to mainstream U.S. society, immigrants can build camaraderie and class consciousness, as illustrated in Chapters 4, 5, and 6. Because transnational workers have few external bonds and little time to acquire them, they depend heavily on the social networks that emerge within segregated workplaces. Segmentation on the basis of identity—color, nationality, ethnicity, and gender—is a valuable source of potential solidarity as it has been among garment, mining, and public service workers in previous generations. But even among immigrants who do not share such identities, social exclusion tends to build deeper, sturdier relationships on the job than those among native-born workers.

To gain influence among immigrant workers, union leaders must recognize that the current workplace blends old and new social ties that may diverge greatly from those within their own organizations, which were formed decades ago to protect different workers in different labor markets. Unions must become more flexible about organizing and collective bargaining and embrace social-network unionism that appeals to diverse workers and workplaces. National unions must also foster the organization of autonomous locals reflecting the ties among workers. Those locals would not be based purely on identities like ethnicity or country of origin, but could also grow from labor-management struggles in the relentlessly changing workplace.

A positive trend seen in current organizing drives by national unions is the changing of jurisdictional boundaries. More unions in low-wage manufacturing and service industries seek to organize workers beyond their old industrial bases. Indeed, unions may need to expand their traditional boundary lines further in order to organize immigrant workers. Fresh leadership by workers in new industries under old jurisdictional boundaries is the key to modern union organizing. However, as we will see, boundary disputes may still staunch efforts to promote worker participation and discourage the emergence of new rank-and-file leaders.

For its part, grassroots immigrant workers' organizing often lacks the resources, muscle, and staying power that national unions can provide and tends to occur on a smaller, more local scale. While grassroots worker control is clearly preferable to centralized control imposed by large unions, small units may not permit transnational workers to successfully challenge employers. To succeed, local strategies must account for the might of corporate globalism.

The next three chapters reveal grassroots organizing by transnational workers in three different labor markets in New York City: the mobilization of Mexican greengrocery and deli workers, the mobilization of West African supermarket workers employed by labor contractors, and the organization of Asian black-car drivers against fleet owners. Union responses differ from case to case. A union may opportunistically compel workers back under its jurisdiction, deliberately ignore workers in restructured labor markets, or fail to help workers form an entirely new, independent local to represent the members' interests rather than those of the broader union. The three case studies show that organizing tends to originate in the workplaces and percolate up to established unions. Even some unions that seldom organize can benefit from "hot shops" already organized by transnational workers, who then appeal to unions for assistance. On the rare occasions when employers do not resist organizing, unions may assist in the legal process of gaining recognition and negotiating collective bargaining agreements.

New transnational workers are not only seen as foreigners by U.S. society in general but are frequently treated as outsiders within labor unions in the industries in which they work. These workers are frequently trapped by inter-union conflicts and by the jurisdictions of national and local unions protecting their turf in the labor movement. As technology and the nature of work change, union leaders lose not only their demographic ties to workers in their traditional industries but their connection to the culture of the work.

One cannot assume that transnational workers will be organized into existing unions. In fact, the period of large-scale immigration from the 1880s through the early 1920s witnessed the creation of specific ethnic and national union structures, particularly among garment and mining workers. Today, the slogan "Si Se Puede" (Yes We Can) is both a union slogan and the cry of Mexican immigrants seeking self-respect in the United States. Organized labor would benefit from a renewed discussion of the many possible forms of inclusion beyond traditional bureaucratic unions that give little autonomy to workers.

4 Mexican Immigrants, Class Formation, and Union Organizing in New York's Greengrocery Industry

Although workers are intimately connected to their employment communities, a huge chasm exists between their workplaces and their neighborhoods. In the United States, workplace politics differ significantly from community politics. Although workers hold a large stake in their employment communities, they have little power in advancing their needs on neighborhood issues that are crucial to the survival of their jobs. For example, what power do workers have in New York City's informal economy when rising real estate values lead to exorbitantly high commercial rents, causing their employers to shut down and move? The relocation of industrial employment to low-wage areas in the United States and abroad has significantly changed the social and economic character of U.S. cities. Industrial jobs in New York's urban factories have almost entirely disappeared and been replaced by retail and domestic service positions with firms that employ workers in nonstandard jobs providing low wages and few benefits.

Recent immigrants have become significant participants in the economy and culture of New York City. Over the past decade, most of the one million new immigrants have entered the local labor market, predominantly in low-wage industries. New Yorkers are quite familiar with these new immigrants who perform many essential daily services. Transnational workers are employed in construction and building rehabilitation; as cooks, dishwashers, and busboys in restaurants; and as taxi drivers, domestic workers, and delivery people (Sassen 1991).

A majority of workers in the informal economy are the victims of exploitative employers and labor contractors who force them to accept nineteenth-century working conditions and wages below the federally mandated minimum. This chapter examines workers in the low-wage Mexican greengrocery industry who bravely rose up and mobilized—at first independently and then through the help of a maverick local union—from 1997 to 2003 to challenge employers' abuse and to successfully restore wages to at least the legal minimum. Some trade unions and labor activists consider government enforcement of federal labor law to be a modest gain, but the elevation of wages and labor standards in the greengrocery industry could not have happened without worker-led organizing drives, backed by a maverick union leader.

The Political Economy of the Greengrocery Industry

The New York City greengrocery is a modern service industry closely associated with the rise of the postindustrial economy that emerged in the early 1970s. Often functioning as a neighborhood deli, the greengrocery is typically a small store employing three to five workers, selling fresh fruit and vegetables, dairy products, beverages, canned goods, snacks, and cut flowers to local residents and daytime workers. In commercial and business districts, larger shops sometimes employing up to fifty workers serve the bevy of office workers rushing in for a quick breakfast, lunch, or dinner— effectively the urban equivalent of a fast-food restaurant in the suburbs. As a rule, grocers in residential districts employ fewer than five workers, while those in commercial districts employ twenty or more. The emergence and growth of the greengrocery industry in New York reflects the horizontally dispersed nature of the city's economic infrastructure which necessitates the establishment of smaller food and retail outlets rather than large supermarkets and big-box stores. The high cost of real estate prevents large facilities in most locations, thus profit margins tend to decline as more stores open in the same area.

Greengroceries are an integral feature of an economy that places extreme time constraints on all workers. Shortened—or at least strictly enforced—lunch breaks and the grind of the workday give consumers few options other than running to the nearby green-grocer to order a salad and sandwich to eat at their desks while working. Because the workday is often extended and greengrocery workers frequently work more than one job, these workers find themselves catching a quick bite on the run between jobs or after work. Since the neighborhood greengrocer often provides ready-made food twenty-four hours a day, seven days a week, these stores have tended to replace conventional supermarkets and restaurants in the lives of busy New Yorkers. By the late 1990s, greengroceries/delis and higher-priced specialty markets were taking busi-ness away from an array of food service establishments—from supermarkets in upscale areas to bodegas and other small markets in working-class neighborhoods.

The rise of greengroceries in the busy commercial and residential neighborhoods of New York in the 1990s has intensified pressure on food service unions to hold on to the older, unionized segment of the industry as labor market share is captured by new estab-lishments. Presumably, workplace standards erode as union labor market density declines. To maintain density, market share, and relevance in the food service industry, unions face the compelling and often maddening task of dealing with the influx of a new set of ethnically, racially, and linguistically diverse immigrant workers who have entered the labor market since the early 1990s.

Ownership Patterns in the Greengrocery Industry

Until the 1970s, small greengroceries and delis in New York City were situated mainly in residential neighborhoods, and typically were owned by first-generation Italian or Jewish immigrants. Lack-ing family members willing to replace them, an aging population of shop owners began to leave this labor-intensive industry in the 1960s, and a new generation of Puerto Rican and Dominican new-comers began to open bodegas that replaced the old neighborhood greengrocers. Korean-owned greengroceries began to appear in New York's African American and Caribbean neighborhoods in the 1970s and soon thereafter spread to all five boroughs (Ilsoo Kim 1981).

Koreans maintain a loose-knit employers' association for retail operators; they typically buy and sell greengroceries to fellow Koreans with loans provided by family and immigrant networks in Korea and the United Stated (Min 1996). These associations were established by the early Korean shop owners, who borrowed money to start and operate the stores and then sold them for a small profit to more recent Korean immigrants, who gradually expanded the scale of these businesses. Like their European predecessors in the industry, the Korean owners initially operated the greengroceries on a "Mom and Pop" basis—that is, with family labor. But during the 1980s, as greengroceries became larger, they began to hire newcomers from Korea to help with the taxing work of unloading trucks; cleaning, cutting, and packaging fruit and vegetables; and stocking and cleaning the stores.

By the early 1990s, Korean owners dominated the greengrocery industry. According to business leaders in the community, a primary factor in the expansion of Korean ownership was their exclusion from mainstream industries that require more advanced English language skills (Young 1999). By 1998, about 80 percent of some two thousand greengroceries in New York City were owned by Koreans, who had found them—along with laundries and small garment-production shops—to be among the few accessible entryways into the local economy (Kim 1999; Interview, Donovan 1999). The ethnic concentration of Koreans as owners in the greengrocery industry expanded during the 1980s and 1990s, although by the late 1990s, immigrants from Palestine, Pakistan, India, and Yemen had also begun to enter the industry.

As demand for low-wage labor intensified in the late 1980s, more educated Koreans became less interested in and less confined to working in groceries. Although Korean owners generally report satisfaction with their co-ethnic employees, by the early 1990s profits generated by the markets were being squeezed by Korean workers demanding higher wages (Dae Young Kim 1999; interview, Korean worker, June 2001). Also, because the business was fairly uncomplicated and loans were easily available, employers realistically feared their workers might borrow the capital to open a store nearby and compete for customers and market share. Despite the pressure on profits, it is not unusual to find many Korean shops operating in the same square block, in some cases only a few doors apart.

Mexican Migration to New York City

Although considerable numbers of Mexican immigrants have lived in the western United States for much of the twentieth century, in New York City their population remained relatively small compared with other Latino groups. Until the early 1990s, Puerto Ricans and Dominicans made up the dominant Latino migrant groups in New York, while Mexicans resided in the city in roughly the same numbers since mid-century. Mexicans first arrived in New York City in significant numbers in the early 1940s in the wake of the Bracero Program, initiated by the U.S. government in 1942 to meet the growing demand for agricultural labor during World War II. This guestworker program brought in migrant laborers as contract workers on a monthly or seasonal basis. The first Mexicans to arrive in the city came from Mixteca Baja, a rural region encompassing southern Puebla, northern Oaxaca, and eastern Guerrero (Smith 1996, 57–104) Reflecting their early settlement and the establishment of a rooted community, immigrants from rural Puebla ("Mixtecans") remain the dominant regional group of Mexicans in New York, accounting for at least 80 percent of Mexican residents in 2000.

In the early 1990s, a mass influx of Mexican immigrants began. The increase in Mexican migration from 1990 to 2000 was nothing short of staggering. In 1990, some 61,700 Mexicans resided in New York City, representing only 3.5 percent of the Latino population of 1.75 million. By 2000, the INS estimated that Mexicans had become the third largest Latino subgroup, increasing during the past decade at a rate of 202.8 percent to 186,872. Officially, Mexicans make up the third largest immigrant population in New York, exceeded only by Dominicans and Chinese (New Yorkers of Puerto Rican descent are U.S. citizens). However, some believe that the city's Mexican population would number from 275,000 to 300,000 if the undocumented population were fully counted (Dominguez 2002; Rivera-Batiz 2003). The 2002 Cinco de Mayo celebration at Flushing Park in Queens is reported to have drawn 400,000 people from the region (interview, Gerardo Dominguez, AMAT, June 12, 2002).

Recent research on Mexican immigration to U.S. cities suggests that stable immigrant communities are promoted through the development of kinship, friendship, and national identity networks that facilitate adaptation to an unfamiliar environment. Mexican immigrants have developed social networks linking communities in Mexico and the United States that provide immigrants with jobs and basic survival needs (Massey, Durand, and Malone 2003; Massey et al. 1990, 147–153; Smith 1996, 57–104). In addition, social networks offer immigrants a sense of belonging to a community while living abroad. As one immigrant worker put it, "I have even greater ties to my friends and family here in New York than I had back home" (interview, Macote [no first name given], November 12, 1998). Massey and coauthors (1990) reinforce this point:

> Compared to the earliest pioneers, recent migrants have many more relatives, friends, and *paisanos* [countrymen] to whom they can turn for information and assistance while abroad. . . . More migrants move to a particular place because that is where the networks lead, and because that is where the social structure affords them the greatest opportunities for success. As more migrants arrive, the range of social connections is further extended, making subsequent migration to that place even more likely. (153)

Beyond these social opportunities, the most crucial factor in the formation of the migrant Mexican Diaspora community in New York City is the demand for low-wage labor in the informal economy. Absent the degradation of jobs once performed by native-born and Korean forerunners, the massive migration of Mexicans to New York would not have taken place (Castles and Miller 2003).

Immigration to New York City as a final destination increased in the early 1990s as xenophobic anti-Mexican sentiment increased and legal restrictions were extended in California and the rest of the U.S. Southwest—traditional destinations of Mexican migration. New York has gained a reputation among migrants as having a higher level of tolerance toward newcomers, due in part to the city's immigrant past. Additionally, passage of NAFTA in 1994 effectively forced Mexican peasants to compete with U.S. agribusiness, which dumped low-cost commodities into Mexico.

Thus, a combination of "push" factors (impoverishment in rural Mexico, hostility toward immigrants in the U.S. Southwest) and "pull" factors (the demand for low-wage workers) has driven Mexican migration to New York City. The recent upsurge in immigration to New York began during the Mexican economic crisis of the mid-1980s, which led to a significant contraction of the national economy, especially in the rural towns and villages of southern Puebla (Smith 1996, 61). With established kinship ties in the city, rural Mixtecans migrated to New York to work as low-wage laborers in restaurants, greengroceries, garment shops, and distribution centers. Robert Smith argues that the ready availability of Mexican food products and the formation of distinctly Mexican neighborhoods throughout New York facilitated the extensive increase in immigration. Initially, most newcomers were single young men and women in their teens and twenties who came to work for a short period—typically from six months to two years—and then return home. In many cases, they lived in overcrowded and substandard housing (Smith 1996, 60–65).

Some union leaders argue that the transitional nature of Mexican workers reduces their attraction to labor organizing, since they intend to stay in the city for only a short time and then return to their families, only to be replaced by newer migrants. However, as working conditions in Mexico have failed to recover from the crisis of the 1980s, an increasing number of Mexicans have remained in New York, raising families and building social networks.

Mexican Laborers in the Greengrocery Industry

Like most immigrant workers in low-wage jobs, Mexicans tend to arrive from rural regions with little formal education. Many are native Mayan speakers not fluent in Spanish. Still, Mexican laborers are in great demand because employers consider them hardworking and subservient. Before union-organizing efforts began among Mexican greengrocery workers, Hong K. Chun, president of the Korean Produce Association, observed that greengrocers hired Mexicans in large numbers because they were willing to work long hours for low wages without complaining (interview, August 20, 1998). Chun said that Mexicans were much more accommodating than were Korean workers, who demanded higher wages and greater flexibility in work schedules.

The prevailing perception among Korean business owners of the docile nature of Mexican workers, reported in a number of books and articles on employer–employee relations, has contributed to the active recruitment of Mexicans to work in the growing number of Korean-owned businesses (Ilsoo Kim 1981). Most workers are recruited directly by business owners through word-of-mouth recommendations by Mexican workers. Other Mexican workers are recruited into the industry by third-party employment agencies. By 1995, Mexican workers could easily find work in a range of industries, from laundries and retail stores to restaurants and greengroceries.

Most Mexican immigrants do not get jobs through word of mouth, but rather by going from one business to another asking for work. The omnipresent image of Mexican day laborers standing on street corners is, in fact, true. More often than not, owners of low-wage businesses find their help among applicants who go out every day pounding the pavement in search of work. However, some immigrant workers do find their way into the greengrocery industry through word of mouth among *paisanos*, or are recruited by Korean employment agencies in Jackson Heights, Brighton Beach, East Harlem, and other neighborhoods where Mexicans tend to reside. Agencies frequently compete among themselves by offering workers to employers at the lowest price possible—usually well below minimum wage (interview, Manhattan employment agency manager, August 14, 1998).

Unfortunately, although the pay is abysmally low, it is significantly higher than what these workers could earn back home in Mexico; it is certainly higher than nothing, which is often the alternative for new arrivals. With this leverage, most greengrocery owners easily replaced their Korean workers with low-wage Mexican labor. It is hardly surprising that undocumented workers in this situation would be less likely to assert their rights on the job than would native-born workers who have other options and can command at least the minimum wage. The enormous inequality between the two groups explains the cultural trait of docility that Korean employers attribute to Mexican workers. Although Korean employers almost always accept Mexican work documents as valid, they frequently remind workers that they are vulnerable to deportation due to their illegal status. The fact that neither Mexicans nor Koreans speak English or another common language camouflages the articulation of dissatisfaction among the workers. Typically, owners and workers exchange few words. Koreans order Mexicans to complete tasks and Mexicans comply. One of the most frequently heard orders is the Korean phrase *bali-bali* ("faster, faster"), uttered, by some accounts, as if to beasts.

There are more than two thousand greengroceries in New York City, employing twelve thousand workers—mostly Mexicans—under conditions similar to those found in garment industry sweatshops. By the late 1990s, most Mexican greengrocery workers who prepared and packaged fruit and vegetables were required to work twelve hours a day, six days a week, with no overtime pay or medical benefits. They received wages well below the minimum, typically earning $250 for a 72-hour week (less than $3.50 per hour). When workers complained about conditions, they were usually summarily fired and replaced with others looking for work. As Mexican union organizer Gerardo Dominguez explains: "Some owners pretend to be friendly to Mexican workers, but at the same time they threaten to cut their throats if they complain. We know workers who complained about working conditions who were put into the freezer for hours. So they usually keep silent about the abuses and their interest in joining a union" (interview, 1998).

For a long time, workers thought they had no recourse but to keep working under these harsh conditions. But in 1996, activist workers founded the Mexican American Workers Association, or in Spanish, the Asociación Mexicano Americano de Trabajadores (AMAT), then known as the Sindicato Mexicano Americano de Trabajadores Mexicano. No existing food service union was interested in organizing workers in the greengrocery industry (interview, union official, 1997). Not until 1998—nearly a decade after these workers first entered the industry—did any union consider them worth organizing, primarily because the shops were small and dispersed throughout the city. That organization was the Union of Needletrades, Textile, and Industrial Employees (UNITE) Local 169. What follows is the story of how a campaign started and how, surprisingly, a union emerged to help the workers. Although many greengrocery workers were recruited into unions of various types, most were not. Still, over a period of five years, through rigorous struggle, organizers and workers in and out of unions improved wages and conditions for everyone in the industry.

UNITE Local 169 and Ernesto Jofre

UNITE Local 169 was founded in 1902 as a constituent of the Garment Workers Union, and in 1914 merged with the Amalgamated Clothing Workers of America (a precursor to the Amalgamated Clothing and Textile Workers Union, or ACTWU). The local was formed by Eastern European immigrants to represent workers employed in the burgeoning men's apparel industry. Its members worked in shops that made hats, coats, sportswear, and other garments. By the 1950s, membership had risen to 10,000, but in the 1960s, membership plummeted as men's garment manufacturing shifted to low-wage states in the U.S. South and to offshore production sites. This trend accelerated over the past two decades, and by the late 1990s, membership in Local 169 had dipped below 1,000 (interview, Jeffrey Eichler, UNITE Local 169, August 1, 2001). Workers represented by this union are especially vulnerable to losing their jobs, since men's apparel is not as sensitive as women's fashions to changing styles that require local production, allowing giant retailers to subcontract work to offshore producers. By the end of the twentieth century, apparel unions were reeling from competition by nonunion firms that paid workers a fraction of the wages once standard in the industry.

To stanch a rapid decline in their membership base and to facilitate a more strategic organizing effort, the International Ladies Garment Workers Union (ILGWU) and ACTWU merged in 1995 to form a new all-purpose garment and textile union UNITE. The new leadership hoped that the combined union, with some 250,000 members, would have more clout with the government and employers, and might thereby prevent or limit the loss of jobs due to globalization.

But even after the merger, union membership among apparel workers continued its downward spiral. In January 2002, UNITE's membership hovered at 200,000. Today, the unionized garment industry is but a shadow of its former self, and UNITE has sought to reduce the spiraling decline in members through high-profile publicity campaigns linking large retailers to the proliferation of sweatshops in the United States and around the world. To raise awareness about abuses in apparel sweatshops, the union helped launch the Global Justice for Garment Workers campaign in August 2001. The campaign claims that more than two million garment workers are employed under sweatshop conditions around the world to serve the U.S. consumer clothing market (Behind the Label, Web site, 2001). Although the campaign is intended to force retailers to respect the rights of garment workers by improving conditions worldwide, its primary effect is to push retailers to increase production in unionized U.S. shops, thereby minimizing the extent of membership loss.[1]

In addition, the national union is actively engaged in organizing members outside its traditional apparel and textile industries. Failing to organize garment workers, UNITE has redeployed its scarce resources into organizing industrial laundries and distribution centers, bringing in some 40,000 new members who have proved pivotal to the union's survival. Under the leadership of president Bruce Raynor, the national union has endeavored to control organizing at all levels of the union. Organizing drives carried out by independent local unions that do not fit the national's industry-based, top-down mission are vigorously discouraged, even though some locals have energetically engaged in dynamic campaigns. UNITE Local 169 waged the most prominent New York–based organizing effort among immigrant workers. From August 1998 to June 2001, the maverick local—a union that pursued an organizing effort independent of UNITE—and AMAT jointly launched a widely publicized independent campaign to organize Mexican workers employed in the greengrocery and deli industries.

Local 169 was led by Ernesto Jofre, a former organizer with ACTWU, from 1991 until his death in March 2001. Jofre had won a hotly contested election for control of the local that pitted him against the national union's handpicked candidate. Long a champion of low-wage immigrant workers, Jofre was a former copper miner and labor activist from northern Chile who had been imprisoned for three years by the Pinochet regime before being exiled to the United States in 1978. After losing his full-time job in the late 1980s, Jofre survived by delivering daily newspapers at night. Working as an independent contractor for a newspaper delivery firm, Jofre was well aware of the travails of new immigrant workers. As part of the nighttime delivery job, Jofre and his coworkers were given individual routes and were required to deliver hundreds of papers. Newspaper delivery workers are required to drive their own cars and pay for their own gasoline; in return, they receive a small percentage of the price of each paper they deliver. When workers met to pick up their papers, they complained amongst themselves about how the job did not pay them enough to survive. But the newspaper delivery workers did not accept their exploitation without demanding improved conditions (interviews, Ernesto Jofre, November 10, 1997; August 5, 1998; October 3, 1999). Jofre recalled how they organized an informal workers' association to demand that the newspaper distributor pay a higher cut for each paper they delivered. Through the close-knit association of nighttime newspaper delivery workers, strong ties of solidarity were established. Ultimately, however, the delivery workers did not have the organizational clout to institutionalize piece rates and other employee benefits, and they failed to find a union that would take on their struggle.

Jofre's experience informed his understanding of jobs in the unregulated economy and reinforced his commitment to low-wage transnational workers as local 169 embarked on organizing campaigns in the late 1990s. He recognized that the organization of immigrant workers into formal and informal associations of solidarity sometimes extracted concessions from employers, but, due to a great power imbalance, were more often ignored. Unlike so many other union leaders, Jofre had a history of labor organizing outside of unions, but he knew that unions could help workers organize by providing the resources needed to consolidate their gains through legally enforceable collective bargaining agreements.

As manager of Local 169, Jofre gained control over significant resources. Even with a declining membership, the local union controlled a robust welfare fund estimated at $20 million, leading many politicians to pursue Jofre for support. Jofre did not want to sit on the union's financial resources, but instead preferred to use the money to build the union by supporting workers' organizing efforts. Jofre's plan was to use the union to assist workers in the community who were already organizing against their employers by providing resources, knowledge, and organizational clout. Jofre was well aware of the transformation of the local economy and the increase in low-wage jobs filled by Mexican immigrants (interview, December 1998). It also helped that the Local 169 offices were convenient to the area targeted by the Lower East Side Community Labor Coalition (CLC), a coalition of community organizations formed in 1996 to improve the conditions of workers in the neighborhood.

Throughout the early months of 1998, CLC members met regularly with Jofre to discuss possible organizing efforts. In the meetings, he stressed that low-wage immigrant workers would be welcomed into the union regardless of their status or the size of their employers. Jofre made it clear that as a recent immigrant himself, he recognized the suffering of transnational workers who struggled at low wages and under poor conditions just to survive in the city. Under his leadership, and in defiance of the national union, Local 169 decided to organize the new immigrant labor force at the city's greengrocers.

The Mexican American Workers Association

Upon its formation in 1996 by activist Mexican workers seeking to improve the economic and workplace conditions of fellow laborers, AMAT led slowdowns, protests, and boycotts of employers who owed workers weeks or even months of back wages. During the late 1990s, Mexican workers engaged in militant protests and strikes in the garment, restaurant, and greengrocery industries to improve their working conditions. Based in El Barrio (East Harlem), the organization had built up an extensive network of Mexican immigrants throughout the city in small greengroceries, laundries, and dry cleaners serving local neighborhoods, where workers have more contact with the public and so are more accessible to organizers.

A defining step was taken in December 1996, when Mexican workers fighting for dignity and equality at Fairway Market, an upscale gourmet New York supermarket chain, initiated an escalating series of actions against management. Although the supermarket had union recognition agreements with the United Food and Commercial Workers (UFCW), the union ignored the Mexican workers, who received lower wages and benefits than the union workers at the chain.

The campaign began when Mexican workers in the produce department—considered the most grueling job in the supermarket—began organizing for wages, benefits, and overtime pay equivalent to what union workers received. Manuel Guerrerro, an organizer in his early twenties from Oaxaca, Mexico, organized meetings at a local park near the upscale Upper West Side Manhattan store. The workers planned slowdowns and distributed information leaflets to local community residents describing the inferior conditions under which they worked.

The negative public attention made Fairway managers take notice, and persuaded them to agree to equivalent wages and benefits for Mexican workers. But the workers' demand for a union of their own was rejected by both Fairway and UFCW Local 1500, the regional food service union representing most of the other workers at the market (interview, Guerrerro, UNITE Local 169, interview August 23, 2001, confidential, 2002). The Mexican workers believed Local 1500 to be conspiring with management to deny them rights equivalent to those of union members. Isolated in the produce department, the Mexicans called for self-representation independent of the union. Over the years, this distrust dissipated as Mexicans joined the other workers to fight management for improved wages and working conditions.

The 1996 Fairway campaign set the groundwork for other militant campaigns throughout the city, primarily among greengrocery workers. The greengrocery campaign began in April 1998 when

CLC joined forces with AMAT to support back-wage protests against employers on the Lower East Side. At a number of restaurants and greengroceries, patrons were asked to boycott the offending establishments. In every case, employers relented and agreed to settlements. The two groups joined forces again the next month to tap into worker dissent against management in the neighborhood's twenty or so greengroceries.

The campaign hoped to move beyond the reactive struggles AMAT had been waging at single sites, and to begin organizing greengrocery workers throughout New York City. Despite success in righting individual wrongs, AMAT's actions had done little to change the pattern of day-to-day abuse endemic to the industry. While an employer could be forced to cough up unpaid wages, the industry-wide practice of paying well below the legal minimum went unchallenged. Organizers hoped that by harnessing worker militancy to a community's power to boycott, they could achieve a more widespread and permanent improvement in wages and working conditions. In addition, community support would protect vulnerable workers from summary firings or exposure to immigration authorities. If successful, the CLC-AMAT-Local 169 strategy could serve as a model for workers, unions, and communities throughout the city.

Organizing in Brighton Beach

In meetings and conversations AMAT conducted with workers employed at greengrocers around the city, many expressed a strong desire to join an organization that could raise their wages and provide protection from employer abuse and unfair treatment. In the Brighton Beach section of Brooklyn, workers seemed ready to move.[2]

The first target was a ten-block stretch along Brighton Beach Avenue where about twenty Korean-owned greengroceries served a local population of recent Russian immigrants. From August through November 1998, AMAT and Local 169 ran a campaign to sign up workers. Hundreds of workers met with union organizers, CLC members, and other local supporters to discuss the campaign. Before workers decided to cast their lot with the union, Local 169 had to convince them that their conditions would be improved through the organization. In particular, workers had to believe that they could win and that their bosses could not have them deported if they organized.

This was not an easy task. In the 1990s, after employers reported undocumented workers who had tried to organize, the INS had made numerous raids on establishments employing Mexicans and other immigrants. For example, in October 1998, as the AMAT/ Local 169 campaign was underway, Mexican immigrants earning $300 for seventy-two- to eighty-hour work weeks at Launderall, a Staten Island laundry, were deported after filing a claim for $159,000 in back wages (Bacon 1998). The raid created a climate of fear among immigrant workers throughout the city. The raids were relaxed only in 1998, after the Clinton administration agreed not to send the INS into shops where workers were engaged in union activity. Still, many workers feared they could be fired by their employers and deported if they tried to unionize.

On any given night during August 1998, dozens of workers employed in Brighton Beach could be seen congregating on street corners, meeting at local diners, and getting together in the homes of neighborhood Mexican workers to discuss the costs and benefits of joining a union. Even after rather acrimonious discussions, more than 75 percent of some five hundred workers—a majority in every store along the corridor—signed union recognition cards indicating that they wanted their employers to recognize the union and bargain collectively for a contract. With a majority of workers signed up, Local 169 presented the cards to the employers and called for union elections, which were held store by store in the winter of 1998.

Once employers discovered this support for unionization, they hired union-busting law firms to oppose the organizing effort. They fired workers who led the drive and intimidated others into ending their support for unionization. In addition, employers sought to dampen the fervor among workers by temporarily raising wages to comply with federal and state wage and hour laws. Wages rose dramatically, from about $2.50 to more than $5.00 per hour, and employers promised to comply with government minimums in the future. Although the National Labor Relations Board (NLRB) forbids employers to raise wages during an organizing campaign, the workers and the union could hardly complain to authorities that the owners were raising wages to the required federal legal minimum.

Most workers considered the effort a success once wages increased and working conditions improved. With NLRB protections so ineffective in securing the rights of U.S. workers—particularly immigrant workers—the campaign failed to convince mobilized workers that they could further defend their interests by joining the union. Although the organizing campaign proved successful at one store, even the strongest Local 169 supporters could not convince their coworkers to vote union. The Brighton Beach drive—though temporarily successful in increasing wages—demonstrated the futility of NLRB elections where employers can violate labor law by firing union activists and intimidating workers with threats of deportation. Despite the failure in Brighton Beach to organize workers into a traditional union, Mexican community leaders emerged to monitor conditions; and as the campaign spread to other neighborhoods, the Brighton Beach employers found it harder to avoid paying the legal minimum wage.

The campaign engendered much goodwill among workers toward Local 169, and brought scores of new activists into AMAT. Even the national leadership of UNITE, which had tended to view the campaign as quixotic, acknowledged that whether or not it succeeded in the short-term, the campaign created significant goodwill among the rapidly growing Mexican population (interview, Edgar Vargas, UNITE International Union, August 24, 2000).

Lower East Side Organizing

During the Brighton Beach drive, activity continued on the Lower East Side. Local 169 hired several Mexican workers as organizers and the union launched efforts among greengrocery workers, while CLC activists built support among church groups and community-based organizations. In the fall of 1998, a parade of more than two hundred people, led by a mariachi band, marched from the CHARAS/El Bohio Community Center in the Lower East Side of Manhattan to every greengrocer in the neighborhood. The protest put employers on notice and showed workers that they had the support of the community and of several elected officials who joined the march.

AMAT, CLC, and Local 169 decided to forego NLRB elections and instead demand employer recognition and collective bargaining after demonstrating that a majority of workers had signed union cards. It was felt that community boycotts could pressure employers to accede to that demand, while at the same time protecting workers from reprisals. The organizing drive to sign up workers in the Lower East Side greengroceries was overwhelmingly successful. Mexican workers were interested in the potential protection the union afforded. Those who signed union recognition cards with Local 169 received ID cards, which were highly valued by Mexican workers who saw them as a way to cash checks, provide identification to law enforcement officials, and achieve a modicum of legitimacy in a strange new city. By late spring 1999, a majority of the 125 workers employed at seventeen greengroceries in the area had signed union cards.

On May 1, workers and community activists held a rally and march to protest working conditions in the stores and to demand union recognition. More than three hundred workers, community residents, and elected officials joined the march, again led by a mariachi band, and again stopping at each store. CLC and Local 169 invited the greengrocery owners to a meeting at the local Boys Club, but only one owner and a representative of the Soho–Greenwich Village Korean Merchants Association attended. A second invitation was totally ignored. The invitations explained that the organizers wished to deal with the stores as a unit and negotiate a neighborhood-wide agreement that would ensure the economic viability of the greengroceries while improving the conditions of workers. CLC indicated that if serious negotiations toward a union contract did not begin, boycotts against the stores would start. Such an agreement, it was hoped, would provide workers a standard contract and local autonomy on workplace issues.

With employers refusing negotiations, the first boycott began in late June 1999 at Adinah's Farms on Avenue C at 2nd Street and at two stores on lower Avenue A owned by the same family: Graceland, a greengrocery, and Gracefully, a gourmet food shop. The stores, owned by Grace Dancyger a Korean immigrant who migrated to New York in the late 1970s, were based on a new business model. "Mr. Kim is characterized by the *New York Metro*, a local newspaper, as a serial deli opener who had a simple business model: find a run-down store, refit it, then replace the staff with better-trained workers before selling or renting the place to the highest bidder" (Ellwood 2004).

The CLC and Local 169 hoped that the boycotts would bring the owners to the table and that an agreement responsive to the needs of workers, owners, and community members could be hammered out. Instead, the owners dug in their heels and resorted to union-busting tactics, firing union activists who publicly opposed them. They blasted loud music at protesters, printed slanderous leaflets identifying CLC and the union with the Mafia and with the drug dealers who had once occupied the area, and, on one occasion, sent four goons in a limousine to physically threaten protesters.

On several occasions, customers also assaulted protesters or tried, unsuccessfully, to provoke violence from the boycott line. In mid-August, workers at Adinah's Farms went on strike to protest the lack of progress in the organizing drive. A majority of workers at the store had signed cards with Local 169, and after the firings the union filed an unfair labor practice charge with the NLRB. On October 25, the campaign expanded the consumer boycott to include 7th Street Fruit and Vegetable, a Lebanese-owned greengrocery on First Avenue.

By late summer 1999, the campaign had received substantial media coverage in the *New York Times, New York Newsday, El Diario, The Villager*, and other papers, as well as on several television stations. An essential element in the campaign's success was the effort to lobby government agencies to enforce wage and hour laws. CLC and Local 169 appealed to the U.S. Department of Labor and to New York State Attorney General Eliot Spitzer. By December 1999, the Department of Labor had issued judgments for back wages against Adinah's, and the Attorney General's office had launched a city-wide investigation of the greengrocery industry. The campaign also received ongoing support from federal, state, and local public officials who used the effort to promote their own political standing. For example, Manhattan members of the New York City Council held hearings on wages and working conditions in the industry that helped draw attention to the plight of Mexican immigrant workers.

The coalition organized daily leafleting at the stores, particularly between 4:00 pm and 7:00 pm, which cut deeply into sales. The pressure brought to bear by consumers in the neighborhood for the most part shielded workers from reprisals by their employers. In December 1999, thanks to six months of community boycotts and the perseverance of the striking workers, the owners of Adinah's Farms finally agreed to recognize Local 169 and negotiate a contract. At Graceland and Gracefully, an agreement was signed for workers that included a provision that guaranteed the owners' neutrality in union elections on December 31, 1999. Daniel Lucas, a worker at Adinah's Farms, said of the victory:

> We have shown other workers in this industry that this can be done. I know that all store managers treat workers the way they treat us. The strike was the only way to show our power and to put pressure on the company. Now that we have won, I feel proud. There are so many workers who are afraid. They can see that we are not afraid and that we won our strike. (interview, December 31, 1999)

By the winter of 2000, two other stores in the neighborhood—Fuji Apple and Hee II Market, both on First Avenue—had agreed to sign contracts. Two months later, a total of six stores on the Lower East Side had signed agreements with the union. These successes led to improvements in wages and working conditions at other stores in the neighborhood, and, indeed, throughout the city, as owners tried to avoid being targeted.

Throughout the campaign, CLC and Local 169 encouraged Korean storeowners to form an employers' association to bargain on behalf of employers in the produce industry. This effort was made at the campaign's inception and continued as it expanded throughout New York City. The idea was that rather than organizing and bargaining store by store, it would be better to solve the problem of illegally low wages and substandard working conditions by reaching an industry-wide master agreement. This, of course, would require most of the workers to sign union cards and most of the employers to negotiate collectively. By the spring of 2000, Mexican workers throughout the city had become aware that they were owed back wages for years of underpaid labor, and they flowed into the Local 169 union hall to join the union and seek back pay.

In the summer of 2000, the pressure on employers increased after Attorney General Spitzer's investigation of the industry's hiring practices concluded that not one store of the dozens examined was in compliance with minimum wage laws. Even the owners admitted that they had not paid workers the minimum wage for many years due to their ignorance of the law, but they insisted that most stores were now paying the minimum hourly wage. Because they had voluntarily raised wages, the owners claimed they did not require oversight from a union. AMAT and Local 169 asserted that given the owners' consistent anti-labor practices, the workers required a strong rank-and-file-run union to enforce the contracts. Unfortunately, although the union, AMAT, and CLC expressed hope that employers would recognize the workers' right to organize, the Korean owners remained divided. Some Korean owners claimed that the Attorney General's office was discriminating against their community, but the office noted that it was also pursuing back-wage claims against non-Korean employers who had violated wage and hour laws, including native-born owners of European descent (interview, Teri Gerstein, Assistant New York State Attorney General, March 15, 2002).

Moving to Larger Shops

An effort to expand the greengrocery organizing campaign beyond its promising origins on the Lower East Side began with the organization of workers at four stores in central Greenwich Village in the immediate vicinity of Local 169 headquarters: Valentino and three stores operated by the Han family—East Natural, Abbigail's, and Soho Natural. The markets, all on Fifth Avenue, catered heavily to office workers in the area and employed two to three times as many workers as even the largest of the Lower East Side stores. The initial target was Valentino Market, a Korean-owned gourmet deli at 13th Street, where a three-day community boycott led to union recognition and, shortly thereafter, a collective bargaining agreement.

Meanwhile, despite early signs of cooperation at Valentino, the effort to gain recognition from the Han family at East Natural, Abbigail's and Soho Natural became a major struggle as the owners hired a union-busting law firm to resist the organizing drive. Although nearly all the workers had signed union recognition cards, the owners refused to accept them as evidence of support for the union. Instead, they immediately raised wages and threatened workers with firing if they supported Local 169. Because the overwhelming majority of the twenty or so workers employed at East Natural signed union recognition cards in support of the union, the local called for an NLRB election. However, that request was withdrawn when better-paid, quasi-managerial employees were transferred to East Natural from other stores, effectively packing the bargaining unit in favor of management.

Workers and community supporters maintained pickets at East Natural, Abbigail's, and Soho Natural until May 2001, when East Natural, under heavy pressure from the boycott and the Attorney General's back-wage campaign, closed down. Though some community members were committed to maintaining the boycotts at the other Han family stores, the situation required building alliances with workers' rights groups beyond the Lower East Side. The boycott lines were expanded and staffed primarily by Mexican immigrants, most of them members of AMAT. Newfound support came also from students at two area schools, New York University and New School University.

Union-Busting Efforts

Before the closing of East Natural, the Han family's union-busting tactics included two separate attempts to bring in other unions that would sign either sweetheart deals or no contracts at all. In July 2000, CLC members went to Abbigail's to inform the owners that boycott lines were being set up that day. While there, they witnessed a manager giving workers union cards from the Service and Industrial Workers Union, a Brooklyn-based non–AFL-CIO union. Then, in October, the Han family formed the Korean Antidiscrimination Association (KADA), a new citywide association of about fifty anti-union greengrocer employers throughout Manhattan meant to block serious unionization efforts. The Han Family and KADA-member stores brought in International Longshoremen's Association (ILA) Local 1964 from Ridgefield Park, New Jersey, which signed recognition agreements at East Natural and a growing number of stores.

In November 2000, ILA Local 1964 teamed up with a group of Korean greengrocery and deli owners to prevent workers from organizing with Local 169. The ILA local told the NLRB that one of its organizers had stumbled upon the boycott line at East Natural, had signed up all the workers in one day, and had received recognition from the owners on the spot. In the following weeks, Local 1964 signed up workers at several other stores that opposed the legitimate organizing drive by Local 169. As an affiliate of the AFL-CIO, Local 1964 gave storeowners the imprimatur of legitimacy, despite the fact that it signed sweetheart deals without the knowledge of the workers. Among the thirty or so stores with Local 1964 contracts, workers said they had no knowledge of the agreements (interviews, Jin Market workers, January 2001; interviews, three workers at markets with Local 1964 contracts, February 2001). According to a Local 169 representative, Local 1964 signed up employers without bothering to get worker approval, which helped owners avoid legitimate unionization with UNITE. Local 1964 continued its campaign, and by the spring of 2003, according to one anonymous source, the New Jersey local had signed agreements with eighty storeowners without the participation of workers.

ILA Local 1964 is a union of some 2,300 members representing a wide range of workers, not on the docks, but chiefly in the warehouse and distribution industries. The union has a checkered history, including allegations of organized crime involvement. In 1989, union president Richard Costello and his son were found shot dead in a murder that authorities never solved (Robbins 2001). In the *Korea Central Daily*, a New York-based newspaper, Jacob Han of East Natural was quoted as saying that Local 1964 was a "counterunion ... more favorable to the employers.... In addition ... the longshoremen's union has promised not to negotiate over wages and allow employees to withdraw from the union two years later" (December 20, 2000).

In a further attack on legitimate worker organization, KADA and Local 1964 hired and paid young male protesters to picket stores that had signed recognition agreements and contracts with Local 169. The threat of a KADA picket line stymied the legitimate unionization campaign by intimidating Korean owners who otherwise might have agreed to recognize Local 169. Ironically, KADA assigned picketers only to Korean-owned stores and did not picket two stores owned by non-Koreans that were unionized by Local 169 on the Lower East Side. Although the anti-union pickets were run by KADA, the protesters were almost entirely African American and Arab youth and young adults (Dewan 2001).

KADA intended to confuse the public by distributing litera-ture in front of unionized stores stating that UNITE Local 169 had "signed sweetheart contracts with a number of employers against the will of the workers in these stores" (KADA leaflet, May 2001). The organization sought to create the impression that anti-Korean bias fueled the conflict. The plan was to evoke the well-publicized 1990 boycott and picketing of a Korean greengrocery in Flatbush that occurred in response to reports that a Korean storeowner had beaten a Haitian woman customer (Abelman and Lie 1997; Claire Jean Kim 2000; Min 1996). Indeed, although many customers aware of the campaign continued to patronize the Local 169 stores, many passersby boycotted the stores, either fooled into respecting the de-mands of minority youth staffing the boycott lines or intimidated by their occasional thuggish behavior.

Local 1964, in its statement to the AFL-CIO, said that its pri-mary motivation in signing up stores was to stop the consumer boycotts, which were interfering with business. This effort to cre-ate a company-dominated union was challenged by Local 169, CLC, and the workers. At a hearing held in Washington, DC, in January 2001, the AFL-CIO ruled that ILA Local 1964 was not the legitimate representative of workers at East Natural Market and that Local 169 retained the right to organize workers there:

> The evidence established that UNITE's strategic campaign to organize greengrocers, and the combination of tactics used under the plan, have proven successful in a number of locations. With this proceeding resolved and only one union in the picture, UNITE stands a reasonable chance of consolidating its support and winning representation of East Natural employees. (AFL-CIO 2001)

Workers organizing at another store nominally represented by Local 1964—Jin Market, a Tribeca greengrocery on Hudson Street, several blocks north of the World Trade Center, which employed about twenty-five workers—signed cards with Local 169 and wore baseball caps at work indicating their support. In mid-January, AMAT and community supporters from throughout the city threw up a boycott line at the store, which was honored by a major-ity of residents and workers in the neighborhood. When Local

1964 appealed to the AFL-CIO, the federation again concluded that UNITE Local 169 had the right to organize workers at Jin Market, despite the existence of a contract between the ILA local and the owners. Under pressure from KADA, the Jin Market closed to avoid recognizing and negotiating with Local 169. Several months later, when the campaign abated, the market reopened.

Not all Koreans opposed Mexican worker organizing and unionization. But local Mexican community leaders reported that anti-union storeowners who equated unionization support with disloyalty to the Korean community intimidated other storeowners who may have been sympathetic to the union cause. According to Cho (pseudonym), a business owner:

> It would be incorrect to view all Koreans as anti-labor. Members of the Korean American community were afraid to get involved in the campaign in support of the workers because of our fear of a backlash. We tried to engage a dialogue between owners and workers, but did not want to be seen as the front organization after things got out of control, because we were afraid of being seen and labeled as pro-Communist by conservative elements in the Korean community. (interview, Cho, October 2001)

Mexican consular leaders in New York City and union organizers seeking to reach a settlement of the dispute corroborate the antagonism of this bloc of Korean owners. Norberto Terrazas, a Mexican consular officer in New York, noted the difference of opinion on worker rights:

> I met with the Korean Consulate in New York but with no success. I told them that Mexicans have a culture of unionism that they also exercise here. They know that the right to form a union is not just a law, but is recognized by the Mexican constitution. We tried to exchange viewpoints amicably with the Korean Consulate, but they showed distrust even for U.S. unions. (interview, April 4, 2002)

Jeff Eichler, organizing director of Local 169, supports this view with respect to the greengrocer struggle:

> The Korean community is hard to influence, and when we organized unions, the owners solidified against us, even attacking Korean owners who signed contracts with us. We tried to make contacts with

> progressive forces in the Korean community such as KIWA (Korean Immigrant Workers Association), but our meetings always had to be conducted secretly due to the harsh repercussions that these groups faced. (interview, August 1, 2001)

Still, even in view of the hardening opposition from Korean employers, by late 2000, Mexican workers came to believe that they could win better conditions with the help of Local 169. As Gerardo Dominguez, a full-time organizer with Local 169, pointed out: "At the very beginning we were trying to convince workers who did not believe that conditions could be improved. In the process of organizing and growing media attention on the issue, workers became more conscious of the unfairness of the conditions they faced" (Dominguez 2002). However, Dominguez also noted that growing wage demands could just as easily have led to replacing Mexicans with other workers. Indeed, in 2000, as the unionization campaign mounted, a number of Korean stores on the Lower East Side and throughout the city that saw themselves as potential targets of the organizing drive began to replace Mexican workers with Koreans (interview, Gerardo Dominguez, June 12, 2002).[3]

Citywide Back-Pay Mobilization

By March 2001, the greengrocery organizing campaign had gone citywide. Organizers went store to store throughout Manhattan to survey and document the state of wages and working conditions for the Mexican immigrant workers who predominated in the industry. But the organizers—many of them workers who had been fired for union activity—also reached out to Korean, Arab, and other non-Mexican immigrant workers. The union gathered information on large-scale violations of minimum wage and overtime laws throughout the city, much of which it turned over to Attorney General Spitzer's office. Local 169 and AMAT then organized an effort to distribute Spanish-language leaflets informing workers at stores throughout Manhattan of their right to collect back wages from employers. The Local 169/AMAT campaign already had developed a track record on the Lower East Side, where several greengroceries had signed back-wage settlements with the Attorney General's office.

The leaflet distribution initiated another wave of workers streaming into the Local 169 headquarters in the spring of 2001 to file back-wage claims against their employers. The National Employment Law Project (a non-profit workers' advocacy organization) and a team of area law school students helped with the paperwork. In the course of processing their back-wage claims at the Local 169 union hall, nearly all the workers signed recognition cards indicating that they wanted the local to represent them vis-à-vis their employers.

For most of the preceding three years, workers had genuinely feared that employers would retaliate if they sought to join a union. In the winter of 2001, for the first time since the organizing campaign began, the fear began to abate among most Mexican workers in the greengrocery industry. Although workers may not have been fully aware of all the improved conditions the union could bring, they began to seek out the union as a source of assistance, rather than avoiding union organizers. The dramatic success of these organizing efforts emboldened workers to sign union recognition cards and testify for back wages at the Attorney General's office.

Attorney General Spitzer's office filed numerous claims for back wages against greengrocers who had failed to pay minimum wages and overtime for a period of several years. Under the provisions of the New York State Unpaid Wages Prohibition Act, which became law on September 17, 1997, employers failing to pay minimum wages must pay workers 200 percent of the amount owed, and the penalty for nonpayment was changed from a misdemeanor to a felony. New York State Department of Labor investigators go back six years for wage violations, rather than the two years required under federal law. The burden of proof shifts from the worker to the employer—a crucial shift because in the majority of cases, employers paid in cash rather than by check and did not keep adequate records. The law also allows labor unions to file on behalf of workers (Gordon 1999).

Local 169, with the help of AMAT, filed claims on workers' behalf against owners who refused to bargain with the union or address the problem of back wages. As a result, workers received back wages at two Lower East Side stores (Adinah's Farms and 7th Street Fruit and Vegetable) and one on the Upper West Side (Lucky Farms). On

November 20, 2001, Spitzer reached an agreement under which members of the Han Family who owned the stores agreed to pay a combined total of $315,000 in back wages owed to thirty-one workers employed at their three markets. By this time, of the three stores, only Soho Natural, which had signed an agreement with ILA Local 1964 to avoid unionization with UNITE Local 169, was still in business (Spitzer 2001). The two other stores chose to close rather than negotiate a collective bargaining agreement with Local 169. The Mexican Consulate took particular notice of the fine imposed against the Korean store owners, which was hailed by New York Consul General Salvador Beltran del Rio:

> Mexican workers, as well as all immigrants, come to New York to work very hard to contribute to the growth of the economy of the city. The extraordinary work performed by Attorney General Spitzer and his team sets a very important precedent in the protection of workers in the city who, regardless of their migratory status, are entitled to the wages established by law and most importantly will benefit by their employers' compliance with those laws. A large number of Mexicans work in the greengrocery industry, therefore, the Mexican Consulate in New York will continue with its efforts to assist and inform those Mexicans whose labor rights have been violated. (Spitzer 2001)

In response to the back-wage campaign, Korean employers began to raise wages at least to the minimum and to address worker complaints of abuse, even in greengroceries not yet targeted for unionization. Many Korean owners attended forums sponsored by Spitzer on conforming to the requirements of U.S. and New York State labor law. By the summer of 2001, wages among greengrocery workers—union and nonunion alike—had risen above the minimum throughout Manhattan. Still, the campaign to organize the workers continued and the Attorney General monitored the industry more closely. Although the law in New York offers the opportunity for workers to collect back wages and significantly improve their conditions, the problem of enforcement remains. As Jennifer Gordon, former director of the Workplace Project, a Hempstead, NY–based workers' center, noted, "Only workers who organize and protest their conditions can improve their conditions through pushing government to enforce the law." Employers, sadly, will not be swayed by increased penalties if workers and their representatives do not pursue campaigns to enforce labor laws (interview, May 13, 2002).

Migrant Organizing and Inter-Union Conflict

Despite the apparent success of the organizing drive among Mexican workers, Local 169 faced pressure from its national union to withdraw from the campaign. As noted, UNITE national leaders, at best, saw the campaign as good publicity for the union, but not as part of the union's organizing strategy, which focused on industrial laundries.

A critical factor in the campaign was the untimely death of Local 169's leader, Ernesto Jofre. By the fall of 2000, Jofre was no longer seen at the union hall, organizing meetings, strategy sessions, or parties for the Mexican workers organizing into the union. Jofre did not want to disclose that he was dying of stomach cancer, primarily out of concern that the national union would try to put a stop to the organizing campaign. But by January 2001, the seriousness of his illness became known, just as the campaign was gaining momentum and hundreds of workers could be seen marching *en masse* in the streets after their day shifts. Tragically, Jofre died in March 2001 as the organizing campaign was taking form with Mexican workers becoming emboldened to challenge their employers and most greengrocery owners beginning to recognize the need to negotiate rather than fight with the union.

In August 2001, five months after Jofre's death, Local 169 was forced to transfer the greengrocery campaign to UFCW, under orders from UNITE international president Bruce Raynor. Meanwhile, ILA Local 1964 accelerated its effort to mobilize owners to sign union contracts, making it the biggest "union" in the greengrocery labor market. Many of the owners who signed contracts without workers' consent had rejected recognition of Local 169 and UFCW Local 1500, which had continued the greengrocery campaign on its own.

UFCW's assumption of the campaign was not without problems. Unlike Local 169, UFCW Local 1500 organized workers independently of AMAT (interview, Pat Purcell, UFCW Local 1500, May 9, 2002).[4] The absence of AMAT left most workers feeling dispirited, since they considered the organization a means through which they could articulate their concerns about wages and conditions in the greengroceries. And months earlier, at the inception of the AMAT/UNITE Local 169 greengrocery campaign, the UFCW had accused the campaign of violating its jurisdiction over the grocery industry, even though UFCW had little interest in organizing greengrocery workers. Using traditional business union methods—paid outside organizers, lawyers, and union resources—such a campaign would be disproportionately expensive, especially given the small size of the establishments involved. With so few workers at so many establishments, the dues money would never cover the union's costs of organizing and representing the workers. But rather than allow the campaign to continue under the purview of Local 169, UFCW had aimed to prevent Local 169 from "showing it up" by organizing within its jurisdiction. Ostensibly, such a precedent would encourage other unions to do the same, thereby undermining UFCW's strength in its core jurisdiction.

Until 2000, UFCW had considered itself a "servicing union"— one that took care of existing members but did not organize new workers into the union. The union was a "receiving union," meaning it obtained its members through agreements that required employers to recognize the union when they opened new stores. Outflanked by UNITE in what it considered its own labor market, UFCW looked to cut a deal that would bring greengrocery workers into its fold. However, Local 169 organizers argued that the food union's jurisdiction claim was debatable, since greengroceries and delis primarily serve prepared food to consumers, while stocking and the preparation of vegetables—traditional tasks for food workers—were merely an adjunct to the main business of the markets (interview, Michael Donovan, UNITE Local 169, August 22, 2001).

Following Jofre's passing, UFCW redoubled its efforts to pressure UNITE's national leadership into turning over the organizing drive, which finally happened in August 2001. In the aftermath of Raynor's election as president in May 2001, UNITE sought to resolve other outstanding jurisdictional conflicts with UFCW and its national president Doug Dority. In effect, UNITE turned the greengrocery campaign over to UFCW in exchange for the right to organize some 2,600 workers employed in 142 Duane Reade retail drugstores in the New York City metropolitan area where UNITE had already established a foothold.

With the seeds planted, UFCW did consider the possibility of organizing greengrocery workers, although it mainly targeted large stores with more than twenty employees. UFCW Local 1500, which represents more than 22,000 members in the New York metropolitan area and the only regional UFCW affiliate actively engaging in organizing in the retail food sector at the time, agreed to take on the greengrocery campaign, with some financial assistance from the national union. The campaign ultimately proved successful, demonstrating the organizing bona fides of UFCW and its ability to police the bottom of the labor market to ensure that wages are maintained in its core supermarkets. Although UNITE Local 169 was strapped for resources, by the spring and summer of 2001 Mexican greengrocery workers in the city had come to the conclusion that the union was serious and was effective in pushing Korean store owners to abide by U.S. and New York State labor laws.

Still, the shift from UNITE to UFCW came at an unfortunate time for the organizing campaign. "UNITE was primed to seize control over the campaign and gain control of the industry, but it blinked," according to Nick Unger, former mobilization director of the New York City Central Labor Council. "If the union had put twenty or fifty organizers into the field, the industry would have been unionized fairly quickly" (interview, August 14, 2002). Even Pat Purcell, organizing director of UFCW Local 1500, said in the fall of 2001 that he had hoped for a joint campaign, combining the knowledge and resources of both unions—a prospect rejected by the national UFCW. What was missing from the UFCW approach was the active participation of the workers and their leaders. The national UFCW, bruised that one of the most well-publicized organizing drives was occurring in its own jurisdiction without its participation, did not want to share the limelight with UNITE Local 169. Additionally, the national union did not want to cede any segment of the food industry to the insurgent union.

The abrupt shift from UNITE to UFCW afforded the Korean owners an opportunity to consolidate power against the unionization drive. Anti-union owners, led by the Han family, accelerated their effort to encourage sweetheart agreements with ILA Local

1964. Korean owners signing with Local 1964 considered themselves absolved from addressing workers' demands, according to Local 169 representatives. Thus, the employers continued to waver on whether they should recognize and negotiate with UFCW Local 1500.

At the same time, the workers had to acquaint themselves with a new union. To ease the transition, Local 1500 hired five organizers from Local 169 who had worked on the campaign, and assigned a total of nine organizers to the effort. During the next two years, the campaign all but collapsed. The shift also created the problem of introducing Local 1500 to CLC and other New York City labor- and immigrant-rights supporters. Under Pat Purcell, Local 1500 genuinely attempted to rebuild alliances with AMAT, CLC, and New York Jobs with Justice, a national labor campaign founded in 1987 to improve workers' standard of living and job security, and to maintain their right to organize. Under Purcell's leadership, a new strategy emerged. Rather than actively wielding the back-wage weapon, Local 1500 would use it as a threat in cases where employers flouted labor laws and refused to bargain with the union. Thus, the hammer of the labor campaign was withdrawn.

One positive result of the shift to UFCW Local 1500 was a broadening of the campaign to larger greengroceries and delicatessens, particularly in the central business districts of Manhattan. The changes initiated by UFCW took the campaign from its neighborhood roots on the Lower East Side to the rest of the city. Most important, however, was the Code of Conduct instituted by Attorney General Spitzer mandating that greengroceries abide by labor laws.

Greengrocers Code of Conduct

Despite the transfer of the organizing campaign to Local 1500 and the predictable tensions between the two unions, AMAT and CLC maintained amiable relationships with Local 1500. Together, the three organizations worked with Spitzer to create a Code of Conduct for the industry.

The Code of Conduct—which governs labor–management relations at all greengroceries—requires all employers to comply with state labor laws, including those regulating minimum wage and overtime wages, meal breaks, maintenance of payroll records, and days off. It also stipulates that owners must grant paid vacation and sick days to long-term employees. In fact, the Code provides better conditions for workers than do existing labor laws. Employers who flout the Code are subject to significant monetary sanctions under the Unpaid Wages Act, as well as promised consumer boycotts by labor–community coalitions and possible unionization efforts. To enforce the Code, the Attorney General's office would monitor stores and make unexpected visits to investigate labor practices. In exchange for signing on to the Code, greengrocery employers would not be subject to expensive back-wage suits filed by workers. The obvious disadvantage for workers was that their employers would not be subject to any back-wage violations that occurred before they signed the Code. This constituted a partial loss for workers—many gave up their right to get back pay if their employer currently complied with wage standards.

The Attorney General hoped the Code of Conduct would improve conditions for workers and encourage more moderate employers to recognize the union. Moreover, the union hoped that the higher standards embodied in the Code would improve conditions for all workers in the industry, whether unionized or not. When the Code of Conduct was announced on September 17, 2002, twenty stores' had already signed on. By January 2003, several hundred stores had signed on, including those represented by unions.[5]

The Ebbing of the Campaign

In early 2002, Local 1500 reported that it had reached recognition agreements with a group of ten stores, partway toward the goal of an industry-wide contract. The union said that two workers from each store were participating in contract negotiations, giving the rank-and-file workers some power to determine their conditions. The Local 1500 contract would be more costly to employers, since it required higher wages and a more comprehensive health care package than did the Local 169 contract, which had addressed the sometimes-tenuous economic situation of the smaller, often undercapitalized stores targeted early in the campaign. Local 169's idea was to bring in as many greengroceries as possible in the hope of negotiating improved contracts in the future as the union gained a larger share of the labor market. In contrast, Local 1500 dealt with larger stores that could afford to pay more. It also had contracts with supermarkets, which face stiff competition from the greengroceries. Thus, it had to be careful not to give the latter an edge by accepting significantly reduced terms, thereby undermining the wages and threatening the jobs of its core membership.

When the greengrocery owners balked at the Local 1500 demands, workers in the stores pressed the union to take action. The UFCW strategy was to conduct one-day strikes at stores where negotiations had stalled. In 2002 and 2003 these strikes took place at targeted stores, supported with leafleting and weekly demonstrations by members of Local 1500, members of other labor unions, and community groups. This pressure finally forced some of the employers to negotiate seriously, but by the summer of 2003, Local 1500 claimed it had secured a contract at only one store, the terms of which included wage increases, a benefits package, and grievance procedures (Greenhouse 2002; Spitzer 2002).

Yet, despite its successes, the greengrocery organizing campaign seemed to run out of steam. By the fall of 2003, UFCW's campaign faded, even though the union continued to claim ownership over it. Local 1500, however earnest, had been constantly diverted by other issues—from organizing rogue supermarket owners to an effort to organize Burritoville, a chain of Mexican fast-food restaurants. In retrospect, the campaign's demise can be attributed in part to the rivalry that pitted UNITE national leadership against Local 169, and later UNITE against UFCW, ultimately undermining the immigrant workers' organizing on the ground.[6]

If we are to measure success by improved wages and working conditions, the greengrocery organizing campaign, directed primarily by rank-and-file workers with the help of unions and community activists, is a victory, since thousands of Mexican immigrants have bettered their conditions. Indeed, the campaign is in some ways reminiscent of the early twentieth century Industrial Workers of the World (IWW) style of organizing without a contract. This organizing led to the enforcement of labor law for all workers, which had long been ignored by small businesses in the informal economy.

Missing is an established rank-and-file organization capable of organizing and mobilizing workers in new battles that are sure to come in the future.

Lessons: Unions Must Support Immigrant Organizing

The reconstituted demographics of the early twenty-first century labor market in New York City is a defining feature of labor struggles in the expanding global economy that now relies largely on underpaid transnational workers. At the dawn of the century, Mexican greengrocery workers perform important functions in the unregulated New York economy where wage standards and safe working conditions are routinely ignored. What typifies the greengrocery labor market segment, and indeed the postindustrial service economy as a whole, is the relentless churning among immigrants who enter and come to dominate these industries as both workers and owners.

In the case of the greengrocery industry, Korean owners hired other immigrants to replace Korean workers who were demanding higher wages and improved conditions. Mexican workers came to be seen as ready replacements, and emerged to dominate the sector in the 1980s and 1990s. The power imbalance between the two ethnic groups allowed Koreans to employ young Mexicans who came to New York in search of employment—no matter how exploitative—that would allow them to earn enough to get by in the city and remit money to their families back home. In the 1990s, the Korean satisfaction with Mexican workers reflected the novelty of the relationship and stereotyped perceptions.

In interviews, Korean greengrocery owners typically portrayed their workers as hardworking and docile, while most Mexican workers portrayed the relationship as exploitative. Owners granted some Mexicans employed at their markets greater authority and higher wages on the basis of favoritism, seniority, English language skills, and work responsibilities (deli work and flower cutting typically paid more than stocking food or preparing fruit and vegetables). Workers on the job for a year or less, however, usually toiled at cutting and packing fruit and vegetables and were paid significantly lower wages. Yet, overall—favored or not—Mexican

workers indicated an almost universal resentment of their employers, a fact seldom recognized by the Koreans.

However, after only five years, the Korean greengrocery emerged
as a primary arena of struggle, as new immigrant workers protested
against poor conditions and demanded more power vis-à-vis their
employers. In a workplace segmented on the basis of race and ethnicity, employers publicly characterized the struggle as an example
of anti-Korean bias, which ultimately proved to be a deceptive ploy
to sidestep the conflict. Indeed, although Mexicans dominated the
labor market, some Korean workers came forward in solidarity to
demonstrate their aversion to the exploitative environment, even
if they were paid somewhat higher wages (interview, anonymous
Korean greengrocery worker, March 2001).

Thus, as the case studies that follow also show, organizers could
tap a reservoir of resentment emerging from the exploitative workplace as they sought to bring the struggle for improved wages and
working conditions to a head. Over a five-year period, the greengrocery organizing effort helped build a consciousness of solidarity
among many workers, who now felt entitled to demand higher
wages and dignity on the job. This spirit was recognized by organizers from workers' centers engaged in back-wage campaigns and
by emerging leaders of Mexican workers' groups—most notably
AMAT, which mobilized workers even before Local 169 agreed to
commit significant resources to the campaign.

However, UFCW claimed the campaign trampled on its jurisdiction. Behind this assertion lay a fear that another union would make
inroads in a series of industries—greengroceries, specialty markets,
and drugstores—that are UFCW's core jurisdiction in the New York
metropolitan area. Were another union to succeed, UFCW would be
shut out of these industries, reducing the union's potential membership and weakening its ability to protect its current members
in the supermarkets by winning wage parity in the new industries.
Thus, UFCW's jurisdictional claim arose from the restructuring of
the retail food industry in New York City. According to Purcell, the
union saw the changes in the industry and the competition posed
to traditional supermarkets as a threat to the union's membership
base, and viewed securing the greengroceries as a way to protect
and replenish that base (interview, February 2002).

The greengrocery organizing campaign demonstrates the stark class divisions in the workplace between immigrant Mexican workers and the storeowners who employ them. Moreover, the campaign attests to the power of worker self-organizing and community–labor collaboration, and some union respect for autonomous forms of organizing. With increasing numbers of transnational workers now convinced that they can prevail against their employers and demand their rights in the workplace, the prospects for building a broader movement for worker rights have brightened. At the beginning, many labor leaders disparaged the greengrocery campaign as a waste of resources. They believed it could not succeed in mobilizing workers in large numbers since the stores were small and dispersed throughout the city. They also believed that immigrant Mexican workers were too vulnerable and intimidated to join such an effort.

Despite the widespread skepticism, greengrocery workers throughout New York City have improved their wages and working conditions and gained new dignity and respect on the job. Even if workers have lost control of the campaign and UFCW Local 1500 cannot organize the shops *en masse*, and simply polices conditions at the bottom of the food chain, this round of the workers' struggle can be viewed as a success. Workers still maintain strong social ties on the job that remain crucial for future organizing.

Local labor leaders, elected officials, and even some outsiders have claimed credit for the campaign, but the enormous undertaking would not have been possible without the efforts of the rank-and-file workers who developed class solidarities within the workplace. The campaign demonstrated that Mexican immigrant workers have the capacity to advance their interests through organizing. It also highlighted the need for unions to adapt their structures to address the pressing problems of low-wage workers in the small shops that comprise the neoliberal economy of New York City. Finally, the campaign is testimony to the ability of workers to translate class conflict on the shop floor into visible struggle in the sphere of politics. In the new economy, work is often conducted in public, not behind closed factory gates, making it easier for workers to rally concerned community residents to pressure employers and government to treat their workers fairly.

Even if viewed a success because wages increased in the industry, the greengrocery organizing campaign is a pyrrhic victory. How could things have turned out differently? The death of Ernesto Jofre at a time when the Mexican worker insurgency was growing was a decisive turning point in the campaign. The union provided resources and protected the autonomous worker organizing from outside threats stemming from inter-union competition. UNITE national leadership did not see the campaign as anything more than "good public relations" for the union and not in sync with its organizing strategy. Winning wars on a shop-by-shop basis was too slow and expensive.

If Jofre had not died, the union's long-term strategy of building a strong rank-and-file presence in the shops could have resulted in both greater immigrant participation and new members for the union. Jofre's untimely death shows how leadership can be a crucial element in campaigns for social justice and suggests that those who think individuals are irrelevant in history could be off the mark. Individuals' actions can be decisive at key historical moments. Building the campaign up until March 2001 helped solidify worker confidence in the power of the union and community, a process that took three years. In the end, it was a "public relations victory" but a failure of union organizing with contradictory results. Mexican workers lost confidence in the ability of unions to deliver the resources and power required to challenge employers, while gaining confidence that victory is a possibility if given a say.

5 Francophone West African Supermarket Delivery Workers Autonomous Union Organizing Outside of a Union

On April 1, 2000, Siaka Diakite, a thirty-two-year-old immigrant from West Africa's Ivory Coast, testified at a forum in New York City that he worked as a deliveryman for a supermarket chain without any guarantee of pay. Classified as an independent contractor, Diakite was paid $1 for each delivery made to Manhattan customers. Typical loads of groceries ranged from fifty to one hundred pounds. On average, Diakite worked sixty hours per week for $110, including tips. Diakite was told by his supermarket manager to do whatever the manager ordered, from bagging groceries to mopping floors. If he refused, he would be fired. At the forum, Diakite equated his treatment to that of a "slave," since he could not speak to anyone or complain about his conditions (Diakite, AFL-CIO Immigration Forum, New York, April 2000).

The term *contract labor*, whereby middlemen subcontract work to laborers, denotes a form of worker exploitation that was supposedly put to an end in the United States in the early twentieth century. What makes labor contracting so exploitative is the fact that the worker has no protection, as he or she is officially in business for him- or herself. Technically, contract laborers exploit themselves.

During the past fifty years, contract labor has come to be associated with migrant and seasonal Mexican agricultural laborers who must meet quotas in exchange for money or a place to stay. Not officially employed by a larger company or labor contractor, the worker determines how many hours and how hard to work. The practice of labor contracting thereby shields business owners from any legal obligations to workers. Considered an anachronism just a few years ago, labor contracting has become a common feature of New York's unregulated informal economy. The practice depends on an ample supply of transnational laborers willing to take on exceedingly onerous types of work. Labor contracting is not normally associated with workers who have union representation.

In the spring of 1998, without any allies or supporters, Diakite and his coworkers began a remarkable organizing drive to improve their conditions, ending in a two-day strike against dozens of supermarkets across New York City. This chapter examines the trajectory of events that led French West African immigrants working for contractors at low wages and under oppressive working conditions to form their own rank-and-file association and challenge their employers, despite (or as argued here, because of) their isolation from established unions. This organizing culminated in a highly visible Manhattan-wide strike by supermarket delivery workers and ultimate affiliation with the union representing other workers at the facility. Deliverymen bag groceries at supermarket and push carts full of food and household supplies to the homes of retail customers.

The effort was a response to a situation in which the nature of work was restructured, workers' rights were undercut through the reclassification of their labor, and the segregation of workers into discrete racial categories negatively affected their ability to take remedial action to improve their conditions through conventional channels. By examining published articles, newspapers, and archival materials, and through interviews with fifteen workers, two organizers, and labor law experts, the chapter considers the role of the union in representing the delivery workers. Labor contractors and supermarket management did not respond to requests for interviews. The chapter examines the origins and unfolding of the campaign, which, due to outside interference by the union chartered to represent the deliverymen in the first place, culminated in a mixed victory for the workers. Finally, the chapter raises questions about the relationship between established unions and independent workers' organizations, reinforcing the book's argument that the restructuring of the labor force has brought about new problems for organized labor requiring new forms of worker organizing. If the labor movement is to grow and flourish, it must recognize and nurture worker dissent that emanates from both formal and informal independent organizing on the shop floor.

The story of the organization of West African deliverymen in New York's supermarket industry illustrates the increasing globalization of the world economy, the restructuring of urban economies, and the emergence of a migratory labor force to fill positions demanded by residents and consumers. How do immigrants from a rural village near Zinguinchor, a city three hundred miles from Dakar, end up delivering food to residents in the most upscale neighborhoods in New York City? While there is a ready supply of native-born workers in New York, the wages and working conditions of delivery jobs have been degraded to such an extent that only immigrants will take this work.

Although there is a growing body of work detailing the influence of new immigrants on the urban economy, investigations of West African immigrant workers in large U.S. cities are glaringly absent from this research. In part, this paucity reflects the fact that West Africans are relatively recent immigrants to the United States, the vast majority having arrived during the 1990s. Knowledge of their working conditions is sketchy, and while a growing number of West Africans in New York City are joining or forming labor organizations, investigations of both union-based and autonomous worker organizing efforts are few (Foner 2001; Kieffer and Ness 1999; Lynd and Lynd 2000; Milkman 2000; Milkman and Wong 2000; Ness 1998; Stoller 2001; Waldinger 1996, 2001, Waldinger and Lichter 2003). Yet the case of the autonomous organizing efforts of French West African deliverymen is noteworthy, as it exposes the evolution of abusive working conditions in supermarkets—an established industry that throughout the 1980s and 1990s gradually blended the formal, relatively high-wage retail food industry with the underground economy of labor subcontracting and avaricious exploitation of immigrants (*Business Week* 1982; Stoller 2001). The remarkable self-organization of Francophone West African deliverymen, despite employer opposition and union ambivalence, highlights the resilience of workers responding to abusive working conditions and racial discrimination.

New York City as a New Destination

The United States is a relatively new destination for West Africans, who for decades had immigrated to Western Europe. By the time the Cold War came to an end in the 1990s, however, a distinctive immigration pattern had developed in response to a convergence of endogenous and exogenous economic and political factors affecting Africa and the developing world as a whole.

As the global economy has expanded since 1980, that of sub-Saharan Africa has largely contracted, with declining growth rates in many sectors of national economies. Standards of living and life expectancy have failed to keep pace with those in much of the world (Jones 1997; United Nations 1995, 1996). This economic plunge has occurred as Africa's population has grown at a more rapid rate than that of any other continent. Between 1965 and 1995, Africa's population expanded by 134 percent, from 311 million to 728 million.

The legacy of colonialism continues to have a profound effect on economic conditions in Africa and on patterns of migration. Although African countries gained formal independence during the second half of the twentieth century, European powers continued to exercise *de facto* military, cultural, political, and economic influence over their former colonies. The promise of self-government for the most part did not deliver economic expansion. Owing to Western European and North American dominance over the continent's economic resources, conditions in many African countries are even worse today they were at the dawn of independence. Africa remains the poorest continent, with the highest poverty rates, the lowest per capita gross domestic products, and the lowest level of industrialization. African immigration to Europe and North America is largely a byproduct of persistent economic stagnation and decline, and the associated lack of opportunity in the burgeoning central urban areas.

One of the most important consequences of the colonial relationship has been the expansion of African immigration to the European metropoles, a dynamic that accelerated greatly following independence in the 1960s. Postcolonial immigration established large and stable immigrant communities in many major European cities, resulting in wider diversity and related social problems (Castles and Kosack 1973).

In contrast, few Africans moved to the United States or Canada during most of the twentieth century. Between 1900 and 1950, only 31,000 Africans immigrated to the United States, the majority from North Africa (Gordon 1998). Later, Cold War competition in the developing world between the United States and the Soviet Union led to expanded political and educational exchange with sub-Saharan Africa, bringing more African students to American universities. From the 1970s through the 1990s, most African immigrants to the United States were refugees fleeing civil war and economic crisis stemming from ethnic conflict. The vast majority of African refugees in that period were rural peasants traveling across the borders of neighboring states in search of a safe haven from war and famine.[1] In the 1970s and 1980s, in the wake of regional conflicts in the Horn of Africa, a significant number of Ethiopian and Eritrean refugees sought sanctuary in the United States.

But in the years that followed, the economic crisis in Africa that began in the 1980s and the closure of European borders to foreigners turned the United States into a leading new destination for college-educated African immigrants seeking higher living standards. During the 1980s, the number of African immigrants living in the United States tripled to more than 360,000, and this population flow accelerated throughout the ensuing decade.

The increase in African migration to the United States was in part a response to tighter immigration laws and restrictions on permanent residency in Western Europe. For example, France, which had been fairly open during the first two decades following African independence, imposed new limitations on African immigration.[2] Stepped-up immigration to the United States also reflected a desire to avoid social unrest in European cities. Uprisings by African immigrants have occurred in the *banlieues*—impoverished working-class suburbs that encircle major French cities. Similar unrest, triggered by years of racism, discrimination, unemployment, and poverty, has occurred in working-class immigrant areas in England, including the Handsworth district of Birmingham, the Brixton district of London, and the Tottenham district of London.

Restrictions on African immigration to Europe increased even as U.S. immigration laws were relaxed (or were largely not enforced) over the past several decades. The U.S. Immigration Act of 1965 gradually ended quotas based on national origin, which had given preferential treatment to Europeans and discriminated against immigrants from the Third World. The 1965 law amended the 1952 McCarran–Walter Act, which permitted 149,667 Europeans to enter the United States per year, while restricting the annual number of immigrants from Asia to 2,990 and from Africa to 1,440 (Reimers 1994). The new law created special provisions for skilled immigrants, and subsequent reforms eased the migration of Third World refugees. This relaxation of restrictions expanded U.S.–African interchanges of all types, including those for the purposes of education, work, and family reunification.[3]

The economic boom of the 1990s and New York City's growing importance as a financial and cultural center of the global economy spurred the rapid growth of African migration to the city. Moreover, New York's reputation as a comparatively safe haven from anti-immigrant bias in the United States further encouraged African immigration. The U.S. census reported that the official number of sub-Saharan Africans residing in New York State more than tripled, from 31,440 in 1990 to 102,153 in 2000, with the population concentrated in New York City. If undocumented immigrants are included, there are an estimated 200,000 to 250,000 West African immigrants living in New York City alone (U.S. Department of Justice, 1998). Others believe that the numbers are significantly higher.[4]

Immigrants from French West Africa specifically are among the most recent newcomers to New York City, having begun to arrive in small numbers in the 1990s. The first major group of Francophone Africans arrived from Senegal in the early 1990s. A second wave of migrants from Mali followed shortly thereafter. Today, these two nationalities form the largest groups of French West African immigrants in the city. Smaller numbers have arrived from the Ivory Coast, Guinea, Gabon, the Congo, and Cameroon. Although statistical data on these populations are not available, interviews with leaders in the community indicate that they may number about ten thousand in the city, spread across neighborhoods in northern Manhattan and the Bronx. Undercover police officers' unprovoked shooting of Amadou Diallo, a migrant from Guinea, on February 4, 1999, is a stark reminder of Francophone West African immigrants' growing influence in New York City during the past decade.

Restructuring Work in Supermarkets

What factors have contributed to the erosion of working conditions in the retail food industry and the entry of undocumented immigrants into that labor market? The typical French West African immigrant to New York City is a male in his twenties to thirties who speaks little or no English. West African immigrants typically arrive in the United States with little or no formal education; many are literate in neither English nor French. The majority of West Africans in New York City fill unskilled employment niches as residential and commercial security guards, livery cab drivers, messengers, food service workers, newspaper deliverers, and street vendors (Stoller 2003).[5]

Like other recent immigrants, many West Africans enter the labor market as "nonworkers," or independent contractors, ostensibly in business for themselves but in fact performing work usually done by employees of a firm. Because U.S. labor law affords protection to all workers, without regard to immigration status or citizenship, the ability of businesses to redefine the labor relationship from employer and employee to broker and independent contractor has severely undermined working conditions by cutting off workers' opportunities for legal redress. Both retail food industry corporate managers and labor contractors benefit financially from engaging immigrant workers who either are unaware of their workplace rights or do not avail themselves of labor protections because they fear repercussions arising from their precarious legal status. While African immigrants play a crucial role as workers in the service sector, employers, contractors, and even unions have pre-vented them from assimilating into the formal political economy, thereby frequently preventing them from being covered by estab-lished wage and work rules.

In New York City, the supermarket industry differs markedly from food retailers throughout the rest of the nation (See Walsh 1993). Due to the high cost of retail space in the city, supermar-kets typically are smaller and provide a narrower range of food and household products. The pressure for space is even greater in residential Manhattan neighborhoods, where commercial rents are higher than in the outer boroughs. Still, despite these differences, New York's retail food industry has undergone many of the same changes taking place elsewhere: consolidation among a small group of large supermarket chains, store closures that increase sales at re-maining outlets, and, during the past two decades, the replacement of full-time union jobs by part-time jobs that pay lower wages and offer fewer benefits. In New York City supermarkets, the ratio of part-timers to full-timers ranges from 4 to 1 to 5 to 1.

The entry of a new immigrant workforce in New York City's supermarket industry has been critical to the restructuring of tra-ditional employer–employee relationships. Two major unions have dominated the New York regional retail food labor market since the 1930s: Retail, Wholesale and Department Store Union (RWDSU) Local 338 and United Food and Commercial Workers (UFCW) Lo-cal 1500. By the beginning of the new century, the two unions' capacity to control retail food wage rates had eroded with the clos-ing of large supermarkets and their replacement by nonunion delis, greengrocers, upscale specialty food stores, and chain drugstores selling food products (see Chapter 4). In response to declining profits and competition from these stores, the supermarket chains—which typically operate on low margins—have cut labor costs by creating part-time jobs that pay much lower wages and provide few, if any, benefits, and by hiring new immigrants who work longer hours under more adverse conditions. Further, supermarkets have urged unions in the industry to help cut labor costs, a key element in expanding profit margins.

In New York City, large numbers of new, undocumented im-migrants who have overstayed their visas have replaced unionized workers in the retail food industry. The most vulnerable workers are employed at independent or franchise stores and are paid in cash "off the books," a term that has become emblematic of the low-wage labor market. Many workers report that they sometimes are not paid at all. Due to their precarious legal status, these workers—often employed as cashiers, stockers, baggers, and deli employees—are afraid to avail themselves of federal- and state-mandated wage and labor protections. At the chain supermarkets in New York City's upscale neighborhoods, most bagging and delivery services are out-sourced to independent labor contractors that almost exclusively hire undocumented French West African immigrants and ignore federal and state labor standards completely. As one worker from Senegal who began delivering groceries for supermarkets in 1995 reported:

> When I started, I was working twelve hours a day, seven days a week, 84 hours a week. We had to depend exclusively on tips. That was my big problem with the labor contractor. I had to agree that I was not going to make trouble with the union or the government. At the end of the week sometimes they don't pay. In the summer [the labor contractor] was not around and his mother said, "We don't have the money. Don't expect to get paid until after the bookkeeper comes back." But they don't have bookkeeper. So when they say they don't have money, or the bookkeeper is sick, that is a lost check. The week after they might give you a check. (interview, anonymous Senegalese deliveryman, September 18, 2003)

During the 1990s, the supermarket industry labor market in New York City was transformed into a "gray market," with one group of predominantly minority native-born workers employed at low wages in the formal economy and another group—immigrants from West Africa—employed in the underground economy where they may or may not get paid. Although undocumented immigrants are officially covered by the same minimum-wage laws as citizens, they are paid well below the minimum (if at all), cannot avail themselves of union benefits such as health insurance and pensions, and do not have access to federal- and state-mandated protections such as disability or unemployment insurance.

In 1999, when West African baggers and deliverymen mounted an organizing drive and an unauthorized strike at supermarkets where RWDSU Local 338 represented other workers, the local stepped in to maintain its exclusive right to represent new categories of workers wherever it had collective bargaining agreements covering some of the other workers in the stores. In April 2003, the Federal Southern District Court in New York City found immigrant deliverymen employed at Gristedes and other stores to be employees covered by federal minimum wage and overtime law (National Immigrant Law Center 2003). Local 338 received widespread praise from immigrant rights organizations for its groundbreaking organizing efforts, despite considerable evidence that the union had actively collaborated in the initial deunionization of the bagging and delivery worker job classifications and did not actively support deliverymen in an independent labor law firm's successful $3 million back-wage lawsuit against Gristede Supermarkets and Duane Reade retail drugstores (National Employment Law Project 2003).

After nearly two decades of exploitative wages and abusive working conditions for baggers and deliverymen in the union stores, Local 338 public relations officer Steve Pezenik told *Newsday* that his union "found many [workers] were earning as little as $1.10 an hour, working a minimum of ten hours a day, and were forced to rent their own uniforms and carts. Most of the victims were *documented* West Africans." Without elaborating, Pezenik added that undocumented Mexican workers are in a more difficult position due to their immigration status, because, unlike Francophone Africans, "[t]hey live in fear every day that the boss will call the INS if they look at organizing" (Vargas 2001).

Even after the West African workers organized themselves and were compelled to join the union, Local 338 failed to cooperate actively in a lawsuit filed by workers through the National Employment Law Project claiming back wages for the half-decade during which labor contractors servicing the supermarkets had underpaid them (interview, Catherine Ruckelshaus, National Employment Law Project, October 2, 2001; Outten & Golden LLP 2001). What emerges from the research is a pattern of union–management cooperation at the expense of workers. In this case, supermarket deliverymen had, during a period of two decades, been all but excluded from the union through the reclassification of their jobs and the local's failure to meet its jurisdictional responsibilities.

Labor Contractors or Foremen?

In the highly capitalized retail food industry, subcontracting provides low-wage replacement workers who perform new tasks or tasks equivalent to those once carried out by workers directly employed by supermarkets. A primary goal of large chain stores is to focus on advertising and marketing and leave production and service functions to subcontracted vendors. But the trend is not as significant as in the large retail chains like it is in consumer goods where outsourcing and offshoring have become the norm.[6]

In the early 1990s, labor contractors in the New York City retail food industry began to engage undocumented immigrants from French West Africa because they were significantly more vulnerable to threats of deportation and therefore willing to work at considerably lower wages and under poorer conditions than were native-born workers. Hiring Francophone West Africans as independent contractors allowed employers to evade minimum wage and overtime requirements and to avoid unionization. As one organizer noted: "We are all undocumented and we are kind of afraid. If we get caught, we all know we could be arrested and deported" (interview, anonymous Malian worker, August 24, 2000). Despite the Local 338 union official's assertion that the workers were legal immigrants, nearly everyone among the twenty-four workers interviewed for this book had overstayed their student or visitor visas. Some had married American women and had therefore gained some legal standing, but most were vulnerable to deportation by the U.S. Bureau of Citizenship and Immigration Services (BCIS). Still, the BCIS has mainly targeted Arab and Muslim immigrants from South Asia and the Middle East. Some Francophone Africans of the Islamic faith interviewed for this study had maintained student visas and have been able to travel with less fear than other immigrants, but after September 11, 2001, restrictions on migration were expanded by U.S. immigration authorities (interview, Khalifa [no last name given], October 14, 2003).

An important feature of subcontracting is the ambiguous employment relationship created between the firm and the workers. Ostensibly in business for themselves, baggers and delivery workers typically are engaged as independent contractors but are directed, ordered, and fired by the store's management. Subcontractors hire the workers, pay them for deliveries, and formally dismiss workers who are in fact discharged by supermarket management. As "nonworkers," deliverymen are told by contractors they are not protected by labor law, and thus escape the notice of government labor agencies and unions.[7] That workers are designated as independent contractors does not matter to the supermarkets. Despite their so-called autonomy, they are still treated as workers. As newcomers to the United States, most workers are unaware that they really are protected by labor laws.

Under this scheme, the labor subcontractor does not dictate the work routine of delivery workers, but is responsible for establishing and enforcing the work rules applied by supermarket management. Nevertheless, most of the seventeen Francophone African delivery workers interviewed for this study said they were essentially told by supermarket managers to perform tasks unrelated to bagging and delivery. As one worker recounts: "One manager at a store asked me to clean windows, to sweep, to mop the floor, something you are not paid for because you don't work for them. They'd even ask you to do the garbage. When customers come, the manager tells you to bag groceries. If you don't do it, you are out" (anonymous interview, August 2003).

Charlie Bauer, owner of City Express Delivery (also known as B&B Delivery Service), initially ran his business out of a Key Food Supermarket in East Harlem and emerged as the first subcontractor of bagging and delivery services in the early 1990s. The City Express Delivery office was located in a neighborhood in which French West African immigrants had settled in significant numbers. To sign up for employment, immigrants applied for work at Bauer's office and were then assigned to jobs in Manhattan, Brooklyn, the Bronx, and Queens. Some workers entered the industry in the early 1990s and worked as baggers and deliverymen in the local retail food industry for up to eight years. After several years, the INS shut down Bauer's office, at which point he simply moved into the basement of a nearby building (interview, French West African worker, October 2000).

Scott Weinstein and Steven Pilavan ran the other major New York City food delivery labor contractor, registered independently as both Hudson Delivery and Chelsea Trucking. The businesses supposedly operated out of Pilavan's apartment on Manhattan's Upper

West Side. Weinstein and Pilavan were more successful than Bauer in gaining contracts with large retail food clients and avoiding government detection.[8] Weinstein's clients included Associated Supermarket, Key Food Supermarket, Western Beef, and Fairway, a chain of three upscale supermarkets. A legal complaint filed by the National Employment Law Project (2000) contended that the migrant workers were treated as independent businessmen so that their employers contributed nothing to Social Security, kept no records of the hours they worked, and paid them subminimum wages and no overtime pay for hours worked in excess of forty hours each week and ten hours in each day.

According to Mamadou Camara, an immigrant worker from Mali who became the leader of the deliverymen's organizing effort: "Weinstein always moved his offices to beat the system—to avoid the INS—and he doesn't want to pay minimum wages. He uses a cell phone number as his business phone, allowing him to change his location to avoid workers who are still owed money" (interview, December 22, 1999). The ambiguity of the relationship between labor contractors and supermarkets confuses the workers as to who their legitimate employer is, thereby making it more difficult for them to organize. One worker described the dual nature of this employment relationship:

> We work for both the supermarket and the subcontractor. The supermarket manager gives us direct orders. But they are the joint employers. We were hired by Weinstein to deliver groceries. But the supermarket manager says we have to bag groceries for shoppers when we are in the supermarket. When there are no deliveries, we are always doing a task for the supermarket, such as helping shoppers with bagging, carrying groceries to the car. The only difference is that the [supermarkets] refuse to pay us for our labor and [the subcontractor] pays us peanuts for lifting and carrying groceries to walk-up apartments. Rain or shine we have to walk sometimes ten to fifteen blocks to deliver these groceries. Any complaint from the customers is forwarded to the supermarket manager, who speaks frequently with the subcontractor. If the customer complains about a delivery worker, the supermarket's manager can fire the worker without consulting the subcontractor. (anonymous interview, December 23, 1999)

Workers are required to wear uniforms issued by the subcontractor that fit as aprons over their clothes and identify them as supermarket deliverers, for which they must pay $15 to the labor contractor. When a uniform becomes stained and tattered and can no longer be used, the deliveryman must pay to have it replaced. Workers also are required to maintain a pushcart, which is rented from the subcontractors for $5 a week. Subcontracted deliverymen work longer hours than in-house employees. They are required to work from the time the store opens in the morning until it closes in the evening, sometimes more than eighty hours per week. Deliveries are made by foot and may be up to twenty city blocks away; they usually take from thirty minutes to more than an hour to complete. According to the workers interviewed for this study, it is extremely difficult—if not impossible—to complete more than one or two deliveries in an hour.

Nelson Resto, a business agent with Local 338, described a typical winter workday for a deliveryman subcontracted to the supermarkets:

> Chelsea Trucking [a.k.a Hudson Delivery] was hired by Food Emporium [a New York–based supermarket owned by A&P] as a subcontractor and claimed not to be aware of these practices. To make a long story short, they were charging these employees for the uniforms, carts, and coats—they never had coats—these guys had to wear fleece. The fleece was warm, but in the winter it got cold—ten degrees below zero—that's ridiculous, pushing 120 pounds on a cart ten, twelve, fifteen blocks. Guys wouldn't even eat until they earned enough to buy breakfast. (interview, September 14, 2001)

Interviews with workers reveal that both Bauer and Weinstein repeatedly maintained two work conditions: (1) the workers were employed neither by the supermarket nor by the delivery agency, but were considered independent contractors in business for themselves; and (2) as independent contractors, deliverymen were told they were not entitled to a minimum wage or overtime pay.

Despite these claims, deliverymen are in fact employees as defined by federal and state labor law: Workers are asked to arrive at a specific hour and stay for a designated period of time; are directed to perform bagging, delivery, and other tasks by supermarket management; and are unable to pass any of the costs of their labor on to the customer. Moreover, with the exception of renting carts and buying uniforms, workers do not invest any capital, nor can they buy or sell any franchise or investment in the operation. Although U.S. labor law is vague in defining the difference between an owner and a worker, according to one interpretation, independent contractors must be subject to the risk of monetary loss (Stalnaker 1993). Even though the deliverymen do not fit even the broadest definition of being in business for themselves, when first hired, most accepted the classification without protest. Subsequently, in violation of labor law, the workers can be subjected to monetary loss and made responsible for renting their carts.

A delivery worker's ability to generate income from deliveries and tips is limited by supermarket managers, who usually ask for more workers than are required to bag groceries, thus cutting into the number of runs one can make. In interviews, twelve workers consistently cited the requirement to bag as well as deliver groceries. The bagging requirement contradicts the supermarket managers' contention that the deliverymen are independent contractors rather than in-house employees. It also contradicts the supermarkets' rationale for cutting previously unionized in-house jobs. In-house unionized workers performed the bagging and delivery operations at Food Emporium until the mid-1980s, when the chain started contracting out the work to intermediaries who, in turn, hired delivery workers—as independent contractors.

The new subcontracting arrangements came in response to what even the Local 338 newspaper reported in the early 1980s as a decline in worker productivity, which had not increased fast enough in the retail food industry despite the introduction of checkout scanners and other labor-saving technology. Between 1980 and 2000, the national supermarket industry pursued alternative labor cost-cutting methods, including contracting work to outside agencies (interview, Pat Purcell, UFCW Local 1500, October 23, 2001; Strunsky 1983a). The subcontracting scheme took hold through the confluence of supermarket industry restructuring and spiraling immigration to New York City. Unable to find any other work after their arrival in the early 1990s, unwary French West African immigrants—desperate for money—were persuaded to perform bagging and delivery at wages that amounted to 10 to 15 percent of the compensation paid to unionized workers in the industry—or no pay at all.

Local 338 and Repression of the Deliverymen

In the early 1980s, reports began to circulate that the supermarket industry would be facing low profitability in the years to come. Although the industry had recently achieved cost savings by creating operational efficiencies, instituting stringent financial controls, closing stores, and introducing technology such as scanners, industry analysts believed that labor costs had to be further lowered to ensure future profitability. At A&P, executives argued that even as these cost-saving efforts ran their course and the company emerged from a long recession, there would be a need to extract greater savings from a mature industry (Great Atlantic & Pacific Tea Company, Inc. 1984).

Upon hearing these reports, Local 338 argued in its newspaper, *Local 338 News*, that despite the negative projections for future growth, supermarket industry profits had accelerated in the early 1980s and that coming out of the recession, the industry was likely to prosper once again (Strunsky 1983b). As an older industry, retail supermarkets typically do relatively well during economic downturns, but profits generally stagnate during economic recoveries as investment goes into newer industries that have not saturated the market.

In May 1983, Local 338 contradicted its earlier position and acknowledged the need to compromise by increasing worker productivity. Citing a study in *Supermarket News*, an industry trade journal, *Local 338 News* reported there was little room for technological productivity increases, and that productivity gains therefore had to be achieved through changes in the nature of work: "With top industrial concerns across the nation stressing the importance of productivity by workers, some employers, especially in the food industry, are linking productivity to human beings, rather than computers, and are talking about 'people power.' . . . [P]roductivity improvement efforts may be shifting away from technology and towards human resources" (Strunsky 1983c).

In addition, the union newspaper cited a study on productivity by the Food Industry Management Program of the University of Southern California, pointing to six general requirements for enhancing profitability. Among these was the need for human resource departments to integrate an "incentives and reward program" into management strategies—unequivocally an antiunion position because it replaces union-negotiated wages, benefits, and job descriptions covering all unionized workers with a reward system for individual workers.

These reports were made as Local 338 was negotiating with regional supermarkets, culminating in the summer of 1983 in what the union called the "best-ever contract," with higher health and pension contributions and wage increases. Union president Emanuel Laub praised the agreement for making no concessions to employers: "In this era of contract give-backs we faced numerous obstacles with employers, chief among which was the proposal that we give up conditions gained over many years. . . . However, from the outset I made a pledge to our members at area meetings and subsequently I told management that there would be no give-backs, and there were none" (Strunsky 1983c).

What Laub failed to mention was that, at about the same time, supermarkets that employed Local 338 members began to contract out bagging and delivery services—jobs that previously had been classified as part of the bargaining unit—as a cost-cutting measure. Evidence of the subcontracting was noted by a union informant who claimed that RWDSU Local 338 had failed to enforce its collective bargaining agreements covering Gristede's supermarkets, which were divided with Local 1500, with each union covering workers at half the stores (interview, Pat Purcell, UFCW Local 1500, October 23, 2001). Two years later, in a column in the union newspaper, Laub took pride in the fact that Local 338 had not engaged in concessionary bargaining that allowed the formation of a two-tier workforce—that is, hiring new workers at rates lower than those paid to employees with seniority (Laub 1985). Though Local 338 officials interviewed about the details of the altered status of bagging and delivery operations in the mid-1980s said they were unaware of the changes in the relationship, previous union contracts negotiated by the union in the 1950s through 1970s covered the deliverymen as workers. In many cases, the union counted workers as members but they were not covered by wages and benefits negotiated in its contracts, a practice the union is reported to continue to this day (anonymous interview, December 2002).[9]

Contracting Drugstore Delivery Workers

In the mid-1990s, the subcontracting of delivery services to independent labor contractors extended beyond the supermarket industry to other retail outlets with high consumer demand for home delivery of goods. At the same time, retail drug outlets began to expand throughout New York City, frequently providing many of the same food and household goods available at supermarkets. Competition among the three major drugstore chains—Duane Reade, CVS, and Rite-Aid—is particularly fierce in New York City, where pharmaceutical and personal items command significantly higher profit margins than do food products. Thus, at prime New York City locations, chain drugstores have replaced supermarkets that could not afford spiraling commercial rents.

Delivery became a major service of the new drugstores, and much of this work was subcontracted to the same independent labor contractors that serviced the supermarkets. Although carrying pharmaceuticals is less physically demanding than carting groceries, drugstore deliverymen earn even less than their supermarket counterparts because there are fewer deliveries to be made. One worker who worked for Hudson Delivery and primarily made prescription deliveries for Duane Reade said that he was forced to constantly engage in work outside the scope of his job without pay and was directed by managers to carry out many of the tasks performed by regular hourly employees, including unloading trucks and breaking down cardboard cartons for disposal (interview, Siaka Diakite, April 1, 2000). The worker, aware of the earnings differential between drugstore and supermarket deliverymen, asked the labor contractor for a transfer to the Food Emporium chain, knowing that he would make more deliveries and thus earn more money.

In January 2003, two hundred deliverymen who were paid less than $3 an hour working at Duane Reade won a ruling issued by Judge Alvin K. Hellerstein of the Southern District Court of New York that entitled the workers to make $5.15 an hour. While the store had the right to contract services, Judge Hellerstein ruled that "it did not have the right to use [outsourcing] as a way to evade its obligations under the Fair Labor Standards Act" (National Employment Law Project, 2003).

Subcontractor Recruitment Networks

The primary means of recruitment among West African delivery workers is through established networks formed by contractors and reinforced by the local community of immigrants. In a practice that has become standard within other labor market niches, employers typically hire one ethnic group as a means of creating uniformity in the workforce. Although almost all supermarket deliverymen in New York City are French West Africans, the two predominant groups among them—Malians and Senegalese—tend to socialize and find work on the basis of their nationality. The isolation of workers from other groups keeps them from finding jobs elsewhere and becoming informed about conditions outside their industry sector. As the delivery workers' organizing effort gained ground, managers attempted to weaken ties among them. One worker identified as an activist at a Food Emporium on the Upper West Side was transferred to another in Tribeca, where he had fewer ties to other workers. Conversations with workers reveal that the contractors regularly shifted them from store to store at least once a year, after which relations of solidarity had to be nurtured and deepened once again.

Camara recalls Weinstein telling him that he "prefers and only employs Africans because we are nicer, follow orders, and have never challenged his motives or actions. I was made supervisor because [the owner] knows I influence the behavior of the rest of the workers" (interview, January 18, 2000). Other workers interviewed said that although they did not like the job, they continued to refer family members and friends because alternate employment was unavailable. According to one worker, "Everyone in our building is either a deliveryman or a messenger. We cannot find work anywhere else but in these kinds of menial jobs" (interview, anonymous Gabonese worker, October 18, 2001).

Workers for both major labor contractors were paid by the delivery. As late as fall 1999, according to workers, Bauer paid as little as fifty cents per delivery, while workers for Hudson Delivery said they were paid from $1.00 to $1.25. Workers employed by Hudson Delivery at Food Emporium markets in 1999 said they took home an average of $70 to $80 for a seventy-two-hour week, working twelve hours a day, six days a week. In addition, the deliverymen said that they earned about $10 to $15 per week in tips. In total, workers averaged about one-quarter of the federal minimum hourly wage, with no overtime pay.

Because pay was based on a piecework system, workers competed among themselves to deliver more groceries to customers, further increasing worker productivity. According to one anonymous respondent from the Ivory Coast who worked for Hudson Delivery at Food Emporium:

> Many of the workers do not see that [the owner] is not paying them the right wages. They feel he is a good person for giving them the job and for throwing a barbecue party for them during the summer. The fact is that Scott [Weinstein] is exploiting us. He started to pay us fifty cents a delivery in 1996, but increased our wages as the years went by, up to eighty cents and then $1.25 per delivery. (interview, October 22, 2001)

Most workers complained that they could not survive on the income, much less send remittances to relatives in their home countries—one of the most important reasons many had traveled to the United States in the first place. The worker cited above, who had been a deliveryman at Food Emporium before being dismissed for helping to organize the walkout, said of the supermarket managers and subcontractors, "They do not care about how we survive on this kind of money. . . . They want you to be always working nonstop, so that they can make more money off of us" (interview, October 22, 2001).

Low pay translates into overcrowded conditions in living quarters. It is not unusual for seven to ten French West African workers to live in the same one-bedroom apartment, and frequently spouses and children share the same quarters, sometimes with multiple families. Said one recent immigrant from Mali, "I cannot afford my own place because I do not have the money. I live with other workers. I do not like it, but I do not have a choice" (interview, Mamadou Bah, June 15, 2000).

The Organizing Drive

The deliverymen's organizing campaign was an autonomous effort on the part of the workers to improve their wages and working conditions. Individual deliverymen complained about their working conditions from the beginning of their employment in the early 1990s. Most of the workers did not know they could improve their conditions by affiliating with an existing local or international union. Being aware of the highly exploitative environment in which they worked, the French West African immigrants ameliorated their abusive conditions through self-organizing on the job.

According to workers' accounts in interviews and legal depositions, both Bauer and Weinstein threatened to report them to the INS if they complained about their conditions to unions, legal counsel, or public authorities. Moreover, the labor contractors told workers they could not trust the union. According to one worker, "We were told that if we signed up for the union, the union would take our cards that we sign and hand them in to the INS (interview, anonymous delivery worker, December 30, 2001)." Still, according to African workers, union representatives completed ignored them while visiting supermarket managers.

The first step in the process of organizing was self-education and consciousness raising. An early part of the effort was to dispel workers' expectations of earning significant income fairly rapidly with the stark reality of the abusive workplace conditions they faced as contract laborers. This reality was exacerbated by their categorization as self-employed entrepreneurs, and therefore as their own exploiters: The longer and harder they worked, the more money they could make. This image conflicted with the reality that they were workers—not independent businessmen—who owned nothing but their labor.

The next step was to identify the perpetrators of this exploitation. Initially, the workers were unclear about which actors were responsible for their dire circumstances: labor contractors, supermarket chains, or customers. The ill-defined status of the deliverymen as independent contractors compounded the problem of identifying the cause of low wages and poor conditions. The pejorative designation "alien" for undocumented immigrants could be appropriated to describe how French West Africans felt about their new environment. In interviews, most found New York City to be truly alien surroundings. As the first wave of immigrants from French West Africa, these workers had no previous reference group from which they could learn to navigate their way around the city and the local labor market, unlike recent Eastern European and Latin American immigrants. Thus, they needed to understand how the labor–management structure in the industry functioned to undermine their power.

In interviews, West African workers said that one of their major priorities in organizing was to improve their conditions of work and increase their remuneration. Some believed that their ill treatment reflected racist attitudes of contractors, managers, and customers. According to Camara:

> They made us feel inferior because of the color of our skin. [Scott Weinstein] said he only employs Africans because we do whatever he will say without complaining. I was not a slave in Africa, and I refuse to be one here. Though I need this job to survive, I also believe that my dignity is important. Scott makes derogatory comments toward workers in English while shaking their hands. Since many of the delivery workers do not speak English, they think he is complimenting their work. That made me angry, and when I told Scott to stop doing that, he tells me to lighten up and continues to ridicule workers in English. It got to the point that I began telling workers to use their days off to go to schools to study English. (interview, February 23, 2000)

The sentiment that race was a primary factor in their poor treatment by managers was articulated by all seventeen deliverymen interviewed.

The third step in the drive was to form an organization capable of confronting the supermarket managers and labor contractors. No outside union-based agency existed that the workers were aware of and could trust, so in early 1999 the organizers began to form their own. The initial rumblings began in the spring and summer of that year, when the deliverymen became vocal about poor working conditions and low wages and aware of their rights as workers. Remarkably, the learning process for these French-speaking workers did not result from outside labor organizations advising the workers of their rights, but from their own self-education in meeting together. A general perception prevailed among both the leaders of the organizing effort and the rank-and-file workers that the only way to change their conditions was to directly confront their employers at the supermarkets with demands for improved wages and working conditions.

The absence of institutional or political recourse contributed to a general atmosphere of on-the-job syndicalism among the deliverymen, and indeed among thousands of other recent immigrant workers hired through labor contractors in New York City (Ness 1998). The workers believed that no existing social or political organization was willing to defend their interests; they therefore had to take action directly at their workplaces. This detachment from existing unions was compounded by the lack of English-language fluency needed to negotiate the terms of their employment. For some, their status as independent contractors contributed to a belief that they had no right to complain to store management, but could bargain only with the contractors.

In the preceding two years, some workers had sought assistance from Local 338—the union that represented other workers in the supermarkets—with no success. Three interviewed workers were aware of the benefits of union membership, but did not know that a union already represented workers in the stores (interviews, anonymous workers, July 8, 1999). In many supermarkets represented by Local 338, workers from other backgrounds frequently are unaware of their status as union members, owing to the failure of the local to service the contract. An example of this neglect was seen in the summer of 2000, when a supermarket stock boy was crushed to death by a trash compactor. When, in the aftermath, UNITE Local 169 stepped in to represent workers at the West Side Market (the store in which the accident took place), the owner claimed that Local 338 already represented workers there.[10] Efforts by individual workers throughout Manhattan and Brooklyn to reach out to other labor organizations had elicited some response, but had not proceeded very far because the stores were already represented by a union, the organizers lacked resources, and the mostly immigrant workers feared retribution from management if they protested their conditions.

The Quest for Legal Redress

When a Senegalese worker complained about working conditions in the supermarkets to the New York affiliate of Jobs with Justice (a nongovernmental organization that had maintained close links with the AFL-CIO since the early 1990s), that group became the first labor organization to hear about the stirrings among delivery workers.[11] The worker was employed at a Gristede's supermarket as a contractor for City Express Delivery. Formerly a flight attendant with a West African air carrier, he had an advanced degree in literature and had lived in the United States since the early 1990s. When he first lodged a complaint against Charlie Bauer, the deliveryman claimed he received fifty cents per delivery, plus tips of less than $10 per day. He said that when he had first entered the industry he knew the wages were exceedingly low and violated U.S. wage and hour rules, but had no alternative and thought conditions would improve. One worker said that before taking the job on, he was told that wages in supermarkets were better than retail clothing stores where many African workers are also employed (interview, anonymous Senegalese worker, September 18, 2003).

Despite the persistence of low wages at supermarkets that contracted work through City Express Delivery, workers at the stores were unwilling to support the Senegalese worker's effort to take legal action against Bauer to collect back wages because they feared losing even the pittance they were making and faced constant threats of deportation from the labor contractor.[12] The Senegalese worker was threatened physically by his coworkers, who feared that if he complained, trouble would befall them all, exposing the entire labor-contracting scheme and denying them their only source of income.

Coworkers at Gristede's supermarkets told him they needed some source of income and feared that even if he complained on his own behalf, they would all lose their jobs. The National Employment Law Project (NELP)—a nonprofit organization advocating on behalf of low-wage workers and the unemployed through litigation, policy advocacy, public education, and support for organizing—wanted to pursue the case through the courts, but coworkers at City Express Delivery supermarkets would have none of it, fearing exposure, loss of work, and deportation (interview, Catherine Ruckelshaus, October 2, 2001; interview, Jaques Legrand Ngouvi, September 23, 2001, interview, Justin Obiang, September 26, 2001).

Nevertheless, NELP brought the case to New York State Attorney General Eliot Spitzer's office. Due to the lack of support among deliverymen, it was difficult to sign up a sufficient number of workers to develop a legal case. Initially, there was nothing NELP could do other than draft a legal complaint and encourage workers to join a lawsuit against their employers. Because most were unwilling to bring a back-wage claim against the delivery company and the supermarkets publicly, and due to a lack of resources at the attorney general's Labor Bureau, the effort to recoup millions of dollars in back pay and bring the industry into compliance with federal and state wage laws stalled and appeared moribund. Lacking reliable outside support capable of convincing the deliverymen that they could win a battle against the supermarkets and labor contractors, leaders began an effort to organize the workers autonomously.

The organization was achieved through the reinforcement of social ties in the stores and neighborhoods where workers lived. With no union or legal assistance in planning an organizing strategy and eventual strike, the campaign advanced due to four primary factors:

(1) The development of a cadre of leadership among the workers, critical in convincing workers of their rights and the need to take action;
(2) The unabated exploitation of workers and the channeling of their indignation and frustration into action;
(3) A worker–community alliance that targeted businesses directly, a strategy that socialized the conflict within the neighborhoods of Upper Manhattan and throughout the city; and
(4) A legal strategy seeking back wages through federal and state labor enforcement agencies.

Mounting Discontent

The mobilization that culminated in the October 1999 strike by supermarket delivery workers began the previous spring as mounting discontent over wages and working conditions gave rise to a series of meetings among workers to devise a strategy to improve their situation. An effort to broker an agreement between the leadership of the nascent African Workers Association and supermarket management failed, and the workers felt they had no recourse but to strike to demonstrate their plight to the community to improve wages and conditions.

Workers at the stores targeted for labor actions were employed by Weinstein's Hudson Delivery; a majority of them were Malian. In early 1998, the workers first sought to negotiate better working conditions with Weinstein. Thirty-year-old immigrant Mamadou Camara from Bamako, Mali, who had entered the industry in 1995 as a Key Food supermarket deliveryman, led the effort. One of the few immigrant deliverymen to have been employed by both Weinstein and Bauer, Camara was fluent in English and had risen through the ranks of Hudson Delivery to become a supervisor at one of the busiest supermarkets in Manhattan—the Food Emporium on Broadway at 68th Street, a large store near Lincoln Center that caters to a high-income clientele (*New York Times* 2000). Having risen through the ranks himself, Camara was sensitive to the conditions faced by the workers.

As dispatcher of the baggers and deliverymen, Camara sent workers out to the predominantly luxury buildings in the surrounding neighborhood, for which he was paid the federal minimum wage of $5.15 per hour, working from early morning until late at night. His job was particularly demanding due to the large number of baggers and deliverymen who worked at the store. Unlike some smaller markets that subcontracted work to City Express Delivery, dozens of deliverymen worked at Food Emporium, as well as at other large supermarket chains controlled by Hudson Delivery.

Camara was not a mere cog in management's continued exploitation of the deliverymen, but rather a consummate organizer who maintained contact with the leaders among the workers, many of whom were fellow immigrants from Mali. According to Catherine Ruckelshaus, the chief NELP litigator:

> Mamadou always was talking with all the workers. Because he's so smart and good at what he does, he had become sort of a supervisor, but not quite, because management knew that he cared and advocated on behalf of the deliverymen. He knew everybody at the store, and having done the same work over the years, knew that the operation wasn't right. He knew that the money they were getting paid wasn't right. (interview, October 2, 2001)

In the spring of 1999, at the urging of deliverymen at supermarkets throughout Manhattan, Camara pressed Weinstein about improving wages and conditions. Weinstein told Camara that his company was receiving so little money per delivery from Food Emporium that he was unable to raise the pay of the deliverymen; instead, he suggested that Camara directly ask Food Emporium management for an increase in compensation. In effect, Weinstein acknowledged to Camara that Hudson Delivery was formed primarily to serve as a front to pass wages from Food Emporium to the deliverymen. According to Ruckelshaus:

> That just shows how Scotty was basically the foreman; he was just a pass-through. He is not another business. He is really just Food Emporium's foreman for the labor-intensive piece of their work. Mamadou went to Scotty the foreman. He's just like a farm labor contractor, a garment shop guy. He is just doing the piece of it that is labor-intensive. (interview, October 2, 2001)

Told by Weinstein that wages and working conditions could not be improved, Camara went to the manager at the Broadway and 68th Street store, who told him that if he incorporated himself as a contractor he could compete against Weinstein for the business. What the manager did not say was that this might well have the effect of bidding down the already meager wages. Unaware of this possibility, Camara was encouraged by the supermarket to incorporate as a business so that he would be on better footing to negotiate on behalf of the workers to improve conditions and increase compensation. But it would be virtually impossible for Camara to pay workers anywhere near the minimum wage. Moreover, he was unwilling to serve as an intermediary like Weinstein and Bauer, further exploiting the workers by taking a cut out of the supermarket's payments before passing them along.

Lawyers for the supermarkets responded to the class-action lawsuit for payment of back wages by asserting that Camara was not interested in the plight of the workers, but was simply trying to compete with Weinstein in the delivery business. In both personal interviews and depositions in lawsuits against the supermarkets and the contractors, however, Camara claimed that he was only one of many workers seeking to improve the wages and working conditions of the deliverymen. As a supervisor, Camara was placed in a contradictory position, but he was unwilling to become a labor contractor. His intention to support the organization of workers is borne out by his statements, corroborated by workers, and—most notably—authenticated through the unprecedented labor organizing effort that culminated in a massive walkout and protest.

The Strike

A&P, Food Emporium's parent company, was unwilling to improve the deliverymen's compensation package, and store negotiators rebuffed the workers' efforts to press for more money. Frustrated by the lack of progress in talks with both Weinstein and Food Emporium, the workers began meeting to plan strikes at several large supermarkets. According to Camara:

> I couldn't do anything else. I thought that the entire [delivery scheme] was crazy. I tried to talk to my direct boss, Scotty, and he said there was not enough money unless Food Emporium pays him more. I went to Food Emporium, and they're not talking to me. So I spoke to the workers, proposed a strike. We had meetings with workers from all the stores on the West Side and the East Side. . . . We went on strike because it is the only recourse we have. I have always talked to the guys about a strike. I tell them that if we can come together as one body and ask Scott to pay us the proper wages he will, but if he refuses we shall go on strike. (interview, November 18, 2000)

Initially, worker appeals for higher wages fell on deaf ears. Some workers went so far as to report the organizing effort to Weinstein. Said Camara:

> With the help of other delivery workers who agreed with me, we joined forces to bring the rest into understanding the importance of the strike to them. I set up six meetings over the course of six months in my house in Harlem. The first time only a few people came. As we started holding more meetings, more and more workers showed up. I passed out a letter written in both French and English to each worker telling them about their rights as a worker and as a human being. I also spoke in my house to them about Africa and the lives that Scott is subjecting them to. (interview, November 18, 2000)

The workers were responsive to this appeal to class solidarity based on cultural and racial discrimination. According to Camara:

> I told them this is not the America we read about in Africa. We are not slaves, but Scotty pays and treats us like [we are] because of the color of our skin. Most importantly, I emphasized to them that it is only through a movement or as a group that they can attain the rights and benefits from our employer. I also asked the workers if they were slaves in Africa. They answered no. My life was good in Africa until I got here doing this job, and the same is true for the rest of them. You have to appeal to their inner and personal side in order for them to agree to come together as a group. (interview, November 18, 2000)

The deliverymen, once organized, went on a two-day strike and boycott from October 27 to October 29, 1999, extensively disrupting the supermarkets and gaining widespread publicity in the local press, including the *New York Times* and Manhattan weekly newspapers. The deliverymen—about one hundred in all—marched from supermarket to supermarket on the affluent Upper West Side and Upper East Side, protesting against their employers and urging a consumer boycott. Their placards exposed their feelings about their working conditions; two read "We Are Slaves" and "Please Help Set Us Free." The *New York Times* pointed to the African workers' naïveté and lack of organizing experience demonstrated by their failure to seek union help with the campaign, without recognizing that the union had already failed to protect them.

The strike represented one of the most audacious labor actions seen in New York City during the past decade by a labor or non-labor organization (Jacobs 1999). Notwithstanding employer threats to fire the deliverymen and report them to the INS, workers continued the public strike and protest for two days. In fact, the strike roused a number of local unions that previously had not been aware of the workers' plight, including UNITE Local 169, which was at the time mobilizing Mexican food workers into a broad campaign against smaller greengrocery and deli owners (see Chapter 4). As a result of the greengrocery campaign, Local 169 had earned a reputation for its willingness to mobilize the most exploited immigrant workers in the city.

The Back-Wage Campaign and Contract

The October 1999 protests extended throughout Manhattan to dozens of retail food and drug outlets where delivery work was contracted out to Weinstein. As soon as the strike began, Weinstein initiated negotiations with the workers. Each night after the protests, meetings between Weinstein and the strikers took place. Dozens of workers turned out to protest on the second day, and they did not go back to work until Weinstein promised to improve conditions through negotiations with the workers.

Once the strike action was completed, the workers sought assistance from UNITE Local 169, which met with the strike organizers and helped them form the African Workers Association. However, RWDSU Local 338 immediately put a stop to the competing union's effort by invoking jurisdictional authority within its supermarkets. Local 169 withdrew its organizing effort, and Local 338 began a process of damage control, including hiring a French-speaking business representative to "cool out" the workers.

During the winter of 1999–2000, the labor contractors were concerned that delivery workers might unionize and claim back wages with the help of outside legal representation. In his sworn testimony Camara stated:

> On or about February 9th or 10th, I received another series of calls from delivery workers who informed me that Scotty and his supervisors were in the stores asking [the workers] to show them immigration documents and to sign papers stating they were independent contractors. Some of the workers did not read or sign statements, but some did, saying they were afraid of losing their jobs. The workers who I called were nervous and concerned. (sworn testimony, March 6, 2000)

In addition to the labor contractors' direct threat to turn the striking workers over to the INS, the workers alleged that after the wildcat strike, Weinstein's lawyer had "rounded up [deliverymen] . . . in vans, [and the workers were taken] into their midtown offices and interrogated" (interview, Mamadou Camara, November 18, 2000). Weinstein regularly checked workers' immigration papers in an effort to intimidate them from filing back-wage complaints in court. The regular scrutiny of their immigration status had the effect of intimidating the workers into continuing their employment at substandard wages and under exploitative conditions, which they saw as preferable to the possibility of deportation.

Because Local 338 already had representation and collective bargaining agreements in the supermarkets, the union did not even pursue elections for delivery worker representation, nor did the supermarket managers call for them. Instead, in the face of public scrutiny, the union initiated collective bargaining negotiations with Weinstein for a separate contract to cover the deliverymen. Four months later, in March 2000, this culminated in a contract that transformed the deliverymen from independent contractors into employees of Hudson Delivery. Rather than being paid on a piecework basis, workers were to receive $4.50 per hour—the minimum wage for workers who receive tips. In federal court, delivery workers at Hudson Delivery and other markets were found to be entitled to these labor standards. In addition, full-time workers became eligible for health coverage and paid holidays. A year later, Food Emporium brought its baggers and deliverers in-house as regular unionized employees, while Weinstein continued to employ deliverymen at other stores.

Local 338 explicitly avoided engaging organizers of the strike and the newly formed African Workers Association, instead reaching out to African workers who were not active in the strike. According to Mamadou Bah, a Malian strike leader working at Food Emporium:

> Well, we have a union representing us now, but the union does not meet with us to see how things are. I see the union and Scott meet all the time, laughing and making jokes together. I do not see any difference, because they are Scotty's friends and not ours. They only take money from our check weekly for representing us. (interview, June 15, 2000)

In interviews, Local 338 representatives maintained that the delivery worker campaign was testimony to the union's new emphasis on organizing. The union spokesperson, Steve Pezenik, refused to respond to inquiries as to why the leaders of the organizing and strike effort were excluded from negotiating a settlement with the supermarkets. Pezenik also said that he was not authorized to respond to any questions surrounding the Gristede's case, or why the union thought workers should not seek full compensation for back wages (interviews, Steve Pezenik and other union staff members, Local 338, September 14, 2001).

Thus, although worker self-activity was the primary force in advancing the union-led campaign to improve wages and labor conditions at the supermarkets, workers—and especially organizers—were largely excluded from union–management negotiations. Nevertheless, worker activists continued to pursue a legal strategy set in motion principally by NELP, which filed lawsuits against the supermarkets and labor contractors for back wages—including the case against Gristede's and Hudson Delivery initiated by the Senegalese worker. The suits alleged that the labor-subcontracting scheme was used to defraud the workers of their entitlement under the Fair Labor Standards Act of 1938 to receive minimum wages and overtime pay. NELP filed a claim against three supermarket chains and a regional drugstore chain on behalf of approximately five hundred workers; the class was subsequently expanded to include about one thousand delivery workers who had been employed by the supermarkets and labor contractors in the preceding eight years.

Organizing and Union Boundaries in New York City's Food Industry

The West African rank-and-file organizing campaign raises important questions about how unions can positively and negatively influence immigrant organizing. Whereas the mobilization and strike demonstrated the militancy and boldness of the deliverymen, the intervention of the existing union impeded workers' potential gains. Indeed, African delivery workers noted that the union business agents that visited the supermarkets never even talked to them. Local 338 responded to the worker insurgency by replacing the initial leaders with new token leaders who could be manipulated by union leadership. Thus, the union prevented the expansion of worker mobilization and became an obstacle to workers seeking to organize to improve their wages and conditions.

This chapter challenges the view put forward by supporters of the institutionalized labor movement that "any union is better than no union." The case study of French West African deliverymen calls this position into question, since it demonstrates that sometimes unions are complicit with management in repressing workers by failing to represent their interests on the shop floor. In this case, delivery workers were unaware that Local 338 had the power to enforce its jurisdictional rights at the supermarkets. Further, this example points to the need for unions to encourage rank-and-file activism and provide support to *all* workers in the establishment, rather than a choice few.

Workers could, in theory, improve their conditions by compelling unions to represent their interests, which the deliverymen in effect did. But while the union in this case responded, it did so by channeling workers' activity into a bureaucratic cul de sac, effectively stifling their further organizational development. The ultimate failure of the insurgency among French West African delivery workers—one where wages increased but true representation was not achieved—reveals a crucial problem inherent to U.S. industrial unionism. Organized labor today does not follow through with the "wall-to-wall" concept of labor representation, which replaced the old nineteenth century AFL concept of craft representation that encouraged multiple unions in a single workplace, each with a discrete craft jurisdiction.

The wall-to-wall concept of unionism could incorporate independent forms of worker representation within the same facility through encouraging multiple forms of rank-and-file representation and organization. As the delivery worker organizing drive demonstrates, the failure to represent on the basis of wall-to-wall units created industrial hierarchies within unions at the same facility, while destroying worker autonomy in narrowly based unions with the artificial patina of workplace and industry-wide representation. Local 338 is a conservative, bureaucratic service union that showed no interest in actually pursuing militant on-the-job organizing to defend and extend workers' interests. The union did not allow the formation of independent representation of deliverymen, blunting the potential power of workers in the grocery industry. Local 338 continues to misrepresent deliverymen by isolating them into craft-like categories.

The African delivery worker mobilization reveals that unions have responded slowly or not at all to the rapid changes in their labor markets. To maintain wage and workplace standards in a shifting labor market, unions must understand how employers have taken advantage of unregulated transnational migration in order to lower labor costs in the seemingly resilient service sector. Unions in the United States *do* realize that labor and capital flows are inescapable, and that they therefore must better understand how employers shape labor markets by hiring new groups of workers who have little connection to the past. However, unions do little to act on the reality by resisting business closures.

Because Local 338 fails to mobilize rank-and-file worker organizations on an industry-wide basis, the union has become increasingly irrelevant to workers as demonstrated by its unwillingness to mobilize independent centers of labor power at individual worksites. Unions need to support independent worker organizing as a way that allows workers to defend their own interests and hopefully rebuild individual unions and the labor movement as a whole.

Union indifference to employer strategies of restructuring and lowering labor costs has not prevented rank-and-file activism and challenges to both management and union power. The delivery-worker insurgency demonstrates that unions can provide invaluable resources and support to isolated class-conscious immigrants organizing against their employers. The ongoing debate about the future shape of national unions must take into account the importance of facilitating independent worker organizing on the job and the vital need to treat workers equally regardless of color, gender, and nationality. Proposals to divvy up labor markets among national unions must take into account the everyday struggles of workers and encourage the formation of strong rank-and-file organizations.

6 Black-Car Drivers: Industrial Restructuring and New Worker Organizing

The previous two chapters' examinations of greengrocery and delivery worker organizing demonstrate that the restructuring of the food service and other industries and the resulting demand for a low-wage, unregulated labor force have established preconditions for mass migration to New York City. Employers and labor contractors have the best of both worlds through a scheme of labor exploitation that both circumvents U.S. immigration law and intimidates workers by using a loophole in the law that is supposed to punish employers who intentionally hire undocumented workers. Most employers hire undocumented workers with little scrutiny of their legal status. It is only after workers organize that employers take advantage of their illegal status to fire them. The unexpected organization of Mexican and West African workers emerged from their resistance to oppressive conditions on the job and from the close ties in immigrant communities cut off from established social networks.

In the greengrocery campaign, UNITE Local 169—without support of its national union—dedicated resources to support and consolidate the surprising militancy among immigrant workers. But the initial success of this hard-fought effort set off competition for new members by other opportunistic unions. In the Francophone West African organizing drive, a union reasserted its jurisdictional rights after workers went on strike against labor contractors and supermarkets. In both cases, wages and working conditions improved as a result of worker insurgency, but most workers were excluded from active participation in determining workplace conditions.

We now turn to the organization of immigrant workers in the for-hire transportation industry, which reveals a similar pattern of initial isolation that spurred the development of class solidarity and worker militancy. Unlike the greengrocery and delivery workers, however, the black-car drivers gained a union that they could call their own. Two factors appear to account for this difference: (1) the industry was relatively new and no existing union had a jurisdictional claim to the workers, and (2) the union cultivated independent organizing by the workers and helped them form their own rank-and-file–led local. The black-car campaign illustrates how unions can successfully work with immigrant organizations to facilitate both greater strength in numbers and rank-and-file solidarity.

A History of New York City's For-Hire Vehicle Industry

Just as in the greengrocery and supermarket industries, globalization and neoliberal economic policies have played an important role in bringing about the creation of New York's immigrant labor force in the personal transportation industry (See Hughes 1999 on supermarket employment trends). To comprehend the starkly oppressive conditions that confront South Asian black-car drivers, we begin with an overview of the development of the for-hire vehicle labor market in New York City.

The city's motorized taxicab industry emerged in 1907 with the importation of sixty-five French automobiles, the first step in replacing horse-drawn hansom cabs. The number increased rapidly to 15,000 vehicles by 1923, and to 21,000 by 1931. The industry was highly concentrated within the Manhattan central business district, led by three companies with large fleets of medallion cabs: Checker, Yellow, and National (Schaller 2001). Gypsy cabs and independent car services provided private car transportation in the outer boroughs.

Historically, labor-management relations in the industry have been influenced by local government policy. In 1937, the New York City Board of Aldermen passed the Haas Act, which capped the number of medallion taxicabs in service in New York City at 13,595, primarily as a means of ensuring the industry's viability during the Great Depression. In the early 1950s, as many owners went out of business, the number of medallion cabs was reduced through attrition to 11,787, but later rebounded to the present number of 12,187. At the time, the taxicab industry was regulated by a Hack Bureau, which was managed by the New York Police Department. Owners consistently were able to persuade public officials to restrict the issuance of new medallions. Since the early 1940s, the value of a medallion has increased dramatically, as only a restricted number of licensed vehicles are legally permitted to pick up street hails in the city. The taxicab license, purchased by drivers for a mere $10 in the 1930s, was transformed into a privilege; by the late 1990s, the average price of a medallion had soared to $275,000 (Zeiger 1998). This created a substantial, yet frequently unmet, demand for alternative forms of private transportation.

By the mid-1960s, the shortage of taxicabs had created a severe for-hire passenger car shortage throughout New York City. Mayor John Lindsay's Taxi Study Panel (1966) concluded that the limit on medallions had contributed to the establishment of about 4,000 private livery companies that used telephone dispatchers for prearranged rides. In 1971, based in part on the Lindsay Panel's recommendations, Local Law 12 was passed by the New York City Council, creating the Taxi and Limousine Commission (TLC) as the regulatory body for both medallion taxis and limousines. As defined by the law, limousines are vehicles that seat a maximum of eight passengers plus the driver and operate only on a prearranged basis; limousines are not permitted to pick up hails from the street (Grava, Sclar, and Downs 1987; Savas, Grava, and Sparrow 1991).

Efforts in the late 1970s by Mayor Ed Koch to expand regulation of the medallion taxicab industry and to bring gypsy cabs under greater government control were only partially successful. Vehicle fleet owners, who wanted the TLC to allow the car service industry to shift from commissions for drivers to a leasing system, were leading contributors to Koch's election campaign. Under the system that emerged, drivers received a minimum salary in addition to commissions (Morris 1985; Rogoff 1980; Vidich 1976). The new law—pushed by Jay Turoff, Koch's original TLC commissioner—contributed considerably to increased taxi and for-hire car industry profits (interview, Henry Zeiger, former rank-and-file organizer in the taxi industry, June 27, 2002).

Changing Policies and Worsening Conditions for Drivers

Since the origin of the motorized taxicab industry in the early twentieth century, for-hire passenger transportation companies, dominated by private owners and operators, have sought to increase profits by influencing local governments to limit competition and depress the wages of drivers. Although for-hire drivers' working conditions have always been poor, they took a turn for the worse in the early 1980s, when taxicab and car service operators persuaded New York City officials to redefine drivers' job classifications, creating some of the most oppressive working conditions in the city. Under the new law, which redefined drivers as independent contractors rather than employees, their standard of living was sharply reduced and their ability to form an effective union was destroyed. The taxi and car service owners and operators had taken the drivers for a ride.

By the turn of the new century, through a confluence of factors favorable to taxi and car service owners and operators, for-hire passenger transit had become one of the most profitable industries in New York City's postindustrial economy. These factors include growing consumer demand from both businesses and individuals for private transportation, the industry's capacity to generate profit with limited capital investment, and local government policies beneficial to operators. Yet as profits in the industry soared throughout the 1990s, wages and working conditions for drivers slid to an unprecedented low. The consequences were apparent to virtually any New Yorker, as thousands of second-generation immigrant drivers protested by exiting the industry. However, with the rapid growth of transnational migration to New York City in the 1980s and 1990s, operators found a ready and willing new workforce to exploit.

The car service operators' manipulation of long-standing local government policy has diminished workers' rights and undermined

poor but stable labor-management relations in the industry by reducing standards for drivers, discouraging unionization, and effectively establishing informal working conditions comparable to
those seen in the Third World. Although passenger standards have
remained largely unchanged, new labor policies have contributed
to the deunionization of the industry, leading to a downward spiral
of wages and working conditions for drivers. Today, the vast majority of workers in the industry are new immigrants who—almost
without exception—remain drivers for fewer than four years, with
little or no expectation of improving their wages or conditions.

How did fleet owners come to dominate the private car transportation industry, forcing out legions of workers in the 1980s?
And how did a segment of the workforce—black-car drivers—
successfully improve their conditions by mobilizing and organizing
into a union? This chapter examines the erosion of labor standards
in the car service industry and the successful effort of black-car
drivers to force owners and operators to change their status from
independent contractors back to employees. This new identity as
employees allowed drivers to join a union composed of recent immigrant black-car drivers, which contributed to improved wages,
better working conditions, and due-process rights on the job.

Taxi Driver Militancy and Unionization Attempts

The willingness of drivers to organize and form a union of their own
had always presented itself through the militancy of the workers
and their desire for representation vis-à-vis management. However,
throughout the twentieth century, bitterly anti-labor fleet owners
in New York City challenged every effort to expand worker power
in the industry. Since taxis first appeared in the city in 1907, this
latent militancy among drivers repeatedly motivated labor leaders
to explore union organizing campaigns in the industry.

Typically, organized union drives surfaced out of independent
worker mobilizations. In 1915, the International Brotherhood of
Teamsters (IBT), Chauffeurs Division, began the first in a series of
unsuccessful efforts to tap into worker militancy. The second effort
to organize taxi drivers was initiated by Mike Quill of the Transit
Workers Union in 1937, the same year the industry was regulated

under the Haas Act. The act allowed medallion holders to sell their taxis, thus consolidating the industry into fewer companies and reducing the power of taxi drivers. Although the union gained recognition agreements from several fleet owners, the organizing drive was ultimately crushed by owners, who threatened union activists with violence and made opposition to organizing a condition of employment (Vidich 1976). Subsequent efforts to organize the taxi drivers by the United Auto Workers, Transport Workers Union, Teamsters, and even the United Mineworkers failed to form a union. Some of the union-organizing drives followed taxi driver insurrections and work stoppages, but all were thwarted by fleet owners who intimidated and dismissed drivers who were active in the campaign.

Though worker self-activity laid the groundwork for rank-and-file organization, campaigns to consolidate this labor militancy and establish lasting unions in the taxi industry repeatedly failed. In the first three decades of the twentieth century, the industry was highly dispersed among many fleet owners, making it difficult for worker organization to translate into legitimate unionization. In addition, the interest in labor organizing encouraged corrupt unions to enter the fray. The failure to form a representative worker organization intensified exploitative conditions for drivers, who usually worked long hours for low pay (interview, Thomas Van Arsdale, May 22, 2002; Ruffini 2002; Vidich 1976).

It was not until 1964 that drivers began to successfully organize into rank-and-file committees. Eventually, this militancy was once again seen as an opportunity by outsiders claiming a desire to ameliorate the conditions of helpless workers. Without financial backing and a strong organizational force, the workers had been unrelenting in their activism, but did not have the power to resist the fleet owners' abuse and could not improve their working conditions (interview, Henry Zeiger, June 27, 2002). Although workers considered union resources valuable to their campaign, they were excluded from the leadership of the nascent organization. In 1965 and 1966, with and without the support of the Community Labor Coalition and the city's leading unions, taxi drivers went on a spate of walkouts leading to their ultimate unionization in the summer of 1966.

Despite the creation of two local unions from 1966 through the 1990s, representing thousands of drivers, autonomous rank-and-file activism continued through the end of the decade and beyond as conditions for workers worsened. The first union, Local 3036, was formed by Harry Van Arsdale and affiliated directly with the Central Labor Council. Later, SEIU Local 74 gained jurisdiction over the industry. Van Arsdale, leader of the International Brotherhood of Electrical Workers (IBEW) Local 3, was president of the New York Central Labor Council from 1957 until his death in 1986. Although the first union bargained collectively with fleet owners, it could not control arbitrary management hiring practices and discipline. Thus, by the early 1970s, the union had assented to a concessionary agreement that was bitterly opposed by drivers, who were split into several factions. In December 1970, taxi drivers went on a fifteen-day strike for improved wages and benefits—a walkout led by rank-and-file activists disloyal to Van Arsdale (Ruffini 2002; Zeiger 1998). Many drivers opposed Van Arsdale's autocratic, top-down style of leadership, which legally restrained the workers' militancy and excluded rank-and-file participation in the daily activities of the local. In 1977, in response to intense pressure from members, Van Arsdale resigned as president, replaced by Benjamin Goldberg, the union's vice president. Although wages and benefits improved marginally (including the establishment of a pension fund that ultimately collapsed), the taxi drivers ultimately rebelled against the style of business unionism perpetrated by Van Arsdale and his successors. One of the most critical complaints concerned the dues structure, which continued despite the limited benefits most drivers gained from membership.[1]

The exclusion of rank-and-file workers from the union led to its collapse and to further erosion of working conditions. At its peak in the late 1960s, the union represented more than 35,000 drivers, but membership declined dramatically throughout the 1970s. According to former organizer Henry Zeiger, the union eventually failed because it looked down on member participation and therefore "couldn't win the respect of drivers in the garages" (interview, June 27, 2002).

The union faced a major challenge when fleet owners attempted to implement a voluntary leasing system in 1979, under which drivers would lease vehicles from the owners. The drivers fiercely opposed the fleet owners' efforts, and voted against the proposed system by a three-to-one margin. However, according to Zeiger, the union could do little to stop the implementation of the new system, which gradually shifted workers to the status of independent contractors not subject to the jurisdiction of the NLRB.

Under the leasing system today, drivers average between $5 and $6 per hour, after accounting for the $80 to $120 they must pay to rent their vehicles for twelve-hour shifts, plus gasoline, insurance costs, and traffic tickets. The leasing system initiated by the TLC in 1979, feebly opposed by Local 3036, eviscerated the union's effectiveness in bargaining, ultimately leading to its demise. By the mid-1980s, the taxi drivers' union was all but defunct, having become completely subservient to the Metropolitan Taxi Board of Trade, the management association in union garages.

Nevertheless, despite the effective demise of their union, taxi drivers were primed to strike while the iron was hot, going on wildcat strikes against fleet owners, the city, and TLC authorities. In February 1998, a rank-and-file committee of taxi drivers formed the New York City Taxi Workers Alliance (NYC-TWA) and by May organized two one-day strikes supported by 98 percent of the estimated 24,000 drivers (interview, Bhairavi Desai, September 23, 2003; Prashad 1998).

The NYC-TWA, led by a committee of drivers, represents the political interests of drivers in raising fares and reducing lease rates, and exposes discrimination and attacks against drivers. The organization has helped mobilized drivers engage in work slowdowns to improve their economic conditions (Wadler 1999). In addition, worker-led efforts that began in the mid-1990s to organize taxi drivers through an independent union were spearheaded by the Committee Against Anti-Asian Violence, which formed the Lease Drivers Association under Zeiger's leadership.

Unable to negotiate conditions for taxi drivers—who were now considered independent contractors—the remnants of Local 3036 subsequently merged in the early 1990s with Service Employees International Union (SEIU) Local 74, a union that primarily represents public school maintenance personnel and has yet to embark on a serious, industry-wide campaign to organize taxi drivers.

Under Local 74's stewardship, driver membership dissipated. The union, which still officially maintains jurisdiction over the medallion taxi industry, asserts that the law making drivers independent contractors precludes it from organizing workers.

Although Local 74 believes the only way to rebuild is through changing the law, the union is not organizing drivers as part of a strategy to achieve that goal. As of late 2003, Local 74 was ostensibly still interested in eliminating the leasing system and changing the drivers' designation from independent contractors to employees. However, it provided only limited support—which tended to take the form of press releases—and most taxi drivers in New York dismissed the prospect that conditions could be improved through conventional forms of unionization.

Origins of New York City's Black-Car Industry

New York City has the largest mass transportation system in the United States, buttressed by private car services that both supplement and complement the Metropolitan Transportation Authority's publicly run rail, subway, and bus lines. The privately run transportation system comprises taxicabs and for-hire vehicles (FHVs), which are vehicles that pick up passengers on the basis of prearranged telephone calls or are contracted by large employers. The New York City Administrative Code defines a FHV as any motor vehicle that is not a taxicab and that carries fewer than nine passengers. There are three major FHV industry segments: neighborhood car services, limousines, and black cars.

In the early 1980s, following the imposition of the voluntary taxi leasing system, the taxicab industry stridently opposed efforts by Mayor Koch's administration to augment the number of private cars and other FHVs serving Manhattan's central business district. In particular, the taxicab industry strongly opposed a recommendation by Koch's Smith Committee to recommend changes for New York City's for-hire vehicle system that nonmedallion cars complement established taxicabs at three Manhattan central business district sites designated as "hack stands" (Richard Smith 1982).

The most significant change to come out of the Smith proposals was the creation of the black car industry through a new TLC law in

1982 that permitted the transfer of 3,200 medallion taxis belonging to radio dispatch services to nonmedallion status. As part of the new arrangement, medallion cabs without radios would exclusively serve passenger street hails, while the new nonmedallion segment of the industry would be converted into radio-dispatched car services, which came to be known as "black cars." In March 1982, the first two of approximately twenty leading black-car companies emerged: Intraboro and Dial. A year later, in April 1983, an estimated nine hundred radios were taken out of taxicabs and put into other cars operated by taxi owners. The taxi operators saved the best customers in the Wall Street area for themselves, gradually replacing the meter fare system with a zone-based, flat-fare rate system. The majority of medallion owners who transferred two-way radios out of taxicabs and into black cars either leased their medallion cabs to other drivers through brokers or sold their medallions altogether.

The new law and New York City's preeminent position as a global business center effectively created a new industry with a growing customer and employee base. The black-car industry expanded dramatically along with New York City's corporate economy during the 1980s and 1990s, serving a growing corporate customer base that wanted chauffeured car service. Unlike limousines—which typically are hired for special events and parties—black cars primarily service business clients on trips to and from work, airport trips, and regional business trips. In addition, as New York's corporate economy demanded longer hours from its employees, the black-car industry expanded further to chauffeur bankers, accountants, lawyers, and even secretaries to their homes late at night.

Black cars provide expensive service to business customers, but less specialized service than limousines. Drivers typically use late-model American vehicles such as Lincoln Town Cars, Mercury Grand Marquis, and Cadillac sedans. Black-car fares are usually paid by corporations, which provide their employees and clients vouchers to pay for rides. Some black-car services also accept credit cards. Like neighborhood car services, black-car fares are computed on the basis of geographic zone, but are significantly higher—typically two or three times as expensive as those of a car service. For example, neighborhood car services typically charge $25 to $30 for airport fares, while black cars charge $35 to $50, depending on the distance. Minimum fares also are significantly higher; black-car services charge a minimum of $15 per ride, compared with the $3 charged by neighborhood car services.

The black-car industry is organized on the basis of franchises, with most cars owned by drivers, who must maintain the basic standards of the car service. The approximately 12,000 employees in the industry are almost exclusively recent immigrants to the city. Between 1982—when the industry first arose—and 2001, the number of registered black cars increased from none to nearly 12,000. By the early 1990s, black cars accounted for 30 percent of all FHVs, but the industry was highly concentrated among about forty-five bases (Schaller 1993). In 1992, for example, 90 percent of all black-car firms had fleets exceeding one hundred cars, compared with only 39 percent of neighborhood car services and 23 percent of premium limousine services; the average black-car base size was 177 cars. This trend continued into the first decade of this century. Most black cars are controlled by car service owners that operate more than five hundred cars; by early 2000, some had close to one thousand vehicles. Between 1992 and 2000, black-car service increased by 39 percent to more than eleven thousand cars; the number of bases, however, increased by only 7 percent, from forty-five to forty-eight (Schaller 2001, 1–2).

The taxicab and for-hire car service industries are extremely sensitive to economic fluctuations in the New York City economy. The number of licensed cars declined during the mid-1980s' downturn, again in the early 1990s, and most recently during the recession following the attacks on the World Trade Center in September 2001. However following the early 1990s' recession, the car service industry rebounded, doubling between the early 1980s and early 1990s with the growth of the city's economy. Even with the limitation placed on the number of medallion cabs permitted to operate in Manhattan, the city continues to have the highest number of taxis per person among major U.S. cities.[2]

Independent Contracting in the FHV Industry

A crucial factor in the development and expansion of the black-car industry in the 1980s and 1990s was the ability of fleet operators to find reliable drivers to service their demanding business customers.

As noted previously, native-born white, black, and Latino drivers left in droves as the taxi and car service industry shifted from a commission system to a leasing system. Without a sufficient supply of drivers, the black-car industry segment could not have expanded from a relatively small two-way radio medallion taxi business to become a multimillion-dollar industry dominated by several dozen operators. Thus, fleet owners had to both expand their customer base and hire and retain thousands of new drivers.

The black-car industry segment is structured in such a way as to reduce operator costs to a bare minimum, transferring as many costs as possible to the drivers. This was achieved through hiring recent migrants from South Asia as drivers and designating them independent contractors. In theory, the drivers were in business for themselves, but in reality the new label was the fig leaf the industry needed to effectively restructure labor-management relations and create a workforce of low-wage drivers. The shift in designation parallels the change in job description that occurred in the taxi industry during the same period, which contributed to deunionization, the departure of native-born drivers, and efforts to recruit new immigrant drivers.

As described above, in the taxi industry, medallion fleet owners began eliminating the employee designation and started to pay a share of revenues through a commission system. Instead of sharing the till with owners, the drivers—now classified as independent contractors—were required to lease their cars on a daily, weekly, or monthly basis. Thus, while the owners were guaranteed their take, the drivers had to gamble that there would be enough customers to pay the leasing fee. When business was slow, drivers had to hustle, speed, and work excessively long hours just to break even. By the mid-1990s, more than one-third of all medallion taxi operations had been subcontracted to lease managers who ran the scheme. In addition to losing their daily cut of fares, the drivers— no longer employees—also lost their health insurance and other benefits. Under the new system, drivers were responsible for gas, fines for infractions, and all other expenses related to operating their cars. The high rate charged by medallion operators (typically $80 to $120 per day) and the deteriorating regulatory environment contributed to high turnover and a continuous search for new drivers.

Black-Car Driver Expenses and Earnings

The upscale, luxury environment for black-car clients in most cases does not correlate with better driver wages or working conditions than those in the taxi segment. Indeed, the black-car segment extracts even more from the immigrant workers who staff the industry and maintains stricter oversight than do taxi medallion owners.

Black-car drivers must purchase a franchise from a company owner or another driver for the right to pick up fares. Franchise fees range from a low of about $3,000 to a high of $60,000. Franchise fees are calculated based on the ability of the car service to generate income for drivers; firms with more customers and higher rates charge more, whereas newer firms typically charge less. Black-car companies that serve Wall Street generally charge franchise fees ranging from $50,000 to $60,000. Still, due to fluctuations in the business climate, this scheme at times fails to meet the drivers' expectations. According to the International Association of Machinists and Aerospace Workers (IAM), the average franchise fee in 2001 ranged from $15,000 to $20,000. Generally, black-car firms can assist drivers in securing bank loans to purchase their franchises. Such loans are usually obtained at prevailing interest rates and paid off to the bank over a number of years.

Interviews with several drivers conducted from the fall of 2001 to the fall of 2003 reveal a general belief that they may not be able to sell their franchises to other drivers or back to the company owners for at least the price they paid, especially in view of the plummeting value of the franchise in the aftermath of September 11, 2001. One driver who bought a franchise in 1995 for $10,000 said he sold it for the same $10,000 some six years later, even though the printed rate then was about $15,000 (interviews, June–July 2001). It is remarkable that black-car service owners can command—and that drivers are willing to pay—such high fees in an industry that emerged only twenty years ago and already has experienced two severe cyclical downturns. However, almost like indentured servants, workers are bound to the company owners until they repay their car and franchise fee loans.

In addition to franchise fees, drivers are required to purchase or lease a late-model luxury car. The average price for such a car ranges from $18,000 to $25,000. To obtain a car, a prospective driver must make a sizable down payment. In 1995, one driver entering the industry was told by an owner that he had to bring $3,000 to get a car and a loan before he could begin driving (interview, August 2001).

Owners assess drivers weekly fees, in exchange for the right to receive radio calls for jobs from black-car companies, which at some higher-end firms run about $2,500 a year. Drivers are required to wear business suits and ties—which can cost hundreds of dollars a year—and are fined for not wearing proper attire. In addition, drivers also must pay a fee ranging from $1.50 to $2.50 for each voucher they turn in. The fee is considered a surcharge for the radio calls from the black-car bases. Drivers turn in vouchers given to them by corporate customers upon completion of their rides, and the vouchers are in turn sent to the corporations for reimbursement. Drivers also are responsible for paying for their vehicle's maintenance, gas, twice-weekly car washes, required cell phones, and Social Security and self-employment taxes. Because the system operates on the basis of company-issued vouchers, drivers rarely receive tips.

Further, owners require black-car drivers to purchase liability insurance, an expenditure that represents a large share of the cost of operating a black car. According to IAM officials, average annual insurance rates in the early 2000s ranged from $5,000 to more than $6,000 per year, depending on the driver's record and the extent of coverage desired (interview, Kevin Lynch, IAM District 15, August 21, 2001). Because the black-car industry typically services corporate and business clients, most firms demand that drivers take out high levels of liability insurance, sometimes more than $300,000 per accident. High premiums significantly cut into drivers' take-home income. Many times, the insurance companies that owners recommend to their drivers are insurance companies the black-car firms own or with which they have an established relationship. In effect, these insurance companies pay black-car service operators a commission for referrals.

Very few drivers can afford to pay these expenses in cash. Thus, to pay for the right to drive a car for an operator, drivers frequently exhaust their savings, borrow from relatives, and go deeply into debt. The system of expenses and fees charged by black-car service owners forces often-unsuspecting drivers onto the street for long hours, usually seven days a week. In return for purchasing a franchise, buying a luxury car, obtaining liability insurance, and paying weekly fees, the driver typically gets to keep about 80 percent of fares, with 20 percent going to the black-car company; no company charges less than 15 percent for the right to pick up its customers (Strozier 1999).

While large sums of money pass through black-car drivers' hands, workers generally do not have high annual incomes. The IAM estimates that the average driver earns approximately $20,000 a year. Some drivers who work longer hours at up-market firms may earn as much as $25,000. On average, the typical black-car driver earns from $4 to $6 an hour, with no overtime pay. In 1998, one driver earning $1,500 per week in fares paid out about 70 percent of these earnings for loans and expenses, grossing about $450 a week before taxes; working eighty-four-hour weeks (twelve hours a day, seven days a week), he averaged just over the federal minimum wage of $5.15 an hour. Another worker who grossed more than $50,000 in 1998 took home only $20,000 after expenses (Strozier 1999, 14).

Because fleet operators often provide loans for the franchise fee and luxury cars, and referrals to insurance companies, drivers feel like they are entirely reliant and indebted to them. Said one driver from Pakistan who borrowed money for his fee, car, and insurance:

> I feel like I am living like a slave. I borrow everything from the owner and he now owns me. Right now, I don't even have enough to live and cannot send any money back home. I drive all day and night and all my money I earn goes back to the company to pay for the right to drive rich customers. They tell me I will be making money, but when? Because I owe so much, I have no choice but to keep driving. (anonymous interview, August 2003)

In the aftermath of September 11, 2001, many drivers have lost almost all their fares while continuing to pay for their cars. One driver reported that many have left the country because they lack the income to pay their debts.

The TLC and Black-Car Drivers

Some of the most common complaints among black-car drivers relate to the TLC's interference with their ability to operate their vehicles, the imposition of high fines, and the frequent issuance of penalties. As noted above, the TLC was created in 1971 to license and regulate New York City's taxicab and car service industry. The agency regulates more than 45,000 vehicles and approximately 92,000 drivers (New York City Taxi and Limousine Commission 2000a).

Although the black-car industry expanded rapidly during the economic boom of the early 1980s, there was little government oversight. With some 7,200 black cars registered in fiscal year 1985, the industry remained largely unregulated, as did the approximately 12,000 cars operated by neighborhood car services. The growth of the for-hire vehicle industry—and the lack of standards governing quality of service, insurance, and safety—led to increased public pressure to establish regulations.

To better enforce standards of operation, the New York City Council in 1986 passed Local Law 76, which mandated the TLC to license vehicles, drivers, and operators that dispatch cars from bases. The TLC, administered by the mayor's office, now regulates both taxis and for-hire vehicles—including black cars—operating in the city. Under the law, black cars are not permitted to pick up street-hail passengers, but may take only prearranged passenger appointments, typically made by telephone. In the ensuing decade and a half, the TLC has promulgated rules and regulations that more specifically set forth standards for operation, service, insurance, and safety in the burgeoning industry.

The TLC requires base owners and drivers to renew their licenses annually and to have their vehicles inspected three times per year. The commission charges licensing fees and assesses penalties against unlicensed and uninsured vehicles and drivers. The TLC also licenses out-of-city for-hire vehicles that pick up passengers in New York for out-of-town destinations. In addition, the commission cooperates with the New York State Department of Motor Vehicles (DMV) to enforce regulations governing drivers' licenses and vehicle registration. Drivers who do not keep their driver's license and insurance in order risk losing their license and registration for periods ranging from sixty days to six months. The TLC insists on strictly enforcing the law, claiming that a significant number of unlicensed company owners and drivers continue to operate in the city. The commission claims that it does not interfere with the FHV industry by imposing burdensome regulations, which would be counterproductive because it would encourage unlicensed operators. But drivers argue that they are regularly stopped by the TLC and issued tickets, sometimes for no offense at all (Syed Armughan ul-Asar, interview, October 26, 2001).

For-hire vehicles must be affiliated with car service base operators, which are held accountable for driver and vehicular infractions. Car service owners and operators, as well as drivers, are fined and face suspension for failing to maintain licenses in good order or for violating laws prohibiting street-hail passenger pickups (Schaller 1993, 25–27). In the twelve months ending June 30, 1992, some 39,000 summonses were issued to unlicensed vehicles, base operators, and drivers, with the vast majority—over 95 percent—issued to drivers.

Black-car and for-hire vehicle operators and drivers frequently complain that the TLC and DMV jeopardize their jobs and livelihoods by suspending their licenses and seizing their cars, even when infractions are not their fault, but rather are due to clerical errors on the part of car service owners or insurance companies. In November 1989, the New York City Council granted the TLC the right to seize vehicles that have a high default rate on summonses or that are operated without a license. TLC records indicate that seizures increased from 674 vehicles in fiscal year 1991 to 1,930 in fiscal year 1992. By 2001, the TLC could claim it seized "about 600 vehicles per month for operating as illegal liveries" and held "over 1,500 hearings per week for violations" (New York City Taxi and Limousine Commission 2000b). In 1992, the TLC went so far as to padlock entire unlicensed car service bases. The TLC claims that since it began seizing vehicles, compliance with regulations has risen significantly, and that within only a few years the response rate to summonses increased from 20 percent to nearly 80 percent.

However, after the first few years, the consequences of seizure fell primarily on the drivers themselves, who must go through a painstaking process to retrieve their cars and rebuild their standing with operators. Although the TLC considers vehicle seizure an effective means of enforcing compliance, drivers—who may or may not be aware of their failure to comply with TLC and DMV regulations—complain that when their vehicles are seized, towed, and impounded by TLC inspectors, the drivers continue to be subject to franchise fees, weekly dues, insurance costs, and high monthly payments on their luxury vehicles. If the driver does not post bond and appear at a scheduled TLC hearing within a period of seven days, the car may be auctioned and proceeds used to pay outstanding fines. At the hearings, many drivers do not have the required documents, which often are held by car service owners. Even with the proper paperwork, drivers have no way to recoup their lost earnings, most of which are used to pay for expenses related to operating the car. Moreover, drivers report that they are penalized by their car service operators subsequent to losing their vehicles, as more desirable routes are turned over to other drivers during their absence from the job.

New Immigrant Workers in the Car Service Industry

Drivers in the black-car industry are almost all recent immigrants who have arrived in New York City during the 1990s. The industry workforce is composed of immigrants from South Asia (India, Pakistan), the Middle East (Lebanon, Palestine, Syria, Turkey), East Asia (China, Korea), Eastern Europe (Russia, Poland, Ukraine), and Africa (Egypt), as well as Latinos from Central and South America. According to one black-car company, many recent immigrants who had been taxicab drivers have entered the black-car industry segment due to the impression that they could earn significantly higher wages. However, the reality that the field can be even more onerous than taxi driving has since reduced the ranks. Even Elite Limousine Plus, a leading black-car operator, acknowledged the bleak conditions for drivers in the industry:

> The available labor pool from which we manned our ranks has shrunk considerably. Recent immigrants who first trained driving yellow cabs have traditionally migrated to our fleets. Drivers perceived the transition to the black-car industry as a source of greater income, more

> prestige, and a safer work environment. However all that has
> changed. . . . After expenses, a shift taxicab driver can take home more
> than a black-car driver. (Elite Limousine Plus 2000)

As with the taxi segment, there are few native-born white, black, or Latino drivers in the black-car industry. Because black cars are so new to the New York City landscape, native-born drivers—with few exceptions—never really entered the industry. South Asians account for at least 60 percent of black-car drivers, and are sought out primarily because of their proficiency with the English language, which allows them to communicate easily with their upscale business clientele.

New York City's South Asian population increased dramatically following the liberalization of immigration laws in 1965, which allowed a greater share of Asian, Caribbean, and Latin American immigrants to live in the United States. According to the INS, the documented South Asian population in New York City increased faster than any other Asian population—by 80.7 percent between 1990 and 2000. The number of Indian Asians, as they are classified by the INS, grew from 94,590 in 1990 to 170,899 in 2000; they now constitute 21.7 percent of the Asian population in New York City, second only to Chinese immigrants (Immigration and Naturalization Service 1998).

While the prevailing impression is that South Asian immigrants—in particular, educated Indians—tend to occupy high-wage professional or entrepreneurial positions in New York, in reality a large and growing number have limited formal education and are employed in low-wage industries. Even if workers are educated, they have few options but to take low-wage jobs. According to Johanna Lessinger, an authority on Indian immigrants in New York City, (1995), Indian immigrants often "work as waiters, deli countermen, shop clerks, newsstand employees, security guards, or taxi drivers. Those who work for fellow Indians as waiters, hotel night clerks, shop assistants, or domestic servants often do so under very exploitative conditions. Indians who do such work live out an immigrant experience far closer to that of poor Dominican, Chinese, or Mexican immigrants than to that of fellow Indians" (18–19).

The one advantage that South Asians have is their English language skills. As one driver explained, the edge South Asians have over Puerto Ricans and Dominicans who have operated car service vehicles and gypsy cabs for many more years is their greater facility in English, rather than any special connections to employers:

> There are so many other people who have been here in New York City for much longer—Latinos or other non–English-speaking immigrants. They are driving car service vehicles, livery cars, or gypsy cabs. So I don't know, I think that the reason more South Asians are in the business is because of their ability to speak the English language. It doesn't have much to do with connections; anybody can do this work. (interview, August 16, 2001)

This driver appears to convey the view that, rather than South Asians pursuing jobs in the black-car industry, the industry has sought out South Asians. Black-car companies, according to another driver, place advertisements in local Pakistani papers:

> Our communities have newspapers that are full of these ads. Taxi or livery owners put ads in our newspapers because they know that we are the people they want. They think that we will not complain about our conditions because things are better here than back home. But here we have to work, work, work, with no rest. (interview, September 2002)

Although black-car companies may have sought out South Asian drivers first, it appears that through these linkages, South Asian drivers have developed unique ties to the industry that have contributed to the consolidation of their dominance in the field. By the late 1990s, although black-car companies continued to seek out drivers through newspaper advertisements, most were recruited through the word of mouth of relatives or friends already employed in the industry.

In general, drivers are made aware in advance of the considerable down payment that black-car operators command and the need to obtain bank loans. Recommendations from current drivers help persuade car service owners to assist new recruits in obtaining the necessary loans and insurance. Typically, such financial arrangements are made through the black-car companies themselves, which frequently take finders' fees or have advantageous arrangements with banks and insurance companies. Unlike the remaining gypsy cab drivers, black-car drivers have access to the money they need through a combination of savings, borrowing from relatives, and loans from fleet owners. But the appearance of wealth among workers in the industry is to a great extent illusory, as they are placed in virtual indentured servitude, working long hours for many years to pay off loans, send money back home, and survive in the city. Indeed the term *peonage* may be more accurate to describe the situation than does the term *indentured servitude*. The latter implies a contract with a specific time frame, while peonage refers to debt-coerced work with no real hope of release.

The Black-Car Driver Organizing Campaign

Why would a workforce composed primarily of South Asian immigrant drivers choose to join the IAM, a union that traditionally has represented machinists, aircraft builders, and airline maintenance workers? Although the black-car organizing campaign can clearly be seen as a union's well-planned effort to take on an industry, it was—like so many other organizing attempts in the current era—essentially started by the workers themselves.

The black-car organizing campaign began in the mid-1990s, when workers began to complain about intolerable conditions that made it almost impossible to earn a living. While congregating at key sites, drivers grumbled about the unlikelihood of paying their bills and taking home enough money to feed their families; very few could afford to send remittances back home to their relatives abroad. According to one driver:

> We usually dropped off our vouchers on Fridays and picked up our checks on Mondays. We were always upset when we got our checks on payday for working twelve hours a day, seven days a week. But we did not suffer alone. Twice a week we would meet as a group in the black-car parking areas to complain about our low pay and find ways to complain to management as a group. (interview, September 30, 2003)

Workers built solidarity and social ties on the job at various sites. According to one activist in the organizing campaign:

> When we began organizing we had no union. We communicated with one another when we were doing pickups and drop-offs on the street. Usually, we had multiple pickups for ten persons or more at law firms,

financial service companies, and insurance companies on Wall Street and in Midtown Manhattan. The buildings are well known to us all: 85 Broadway, 125 Broadway, 200 and 245 Park Avenue. We also met waiting to pick up passengers at airports, who we drove home to New York and the suburbs. (interview, September 24, 2003)

Drivers commonly could be found between jobs parked under elevated highways—such as FDR Drive at 34th Street or near the South Street Seaport—where they often rested for a few minutes between Wall Street and midtown pickups. One driver recalling the organizing drive noted that the long lag between jobs gave workers ample time to debate ways to improve their conditions through organizing:

> We all waited under the elevated FDR Drive near the South Street Seaport for calls from the dispatchers. Under the drive, we always had a lot of parking and, most importantly, privacy where we could sleep in our cars and eat before driving to the next job. Most of the time we complained about the fees charged by fleet owners and the unfair fines that we would get from the Taxi and Limousine Commission. That was where all the organizing began—we had lots of time on our hands and began talking about forming a collective organization. (interview, October 2, 2003)

In 1995, drivers at Elite Limousine Plus, a large company based in Long Island City that controlled about 650 cars, organized themselves to demand a reduction in fees assessed by the company. Syed Armughan ul-Asar, a leader of the organizing drive who emigrated from Pakistan in 1991, and several coworkers decided that they needed a union. After holding a number of meetings, the workers reached out to Craig Livingston, a New Jersey labor lawyer, who suggested the aggrieved workers appeal to IAM District 15.

When the drivers first approached IAM, no union was then operating in the black-car industry. Moreover, recognizing its strategic ability to organize these workers, IAM was willing to expend the required resources and engage in a long campaign that began informally in 1995 and continues to this day. In 1996, with the assistance of IAM, the workers created their own local union—Lodge 340—a dormant local that had no members. Within a year, the drivers and their new union organized four hundred members and embarked on organizing campaigns against the black-car fleet owners.

Employees versus Independent Contractors

The overriding predicament in the workers' effort to organize was the classification of black-car drivers as self-employed independent contractors rather than employees. Viewing the drivers as independent contractors, Elite did not pay federal payroll taxes (including the employer's 7.65 percent share of Social Security contributions), federal or state unemployment insurance premiums, or workers' compensation premiums. Nor did the company cover employee benefits such as health insurance, life insurance, paid vacations, sick leave, or retirement benefits.

Historically, independent contracting has been performed by professionals who are in business for themselves and carry out services for many clients. However, in an effort to reduce labor costs, the practice of replacing employees with independent contractors has become widespread among businesses in the 1990s. The IRS uses a test to determine employee status. Workers are classified as employees if they are directed or controlled in the manner of their work. The IRS states that if workers are required to appear at a specific time and place to perform a specific set of duties, they are employees and not contractors. Despite the legal risks of misclassifying employees as independent contractors, large and small firms alike have increasingly done so in order to cut costs. According to industry consultants for employers, designating workers as independent contractors can significantly increase business profitability and offer flexibility that cannot be obtained when workers are hired as employees. A firm can save from 20 percent to 30 percent in payroll costs, and employers are insulated from lawsuits related to wrongful termination and job discrimination. On a national level, the number of independent contractors has increased dramatically; by 1997, according to IRS statistics, more than eight million people filed tax returns as independent contractors. The most notorious case is Microsoft's use of long-term contractors—who came to be known as "permatemps"—in about one-third of the positions at its Redmond, Washington, corporate headquarters.

In the black-car industry the term *independent contractor* is more ambiguous, as drivers own their vehicles and generally are working in the field, theoretically picking up individual customers or clients. Nonetheless, under the IRS test, the drivers should be classified as employees: They are directed by black-car operators where and when to pick up and drop off passengers, and are required to wear a suit and tie. Moreover, corporate customers have no relationship to the drivers, but are in fact clients of the black-car companies, which are paid in advance for rides. Drivers typically are reimbursed by the operators, who pay the workers in cash upon presentation of vouchers.

The Elite Limousine Plus Campaign

Convinced of the drivers' status as employees and not independent contractors, Kevin Lynch, organizing director of IAM District 15, embarked on an effort to organize the workers at Elite Limousine Plus, thereby initiating an organizing campaign among the 12,000 drivers employed in the black-car industry. According to Lynch, immigrant black-car drivers are no different from previous waves of immigrants working in low-wage industries that have organized and formed unions to protect their interests. The fact that most workers in the industry have advanced educational backgrounds reinforces their desire for respect on the job and facilitates organizing to improve their working conditions (interview, Kevin Lynch, August 21, 2001).

District 15's organizing campaign remains one of the largest unionization efforts in the New York City private sector. Until September 11, 2001, the union expected to organize over half the 12,000 drivers in the black-car industry by 2003, as more and more companies were agreeing to recognize the union. The primary focus of the campaign has been to improve drivers' wages and working conditions and to create a benefits system. With an organizing committee in place at Elite, the union reached out to drivers congregating at airports and in Manhattan's central business district. The drivers, according to union organizers, were receptive to organizing appeals and signed union recognition cards in droves.

In late 1995, the organizing effort's first goal was to persuade the NLRB to reclassify drivers as employees of the companies for which they worked. This reclassification would allow the IAM to organize the workers into a union. One of the first test cases was at Elite, whose owner Shafquat Chaudhary—a Pakistani who had once been a taxi driver himself—fought the reclassification effort. In 1997, the IAM won an NLRB decision that transformed the independent contractors at Elite into employees. Two years later, a new worker-led union—representing five hundred members—signed its first collective bargaining agreement with Elite. The victory was an important one for the international union and "set the stage for IAM representation of limousine drivers at many major black-car companies" (International Association of Machinists 2000). The Elite victory gave the union the legitimacy it needed to organize firms one after the other, and paved the way for recognition and collective bargaining throughout the industry.

Organizing Victory

The collective bargaining contract negotiated by IAM for black-car drivers became boilerplate due process and grievance procedure language for most union contracts in the industry. The contract covers voucher fees and percentages for fares, and includes a health benefit plan for full-time drivers who submit a requisite number of vouchers within a quarterly period; however, it does not include health benefits for the drivers' families. In addition, the contract provides for payments into a life insurance plan and for free legal representation for workers fighting tickets and fines before the TLC. Other benefits include vacation and sick pay.

Beyond the contract itself, the rank-and-file leadership of IAM attempted to improve the conditions of all workers in the black-car segment by establishing an industry-wide worker disability plan. In April 2000, as a result of union pressure, the TLC mandated that all black-car base owners must comply with provisions of New York State law requiring owners to contribute to workers' compensation as a condition of obtaining a license. The funds are obtained through taxation of fares charged to corporate clients that pay through vouchers. While the law creating a "black-car fund" applies to most operators, it does not apply to car services in which cash is exchanged between customers and drivers. In addition, the TLC also established a task force to review how workers' compensation issues impact the entire livery industry (New York City Taxi and Limousine Commission 2000b).

Thus, IAM and the members of Local 340 are seeking to influence the behavior of livery and car services with which it does not have established contracts or bargaining relationships, even beyond the black-car segment of the industry. This broader vision represents a new model of organizing in an industry that has not been unionized for a long time, yet retains a history of rank-and-file militancy. This concept of worker organizing seeks to offset the preceding twenty-year period, during which industrial restructuring, reclassification of work, and suppression of worker rights in the for-hire vehicle industry held sway. IAM and the black-car drivers have worked in both the legal and political spheres to advance the conditions of all workers in the industry, unionized or not. The Local 340 campaign gained new members and goodwill among workers, and set the stage for further improvement of conditions, with the worker-led union taking on a significant role as a major force in organizing and defending drivers throughout the industry.

Despite all the disruption in the industry, ul-Asar, who became manager of Local Lodge 340, is still attempting to extend the organizing drive beyond more established black-car companies, arguing that the union is the only mechanism available to prevent anti-labor companies from discriminating against drivers on the basis of ethnicity or other forms of favoritism:

> We would like to help anybody who wants to come and ask us if we can do something for them. Right now we have our targets, but we are ready to organize anybody who comes in where there are victims and there is more immediate need—where workers are not treated well. . . . The base owners determine who will get good jobs. If you . . . are lucky enough into getting a local call that becomes an out-of-town job or a time call that naturally is a good job. But you have to do any kind of job that is asked of you by the dispatcher. You could not stop. (interview, Syed Armughan ul-Asar, October 26, 2001; December 10, 2004)

The Aftermath of September 11, 2001

In the wake of the September 11 terrorist attacks on the World Trade Center, workers in the black-car industry faced a major economic setback as ridership plunged dramatically. In addition, because

90 percent of all drivers are immigrants—the vast majority from South Asia (Pakistan, India, Bangladesh)—the workers also were dealt a staggering political blow as federal, state, and local government authorities began to bear down on them with accusations of association with terrorism (National Employment Law Project 2002).

Demand in the black-car industry is strongly linked to the state of the local economy. Thus, the economic downturn in 2000 and 2001 contributed to the contraction of the industry as businesses curtailed expenses and reduced the use of black cars to transport employees and clients to and from their workplaces. Moreover, the stock market downturn also reduced business travel to New York City, contributing to a decline in airport customers. In 2000, the black-car segment was estimated to have about 12,000 drivers; 2001's looming recession had decreased the number of drivers to about 11,000. The collapse of the World Trade Center pushed the local economy into a full recession and created turmoil in the black-car industry.

While the number of drivers with cars remained steady at 11,000, the industry could sustain only 7,000 drivers in 2001 and 2002. Plans to organize thousands of drivers were put on hold, and Lodge 340's main focus shifted to a broad drive for emergency government assistance for workers displaced by the terrorist attacks and the deepening recession. The union advocated for the federal government to compensate drivers for lost business, and helped workers gain grants ranging from $2,000 to $10,000 to help cover car payments, insurance, and health benefits. The union also undertook a major effort to press the TLC to raise passenger fares by 4 to 5 percent and to ensure that the entire increase went to the drivers.

With more than one thousand dues-paying members, Lodge 340 remains a powerful force in the black-car industry. Thus, as IAM is on the precipice of gaining industry-wide recognition, the worker-led union is a key player in determining a hiring-hall mechanism for doling out available jobs to workers who had invested and borrowed thousands of dollars to enter the field. The widespread recognition of Local 340 as representing drivers initially conferred a greater degree of legitimacy among black-car companies as the union worked with owners to demand that public officials provide restitution and as it defended the rights of workers in arbitrating the distribution of jobs.

In the weeks following the September 11 attack, drivers worried that ridership would decline to a trickle, intensifying pressure on workers to both repay their loans and eke out a living. But by October 2001, it became clear that the immigrant drivers faced another serious challenge. The federal government began to bear down on drivers from South Asian, Middle Eastern, Arab, and Muslim backgrounds, arresting and deporting thousands who lacked proper documents. According to union manager ul-Asar:

> Pakistanis are at the front line, but South Asians in general and Arabs in particular are subject to deportation. On average, about two hundred to three hundred Pakistani guys were deported every week. Initially we were appealing to FEMA [Federal Emergency Management Agency] and the Red Cross for disaster assistance as a result of the financial crisis in the industry. But the main problem among drivers quickly became the fear of government detention and deportation. (interview, October 26, 2001)

Now that federal authorities require immigrants from Muslim countries to register with the government, employers have been emboldened to resist worker organizing efforts. In the wake of the government crackdown, fleet owners have become more averse to recognizing worker organizing and signing contracts with the union. As an example, September 11 cost almost four hundred workers at New York City Two-Way Radio membership in the union. After holding meetings with drivers at mosques, churches, and other public gathering places, Local 340 was confident that it would win recognition. But the campaign was lost after the Brooklyn-based fleet owner warned that drivers would be reported to the federal government if they voted in the union.

Despite the government onslaught against immigrant drivers in the industry, workers remain resolute in appealing to the union. In response to the backlash against drivers from South Asian, Middle Eastern, Arab, and Muslim backgrounds, IAM is supporting the local union's ongoing efforts to get working papers and green cards for workers. In addition, black-car drivers have gained the support of organized labor in New York. Brian McLaughlin, president of the New York City Central Labor Council, has publicly denounced federal government programs targeting workers for detention and deportation on the basis of their ethnicity or religion. Statements such as these and the publicity they have generated have done much in convincing many union members and most customers that immigrant workers from South Asia are not a threat to public safety and should not be racially profiled. (See Chapter 7 for a fuller discussion of the effects of September 11 on immigrant workers.)

Conclusion: Components of the IAM Black-Car Organizing Campaign

The success of the black-car union-organizing effort derives both from the militancy among immigrant drivers that spurred them to demand better conditions and from the existence of an established union that provided critical resources but did not interfere with worker control over the direction of the campaign. The IAM black-car organizing model suggests that success may best be achieved when unions provide resources to workers and at the same time grant them autonomy. In summary, three primary elements contributed to the success of the IAM black-car organizing drive: (1) worker solidarity in an industry dominated by South Asians that was in place even before unionization, (2) the absence of interference from competing unions defending jurisdictional turf or opportunistically entering the campaign, and (3) union monetary and legal support for independent worker organizing that led to the creation of the drivers' own rank-and-file-led local. The black-car campaign illustrates how unions can successfully work with immigrant organizations to facilitate both greater strength in numbers and rank-and-file solidarity. The national union's willingness to support an independent immigrant organization, unlike UNITE and the UFCW in the two previous case studies, suggests that a combination of rank-and-file autonomy and union resources predicts the most favorable outcome in efforts to organize the new immigrants who form a large and growing segment of the U.S. workforce.

Worker Solidarity

The IAM organizing drive benefited greatly from the concentration in the black-car industry of South Asian workers from similar ethnic backgrounds. This ethnic concentration arose in part due to black-car fleet owners' preference for English-speaking Pakistani and Indian nationals over non–English-speaking immigrants, and in part because the local native-born population has neither access to the capital needed to become drivers, nor the desire to work for exceedingly low wages. The owners' propensity to hire South Asians reinforced and expanded this ethnic group's presence in the labor market through family and kinship ties, and led to a distinctive working class culture among the drivers. To build on these ties, Local 340 set up its headquarters in Queens, near areas where many South Asian drivers live.

Despite the preponderance of South Asians in the industry, it would be a mistake to assert that ethnic ties alone suffice to organize new members. Clearly, it would be a stretch to assume that Pakistani and Indian drivers, although sharing knowledge of the English language, would act on the basis of a common heritage imposed by British colonial rule. The majority of South Asian workers are Muslims from Pakistan, which is a factor in the drivers' solidarity, but there is little evidence of tensions between Christian, Hindu, and Muslim drivers. In addition to ethnic and national ties, the organizing victory arose out of the emergence of a common work culture that stemmed from the oppressive conditions in the black-car industry. This shared culture of long and hard work, arbitrary treatment by dispatchers, and TLC abuses helped engender a class identity that the union was able to emphasize and encourage workers to act upon.

Inter-union Competition and Jurisdictional Boundaries

The success of the black-car organizing drive resulted in part from the novelty of the industry. There was no jurisdictional resemblance between black-car drivers and other union members in the New York region. Taxi drivers, although ostensibly still claimed by

SEIU Local 74, were no longer organized in an established union. Rather, the drivers were mobilized by the New York City Taxi Workers Alliance—an independent organization that considered collective bargaining agreements to be inimical to the best interest of workers—and engaged in wildcat strikes and walkouts to demonstrate their power when fleet operators were most vulnerable.

Black-car drivers made up a wholly new, unorganized labor force—a product of changes in the industry, which in the early 1980s had transformed medallion taxi drivers with two-way radios into black-car drivers exclusively servicing the Manhattan central business district. In effect, the taxicab and car service industry had created a new product line to supersede an older commodity, and as a result was able to extract greater profitability from workers as it streamlined the delivery of services to upscale business clients. As a result of these changes, an entirely new workforce was recruited from New York City's rapidly growing immigrant population. The new labor market—primarily made up of recent South Asian immigrants—was considerably dissimilar to its predecessor, which comprised native-born white, black, and Latino drivers. The new black-car drivers shared some ethnic commonalities, but more important, shared a common work culture as superexploited so-called independent contractors who could barely eke out a living.

The international union and IAM District 15 embarked on a highly centralized organizing drive without a competing local unit claiming craft, industrial, or geographic jurisdiction. Moreover, no local unions could claim the right to receive these workers. While rival service sector union leaders could admire or even covet the extraordinary attainment of the black-car workers organized by District 15, no union—including the remnants of the old taxi drivers' union—could claim a competing jurisdiction in this industry segment.

A New Local

Local Lodge 340 was created by and for black-car drivers exclusively, and led by activist workers themselves. According to Lynch, "The entire organizing effort was directed at bringing real power to workers employed in the industry with as little interference from outside as possible" (interview, August 21, 2001). Although the black-car organizing campaign was directed and financed at the national and district levels, there was no need to convince an existing local with other priorities to expend resources and take on the fight. The campaign, while centrally approved, took advantage of the autonomous organizing initiated by rank-and-file drivers at car service firms. The creation of a new local allowed for a direct link between union organizers and strategists and worker activists, who were integrated into the campaign and became leaders of the local that emerged.

In contrast, an existing local with an established industrial labor market presence and dues structure might not easily have incorporated newcomers into its organization. Under such circumstances, union leaders might have had to justify using scarce funds for an organizing effort among workers in an industry outside their usual jurisdiction. All too often, unions that organize outside their traditional jurisdictions in industries that have experienced restructuring and deterioration of wage scales face the problem of trying to negotiate contracts without undermining prevailing union pay scales. Moreover, the black-car drivers did not inherit an inept union controlled by outsiders with no direct stake in defending and improving the drivers' conditions. In the black-car industry, IAM benefited from the absence of a preexisting labor–management accord and could organize from the market baseline, thus improving conditions in the industry and engendering confidence in the union.

IAM's support for the black-car drivers represents a successful union-based strategy for organizing workers in the new informal economy of New York City. The union effectively adjusted its structure to the new industrial realities, and used both rank-and-file mobilization and NLRB actions to redefine and unionize a new workforce. This centralized yet participatory structure proved critical to the dramatic initial success and the bright prospects for organizing the majority of workers in the for-hire vehicle industry.

7 The Post–September 11 Economic Crisis and the Government Crackdown on Immigrant Workers

On a late afternoon in August 2003, Mohammad Waseem, a driver for Skyline Car Service, waited in the concourse area of Newark International Airport holding a placard with the name of a female passenger scheduled to arrive. The company had dispatched him to drive the customer to her destination, for which he would receive a voucher that he could redeem for cash at the end of the week. Skyline pledges first-class service: Drivers are required to greet customers, escort them to the baggage claim area, carry and store their luggage in the trunk of the car, and drive them to their destinations in style in late-model luxury cars.

The twenty-six-year-old driver never suspected that the young businesswoman he greeted at the airport would be his last customer. Waseem cordially followed through with his usual daily routine, but when the young woman asked if she could smoke in his new car, he politely declined because regulations prohibit smoking in cars. He suggested, instead, that he would wait while she smoked her cigarette outside and then he would drive her to Manhattan. Unprepared for the woman's ensuing angry tirade, Waseem kept his cool and remained silent. Approaching her destination, the woman asked Waseem to tell her his religion and nationality.

Dutifully, he replied that he was a Muslim immigrant from Pakistan. In response, the woman called him a terrorist and said that he should be arrested and deported. Waseem said nothing. The woman wrote down his name and complained to Skyline management that he was rude, discourteous, and dangerous. The next day, Waseem was fired by Skyline, left with his car and insurance payments, without work in an industry in which jobs were very hard to come by. Waseem's experience is no exception to the rule, but rather occurs routinely in New York City. In fact, Waseem is fortunate that he was not arrested by government authorities, detained for a long period, and summarily deported. In November 2003, unable to find work for almost three months, Waseem returned to Pakistan on his own accord.

This chapter brings the immigrant workers' struggle in New York City up to date by examining the disastrous consequences of September 11, 2001 on organizing campaigns initiated since the mid-1990s. Despite considerable obstacles, immigrant worker solidarity and resistance to business continues and grows among greengrocery workers, deliverymen, black-car drivers and workers in new labor markets. Although the government crackdown has hurt all immigrants—in particular South Asian, Middle Eastern, Arab, and Islamic workers—and a new business offensive has sharply curtailed organizing campaigns, workers continue to organize to improve wages and conditions. This chapter demonstrates that workers remain resilient even under the dire conditions they now confront in New York City.

Everything changed for New Yorkers—particularly immigrant workers—in the aftermath of September 11, 2001, when terrorists commandeered two commercial airliners and crashed them into the twin World Trade Center towers, killing nearly three thousand people. It is almost impossible to make the leap from sympathy for the victims and families of the September 11 disaster to concern for immigrant workers, who—like Waseem—face daily discrimination from ordinary citizens and continual surveillance by the federal government. This book cannot do justice to the travails of the families of those who perished or the survivors who witnessed the disaster and are fated to remember it for the rest of their lives. Rather, this chapter examines how September 11 has changed the work, lives, and future of transnational workers employed in New York's unregulated service economy, particularly workers in the greengrocery, black-car, and supermarket industries.

Twin Disasters for Immigrant Workers

Immigrant workers sustained two devastating reversals in the wake of September 11. First, a long and sustained economic crisis ensued among the small businesses that support the hospitality industry, a mainstay for undocumented workers. Second, the events spurred a government crackdown on undocumented immigrants, leading to increased public discrimination and violence in the days, months, and years following the terrorist attacks.

These dual blows reversed the tangible—if imperfect—political, legal, and economic gains achieved by transnational workers during the preceding decade. Almost immediately after the attacks, employers withdrew even modest economic advances and reimposed despotic working conditions on the largely unregulated labor markets of immigrant workers. This turnaround overwhelmed transnational workers who had in recent years become more resilient and confident that raids, arrests, and deportations by federal immigration authorities were on the wane. Their optimism was justified by a nearly threefold decline in arrests from 22,000 in 1997 to 8,600 in 1999.

In part, the calm before the storm reflected the real need for immigrant labor in the United States. During the economic bubble of the late 1990s, business leaders viewed undocumented immigrants as an indispensable source of cheap labor. Because these typically low-wage workers offered the lure of reduced labor costs, many employers in manufacturing and service industries welcomed and even recruited them (Piore 1979; Waldinger and Lichter 2003).[1] By the turn of the century, transnational workers became part of the fabric of workaday life in New York City.

Even the *New York Times* was obliged to devote substantial coverage to the subject, moving immigration from a narrow labor issue to front-page news in the national and business sections. Undocumented workers were no longer seen as unusual exceptions to the rule but, according to reporter Louis Uchitelle, were commonplace in the economy and acted as an important force in holding down wages for native-born workers:

> The new leniency helps explain why overall wage increases have been less than many economists and policy makers had expected, given an unemployment rate of only 4 percent and a strong demand for people to fill jobs that pay $8 an hour or less, which is 25 percent of all jobs in the U.S. Immigrants—legal and illegal—have fed the pool of people available to take even lower-paid jobs. (Uchitelle 2000)

The federal government's response to the September 11 attacks reversed many of the gains of low-wage immigrant workers, undermining important economic advances in unregulated segments of the economy. Workers fearful of scrutiny are less likely to lodge complaints against their frequently unscrupulous employers.

A Deepening Economic Crisis

The New York City economy was thrown into chaos by the fallout of September 11, intensifying a recession that had already increased unemployment in sectors typically occupied by immigrants. Undocumented transnational workers with limited legal protections landed in an even more precarious position. The most direct economic harm to immigrant workers was extensive unemployment as small and medium-sized firms shut down temporarily or permanently after the attacks. Those employed in businesses in the World Trade Center (subsequently called Ground Zero) and the surrounding area suffered the greatest cost, as buildings in the area were destroyed, workers were laid off *en masse*, and many establishments closed. The government's emergency lockdown of Lower Manhattan blocked commercial activity, hurting small and middle-sized manufacturing firms—the majority of which operated in the unregulated economy.

The economic turmoil emanated out from Lower Manhattan to encompass the entire city and deepened the impact of the national recession. The collapse of business activity exacerbated the stock market's already dramatic drop, with particularly harsh consequences for the many transnational workers who serviced Wall

Street. As some semblance of order returned during the next two years and the stock markets staged a recovery, some workers were rehired—albeit at lower wages and with less secure positions. Other businesses in the Ground Zero area employing immigrant workers closed permanently and have not returned. Two years after the terrorist attacks, in September 2003, New York City's official unemployment rate had risen by two percentage points to 8.1 percent. If this figure accounted for those who have given up searching for work, the unemployment rate would be twice as high.

The number of small firms employing low-wage immigrant workers dropped significantly after the attacks, especially in the apparel, food service, transportation, and leisure and hospitality industries. The economic pall that followed September 11 also wreaked havoc on workers legally employed in all sectors of the economy, including unionized education, health care, and construction jobs, and others loosely associated with public funding. In April 2003, New York City mayor Michael Bloomberg laid off 5,401 municipal workers to help close a budget deficit in fiscal year 2003–2004.

The loss of work—sometimes in jobs set up before coming to New York—has added to the economic desperation among transnational workers who have made a long trek to the United States. Typically, Asian and African immigrants must have some assurance from friends or relatives that they have a job waiting, considering the great cost of the trip and the possibility that they will not return for many years. Interviews following September 11 reveal that fear of detention and deportation by U.S. immigration authorities has created unease and fear among workers. In addition, many workers complain that they are unable to make remittances back home due to the sluggish economy, lack of work, and high cost of living in New York City. For example, in exchange for staying in the basement of an apartment in Astoria, Queens, three construction workers from Central America have worked ten-hour days without safety protections for a contractor rehabbing a building in Harlem (interview, anonymous representative of workers, November 4, 2003).

While no private labor market in New York City has been completely immune to the economic effects of September 11, some have been hurt more than others. Those hit hardest by unemployment are workers in the hospitality and entertainment industries that rely on a stable flow of visitors—businesspeople and tourists, who use private transportation, stay at hotels, eat at restaurants, and are entertained at theaters, music venues, museums, and sporting events. The vast majority of workers in the hospitality industry are low-wage immigrant workers. Everything came to a halt after the terrorist attacks as visitors stopped coming to the city. Even the so-called "bridge and tunnel" regional visitors from outlying counties stopped traveling to the central city. Remarkably fewer people who live within the city's borders visit the city's major attractions due to a lack of money or, after September 11, vague fears of death and destruction. For-hire vehicle drivers, many of whom are Muslims from South Asia, have also been especially hard hit by increased discrimination and stereotypical accusations that they are associated with terrorism. However, Mexican workers in greengroceries and Francophone Africans in supermarkets—typically recession-proof industries—have not experienced the colossal decline in work and income endured by black-car drivers and others in the hospitality industry.

Debt Peonage and For-Hire Vehicle Workers

Among the three labor markets studied, the for-hire vehicle industry is weathering the steepest decline following September 11, owing to its dependence on corporate firms in Manhattan's Central Business District and customers using the three major airports that serve the city. In the days following the terrorist attacks, all drivers were barred from entering the core business district in Lower Manhattan south of Canal Street. For an additional six months, government restrictions were imposed on all motorized traffic other than emergency vehicles in the Ground Zero area, including the Financial District. The steep decline in airline passenger traffic after September 11 eroded the black-car business even further. Ridership plunged by 75 percent in the weeks and months following the attacks, and economic conditions in the industry had not improved enough for many workers even two years later (interview, Syed Armughan ul-Asar, September 27, 2003).

As noted in Chapter 6, the structure of the black-car industry, in which drivers are required to borrow heavily to pay franchise fees, purchase late-model luxury cars, and pay for automobile insurance—frequently from the same fleet owners that employ them—has left workers in particularly dire financial straits. Although business plummeted after September 2001, franchise fees, car loans, and auto insurance premiums were not forgiven.[2] The dilemma of black-car drivers starkly resembles that of indentured servants obliged to work off their debts to buy freedom from their masters, with the exception that many of today's black-car drivers have no hope of freeing themselves from fleet owners.

Many workers, desperate to stay afloat, say they now work even longer than the twelve-hour-a-day, seven-day-a-week schedule they had grown accustomed to over the years. One driver interviewed in September 2003 could only be reached on his cell phone between the hours of 3:00 am and 11:00 am. The wretchedly fatigued driver told me despairingly, "I am on the road at 11:00 am to pick up my first customers, and I must keep driving until three o'clock in the morning, and still I don't make enough to pay all my bills" (interview, September 29, 2003). A driver at one company said that several of his co-workers, unable to meet their payments, had, like Waseem, given up and returned to Pakistan. And the financial morass was the least of the drivers' problems as the U.S. federal government and local agents initiated a swift and unrelenting campaign of interrogation, detention, and deportation (discussed below).

We Are Not Family: Mexican Workers in New York City

The recession and the economic effects of September 11 have, in particular, harmed Mexican workers in New York City through rising unemployment, a business counter-offensive, and the lack of government support or recognition for the work of transnational workers. However, migration has grown as the demand for low-wage labor in New York remains strong and conditions deteriorate in Mexico.

Unemployment

The turmoil caused by the September 11 attacks undermined the already precarious financial situation of undocumented workers from Latin America who remain in the underbelly of the New York regional economy. While the food industry is typically recession proof, nearly 3,100 Mexicans lost their jobs in the Ground Zero area due to declining business and the closing of dozens of firms such as greengroceries, retail outlets, and newspaper stands. The drop in travel to the city led to empty hotels and restaurants, which also employ a great number of workers from Mexico and Central America. In the restaurant and hospitality industry, immigrant workers typically work in "back of the house" jobs as cooks, bussers, dishwashers, cleaners, and delivery workers. Hundreds of thousands of Latin American workers in the New York City area who lost their jobs or whose income was severely reduced had no place to turn (Cason and Brooks 2001).

Even before September 11, growing unemployment resulting from the late 1990s' recession caused thousands of immigrant workers to return to Mexico. Still more left in the two years after September 11 when the once-flourishing service sector failed to recover to the levels of the 1990s. The slow and tenuous national economic recovery has not been accompanied by a commensurate increase in employment, and hundreds of thousands of immigrant workers in the New York region have joined native-born workers in the tedious search for work. Officially, from January 2001 to March 2003, 226,100 jobs were lost in New York City. Unemployment is concentrated in the restaurant, hotel, and retail industries where immigrants tend to work in greater numbers (Bernhardt and Rubin 2003, 1). In late 2002, so many restaurants closed down that one employer reported "four to five Mexicans" walking in each day asking for work (interview, manager, Gonzalez y Gonzalez Restaurant, April 4, 2002). Those lucky enough to find restaurant jobs were frequently hired on a casual basis as part-time, temporary, or day laborers.

Business Offensive

Despite or perhaps because of the hardship, U.S. employers are exploiting immigrants more than ever. The economic repercussions of September 11 have transformed immigrant workers, once likened to "members of the family" by Korean greengrocery owners, into, at best, distant relatives. The terrorist attacks demonstrated that transnational workers were most vulnerable to exploitation, and revealed the degree of disdain employers, public authorities, and private citizens have for them. Businesses seized on September 11 as an opportunity to reverse the legal and wage gains of immigrant workers by threatening to turn them over to immigration authorities and imposing a more despotic workplace. Whereas before September 2001, businesses would often simply repress migrant worker dissent, afterward—with a large reservoir of unemployed workers to draw upon—the common response to worker complaints was immediate dismissal (Ching Louie 2001).

Government Apathy

Adding insult to injury, the appeals for assistance from immigrant workers' representatives were largely ignored by the U.S. government and charitable organizations. In general, the government has been apathetic regarding the economic crisis faced by undocumented workers who have faithfully worked for low wages during the past decade. Even though migrant workers are essential to the New York economy, the government provided immigrant workers with little emergency assistance or aid. Displaced undocumented immigrant workers in Lower Manhattan were ineligible for unemployment insurance or relief funds to tide them over until they could find new jobs. As Sasha Polakow-Suransky observes, undocumented immigrants are also hesitant to come forward for fear of deportation:

> Most are reluctant to risk what little security they have as illegal immigrants for a chance at the relief available. Those who do come forward face the sometimes impossible task of proving that they or their family member worked in lower Manhattan at the time of the attacks, a precondition for all benefit programs. Those who can clear that hurdle must confront the grim reality of what the government can actually provide. Most programs operated by the Federal Emergency Management Administration (FEMA) are not available to illegal immigrants, who are also denied federal-disaster unemployment funds and New York State unemployment benefits. (Polakow-Suransky 2001, 11–12)

In addition, government authorities typically let up on enforcement of labor laws, due to the large number of unpaid back-wage complaints by immigrants and legal claims filed by workers with the State of New York.

Federal assistance programs providing emergency funds to businesses distressed by the terrorist attacks reveal the pervasiveness of New York's underground economy. Businesses in the unregulated economy typically do not keep wage and other financial records, and are ineligible for government disaster funding. Among the small and medium-sized businesses in Lower Manhattan that were eligible for federal disaster relief, only a small percentage actually applied for and received assistance. Instead, emergency funding disproportionately went to corporations.

Two years after the September 11 attacks, more than a third of the $539 million in federal emergency funds secured by New York State legislators and intended for small businesses had gone to large corporate investment firms, financial traders, and lawyers who did not suffer as great a financial loss. According to the *New York Times*, "Far smaller amounts went to restaurants, retailers and other small businesses, many of them dependent on the foot traffic that largely disappeared from Lower Manhattan after the attack" (Wyatt and Fried 2003).

Desperate for help, the Mexican community marshaled its minimal resources to help transnational workers especially in need. For some immigrant workers, several New York–based Mexican community groups such as Tepeyac, Casa Mexico, and the Mexican American Workers Association (AMAT) and IAM Local 340 have provided help in obtaining government benefits and job training, and have continued to assist in nonpayment of wage claims. The organizations also publicized the great hardship that Mexican immigrants in New York suffered as a result of the collapse of the World Trade Center and the deleterious consequences for the well-being of workers' families back home. More than sixty Mexicans in New York who worked in and around the World Trade Center remain unaccounted for, according to Brother Joel Magallán, director of Tepeyac. Yet assistance from national affinity organizations provided only a small proportion of the income lost as employers dismissed workers, shortened their hours, and cut wages.

New Demand and Rising Poverty

Yet as conditions continue to worsen for workers and peasants in Mexico and demand for low-wage workers grows, many have returned willy-nilly to New York City and other destinations in the United States. Because Mexicans tend to migrate to locations where they have friends and family, many have stayed or returned to New York, even though conditions have deteriorated and full-time, steady work is not readily available. According to one Mexican food service worker: "Even part-time work is better than no work back home" (interview, April 8, 2003). Over and over, workers report the need to send remittances to their families in Mexico for food, clothing, shelter, education and other basic necessities (interview, Juan Haro, March 11, 2003). After oil revenue, remittances from nationals working in the United States is the second most important source of revenue for the Mexican economy, accounting for $14.5 billion in revenue in 2002, according to a report released by the Inter-American Development Bank and the Pew Institute in October 2003. The report noted that 20 percent of all Mexicans receive money from immigrant workers in the United States. The pace of migration to New York has declined since the late 1990s, but in the ensuing years, many immigrants are returning to the city working in unregulated, low-wage jobs. Despite enhanced border security, the report concluded that immigrants are not deterred from coming to the United States due to the continued demand for low-wage labor (Thompson 2003).

The U.S. Government Assault on Immigrant Workers

Perhaps the most pernicious development in the aftermath of the attacks of September 11 has been the immediate, harsh reaction by the U.S. government, which has targeted undocumented immigrants from selected countries for punishment. Shortly after the terrorist attacks, the government launched an attack of its own on the civil liberties of undocumented immigrants and foreigners who overstayed their visas to work in the United States. Just forty-five days after September 11, on October 26, 2001, President George Bush signed into law the USA PATRIOT Act, which recklessly impedes the civil liberties of all Americans, but especially targets immigrants from countries with large Muslim populations.

The USA PATRIOT Act gives the federal government far-reaching surveillance powers at home and abroad. In short order, immigrants were bearing the brunt of an extensive, protracted U.S. Department of Justice campaign of spying, detaining, and deporting foreigners deemed to be security risks—usually for no other reason than their ethnic or religious background. As the government has grasped at straws in its attempt to capture persons with links to terrorist organizations, innocent people of South Asian, Middle Eastern, Arab, and Muslim descent have been intensively scrutinized, and unknown thousands have been detained and deported. The campaign has cast a pall over both legal and illegal immigrants of Muslim descent who know fellow nationals who have been detained for long periods without charges and, if lucky, deported.

Since September 11, U.S. authorities have steadily expanded efforts to enforce federal immigration laws, and have targeted noncitizen immigrants and even citizens from immigrant backgrounds for scrutiny under federal and state labor statutes. Government authorities specifically target immigrants from South Asian, Middle Eastern, Arab, and Muslim backgrounds more than other populations, although many people wrongfully believed to belong to these groups have also found themselves the recipients of private and government scrutiny. All persons who have migrated from a select group of countries must be fingerprinted and register with the local office of the Bureau of Citizenship and Immigration Services (BCIS). Due to its large population of immigrants from South Asia and the Middle East, New York City has become an epicenter of government surveillance, detention, and deportation.

Detention centers have been established in Brooklyn and New Jersey to interrogate persons who ultimately *have not* been found to have a record of engagement with criminal organizations. Often family members are not provided with information on the whereabouts and status of detainees. Some immigrants are detained without charges and may be denied legal counsel. Lawyers representing imprisoned immigrants often are not granted evidence of the charges, and thus can do little besides check in on their clients. Typically, after innocence is established, immigrants are deported for improper documentation. Under the Homeland Security special registration program, from November 2002 to May 2003, some 85,000 Muslim and Arab residents in the United States were interviewed, fingerprinted, and photographed (Swarns 2003). According to the New York Immigration Coalition, as of September 30, 2003, some 13,799 immigrants out of 83,519 men registering with the Department of Homeland Security are facing deportation, and another 2,700 have been detained without any charges of a relationship to terrorism (Cheng 2003; New York Immigration Coalition 2003). Many more have left on their own to avoid harassment and interrogation. But the government's efforts have yet to lead to any evidence of a conspiracy among immigrants in the United States (Dworkin 2003).

The government offensive extends to any immigrant workers who fit their profile. Bhairavi Desai, executive director of the New York City Taxi Workers Alliance (NYC-TWA), reports that since September 11, drivers regularly have vanished off the streets without any accounting for their whereabouts. According to Desai, taxi drivers are working in the shadow of federal authorities who are monitoring their every move:

> Right after September 11 the FBI had a staff going through the papers of drivers. Now the INS and FBI are going out to garages of taxi and black-car drivers and checking on their immigration status. Many drivers are picked up after being singled out by passengers as terrorists. I have been told by one owner that the Department of Homeland Security has a permanent staff at the Taxi and Limousine Commission targeting mainly persons of Asian or Southwest Asian descent.
> (interview, Bhairavi Desai, September 23, 2003)

Racial and religious profiling by local, state, and federal officials has severely undermined New York's black-car industry, leading to increased enforcement actions against drivers who already endure police stops and tickets for driving violations they assert they did not commit. Ul-Asar Armughan, of Machinists Local 340, points out that, "There has been a lot of government harassment, personal bodily attacks, discrimination from landlords and commercial establishments, and racist remarks against our drivers by customers and even other drivers (September 27, 2003)."

In addition to stepped-up enforcement and deportation, the government has discontinued most conventional forms of immigration to the United States from South Asia, the Middle East, and countries with large Muslim populations. It is nearly impossible for most people from these countries to receive a work, tourist, or student visa. Since January 2003, nationals from a large and growing number of Muslim countries in Asia and North Africa are now required to register with the U.S. government on a weekly basis.[3]

On July 23, 2003, the BCIS inaugurated a new, more coercive, administrative rule called *special registration*, which requires persons from designated countries residing in the United States to undergo in-person interviews with immigration officers upon entry into the United States and to notify authorities of any changes of address, employment, and schooling.

The federal government's secretive and unabashedly hostile policies have had a chilling effect on selected foreign nationals and immigrant workers in the informal economy. In immigrant communities, rumor based on fact and fiction is flowing about the degree of government surveillance. Workers are more reluctant to grant interviews, out of fear of being reported to the government. Most transnational workers from South Asia and West Africa who do not have legal status are not talking at all. Many workers believe, rightly or wrongly, that the Department of Homeland Security has set up operations through the FBI in local community centers, mosques, and places of employment. The fear of deportation among Mexicans and other Latin Americans is not as pronounced as it is among Asians and some Africans. Because Mexicans have become a crucial part of the New York City labor force, though some fear deportation, more fret about poor working conditions or worry about finding work.

In the months and years to come, government repression against immigrants from target regions can be expected to continue, as evidenced by statements from federal officials that aggregate all Muslims together as terrorists, fanning the flames of intolerance on the part of the public. After thousands of arrests, the federal government had no convictions three years after September 11, 2001:

> So Ashcroft's record is 0 for 5,000. When the Attorney General was locking these men up in the immediate wake of the attacks, he held almost daily press conferences to announce how many "suspected terrorists" had been detained. No press conference has been forthcoming to announce that exactly none of them have turned out to be actual terrorists. (Cole 2004)

Relentless government efforts to scrutinize selected populations continue unabated, despite lack of evidence of illegal activities. The growth of domestic surveillance in the name of national security is disquieting to constitutional scholars, who argue that the crackdown violates protections in the Bill of Rights that are so important to American democracy.

Civil Society's Assault on Immigrants

In addition to the growing federal government crackdown, more and more South Asian, Middle Eastern, Arab, and Muslim immigrants have come under attack from private citizens as well. Some victims of violence have been U.S. citizens or immigrants from other regions. In the week following September 11, New York Police Commissioner Bernard Kerik reported fifty-six physical assaults and verbal bias incidents in New York City against Arabs. Ironically, Israelis of Middle Eastern origin and Sikhs from South Asia had also reported police stops and verbal and physical assaults from individual citizens (Berkey-Gerard, Robinson, and Viado 2001).

One food store worker in his early twenties from Yemen told me that he was verbally and physically attacked by gangs of young white men even before the events of September 11. Just a week after that date, the young man was knifed by a white man wielding a box cutter shouting racist epithets against Arabs and telling him to go back home. What the attacker did not know is that his victim was a college-educated American-born U.S. citizen who happened to be of Yemeni ancestry. Even after sustaining cuts on his torso and forearm, bleeding so profusely that it could not be hidden, he was still too afraid to report the incident to the police for fear of being arrested (interview, Yemeni grocery worker, September, 28, 2001). In the two years since September 11, at least ten immigrant workers from South Asia working in the black-car industry did not report acts of violence (some of which resulted in serious injury) to the police for fear of recrimination.

Two years after September 2001, it is disturbing that verbal and physical attacks by private individuals against immigrant workers have continued. In September 2003, the black-car drivers union held a press conference detailing verbal and physical assaults on workers. One middle-aged Pakistani man who has resided in the United States for fifteen years was beaten up so badly by a motorist that his arm was broken in two places. In the heat of the summer, the driver was attacked as rush-hour traffic slowed to a halt on FDR Drive on Manhattan's East Side near 96th Street. The driver reported that a motorist in an adjacent car walked over to his car, punched him, and then beat him with a baseball bat. The black-car worker was unable to drive for at least four months. The victim was so suspicious that he believed his telephone line was tapped by federal authorities, and would only talk to me in person (interview, anonymous black-car driver, October 8, 2003).

Not all New Yorkers are xenophobic, ungrateful bigots who despise South Asians, Middle Easterners, Arabs, and Muslims. In the weeks after September 11, amid the public displays of mourning, many local community defense groups—often made up of people who did not belong to targeted populations—emerged in New York City to protect Arabs and Muslims from public and private attack. Several watch groups formed in neighborhoods that had recognizable mosques such as the East Village and Harlem.

Attacks on South Asian, Middle Eastern, Arab, and Muslim immigrants tend to be disorganized and random, and are rarely reported in the media. Immigrant workers and other targeted populations are responding to rising government recrimination and private assaults by "circling the wagons" in neighborhoods that have higher concentrations of members of the target groups. In the past two years, even as many South Asians have left the U.S. in fear of official and unofficial vengeance, those who have remained in many cases move into homogeneous neighborhoods in Brooklyn and Queens where they find greater safety in numbers. The ghettoized working-class South Asian neighborhoods reinforce religious and national identities, as well as the work and community ties so essential to the development of labor solidarity. The trend represents a potential reversal of the historical pattern of ethnic settlement in U.S. cities presented in *City Trenches*, Ira Katznelson's (1991) classic work on urban America. It remains to be seen whether the acceleration of globalization will concomitantly create work and neighborhood ghettos resembling those that were more prominent in cities at the turn of the twentieth century—communities that, as argued here, play important roles in spurring class action.

Post–September 11 Immigrant Worker Activism

As noted, Mexican and Central American workers continue to migrate to New York City, given the relative ease of traveling back and forth across the border despite the rising risk of interdiction by border patrol agents. Because these Mexicans have never applied for visas, as have most other immigrants, they are significantly more difficult for the government to track. Moreover, government and businesses increasingly recognize the economic importance of low-wage transnational workers from Mexico, and have not applied the same level of surveillance directed at other immigrants. In the greengrocery industry, the State Attorney General's Code of Conduct, which now compels employers to comply with federal and state minimum wage and overtime laws, is viewed as a model to be emulated in other industries. Since September 11, workers inside and outside unions have established informal representative organizations that report violations to the government and challenge employer abuses.

Although Mexicans remain fearful of losing their jobs in a tight labor market, they remain willing to challenge employers for improved wages and working conditions, even if it means losing work. A possible explanation is that the federal government is not clamping down on the rights of Mexicans and Central Americans as hard as it is on Arab, Muslim, South Asian, and Middle Eastern workers.

Nonpayment of wages is rampant in the restaurant industry, although significant awards have been made to workers after protests and legal efforts by workers' organizations (interview, Saru Jayaraman, October 4, 2003). The militancy that first took shape among Mexican greengrocery workers in 1998 expanded into new industries, as struggles exploded in the restaurant industry and beyond. For example, in 2003, members of R.O.C.-NY (Restaurant Opportunity Center of New York, an immigrant workers' center loosely affiliated with the Hotel Employees and Restaurant Employees union) won three back-wage claims in New York City totaling almost $250,000 from three employers through protest actions and lawsuits; the center has grown to five hundred members (Jayaraman 2003). Also, in June 2003, Casa Mexico and AMAT launched a campaign to organize some 1,500 workers in the laundry and dry cleaners industries in Manhattan. In July 2003, New York State Attorney General Eliot Spitzer announced a settlement with a laundry to reinstate and provide back pay for illegally fired workers who organized against an employer in the city's Lower East Side (Office of New York State Attorney General Eliot Spitzer 2003). Still, while labor militancy remains strong, the economic crisis in the hospitality industries has eroded strikes and job actions among Mexicans who depend on stable jobs, which are now significantly more difficult to come by.

Francophone West African supermarket delivery workers have not experienced the same economic impact as workers in labor markets that are more sensitive to recessionary swings. Because their union—the Retail, Wholesale and Department Store Union (RWDSU), a division of the United Food and Commercial Workers (UFCW)—continues to neglect their concerns, the workers organize on the basis of social networks established at work and in their isolated national communities. One major obstacle the workers face is the difficulty the government has imposed on travel to the United States. Most workers are not happy with the changes, but in the wake of September 11, they have little recourse.

Black-car drivers from South Asian, Middle Eastern, Arab, and Muslim backgrounds, weathering both an economic crisis and government oppression, have strengthened their level of class solidarity, relying on membership organizations coordinated by the union and stronger community ties. The dual economic and government crises have further galvanized ties among these immigrant workers and encouraged them to fight for their economic and political rights. IAM Local 340, the Black-Car Drivers Union, is finding ways to reduce the financial burden on drivers who have lost income by encouraging fleet owners to apply for government aid and share the benefits with workers. Moreover, as noted in Chapter 6, the union is calling for a fare increase that would accrue fully to the workers.

Currently, Local 340 identifies cases of government repression and private discrimination against immigrant workers and monitors the political environment, holding public events, filing charges on behalf of drivers, and organizing workers—a considerably more difficult task considering the ongoing backlash against its drivers. The organization of black-car drivers does not work exclusively to establish recognition and collective bargaining agreements with fleet owners. It also represents drivers who have yet to receive employer recognition but are in need of all forms of assistance. Nonunion black-car employees of large New York fleets are organized even if they do not have bargaining relationships with employers through Local 340. The union assists workers inside and outside the union in ameliorating their economic situation and defending against government and private retribution.

The business offensive against organizing efforts of immigrants targeted by the federal government only sets back the labor movement. The Immigrant Workers Freedom Ride, a caravan of workers that traveled across the nation in September and October 2003 to publicize the need for amnesty and labor protections for foreign workers, demonstrates that the AFL-CIO and more unions are resisting efforts to profile immigrants as terrorists. Inspired by the Freedom Riders of the Civil Rights Movement, the Immigrant Workers Freedom Ride gained widespread attention throughout the United States (Wypijewski 2003). Remarkably, the New York City Central Labor Council is portraying immigrants as victims of both September 11 and the new government crackdown. While the events of September 11, 2001, have jeopardized the gains made by immigrant workers during the past decade, unions in New York have opposed the government reaction by calling attention to the importance of defending immigrants from agressive government policies of racial profiling, surveillance, detention, and deportation that have been instituted under the USA PATRIOT Act and other federal legislative actions. The Freedom Ride, sponsored by organized labor, clearly established that unions were taking the side of exploited immigrant workers against government coercion.

8 Parallel Organizing: Immigrants and Unions

Any labor organizer deeply engaged in a campaign to establish a union knows the decisive moment foreshadowing the outcome of the struggle—a moment when success or failure appears on the horizon with all that is victory or defeat. If the workers win a union, negotiations with management commence—lose and you move on to another organizing campaign or give up. But unlike professional organizers, win or lose, most workers do not have the option of exit, as most must continue working on the job no matter the outcome.

Transnational workers who have recently migrated to New York City almost never have the option to move on to another job, since employers typically channel new immigrants into labor market ghettos segregated in the informal economy. Desperation alone is not enough to explain militancy. It is surprising, then, that immigrant workers in New York City, given the obstacles they face, mobilize to improve wages and conditions. Despite widespread belief among labor unions that September 11 severely eroded immigrant labor capacity for a broad mobilization in New York, highly visible strikes in the unregulated economy have persisted and even grown in the two years since. The only difference now is that workers wage most strikes in markets, restaurants, and laundries autonomously, without the sanction or support of unions.

Transnational Workers and Industrial Restructuring

Political economists who emphasize the emergence of a new global economy imply that free market forces have suddenly swept away government regulation of national economies and labor markets. Globalization and the expansion of transnational labor is not a new feature of the world economy, though they have become significantly more important from 1970 to the present, as corporations have restructured and the U.S. labor movement has deteriorated. The recent expansion of global labor markets should not be confused with a universal, albeit uneven, process that began centuries ago.

Nonetheless, the expansion of a transnational migrant labor force working in newly restructured labor markets in the Northern Hemisphere is a relatively new and distinctive feature of the global economy. In the United States, New York City has become ever more reliant on immigrant labor working in low-wage unregulated businesses and domestic services. Neoliberal globalization has produced a new class of transnational workers in the city and undermined the city's unionized labor markets.

Unions are not blameless in this process. The legacy of union concessionary bargaining and the rise of two-tier wage and benefit hierarchies in the 1980s, which protected a core of senior workers at the expense of younger workers, have come to haunt organized labor. Unions may have protected that older cohort of individual workers, but they have not preserved living-wage union jobs for those entering the workforce in succeeding decades. Most of those protected by the unions have by now retired and been replaced by newcomers working in jobs that do not provide equivalent wages, benefits, and security. By the 1990s, the power of unions to defend job standards and the social wage provided by government had been eroded even further than in the previous decade, as many unions lost touch with the new workers entering their industries.

The reliance of the current New York City economy on transnational labor is markedly different from what prevailed in previous eras. Today's labor force arrives from locations throughout the world, rather than from one or two regions, as in the late nineteenth and early twentieth century. Whereas Eastern and Southern European immigrants predominated at the turn of the last century and many found employment in basic manufacturing industries, today's immigrants work in a more diverse set of high-tech and low-tech labor markets, making it even more difficult for workers to unify as a class across ethnic and national lines. The sudden expansion of immigration to New York City in the 1980s and 1990s has supplied the workforce to fill unregulated low-wage jobs in the informal economy, a development that has had a profoundly adverse effect on the viability and prospects for a revitalized local and national labor movement.

Today, immigrant workers labor under once-extinct forms of labor-management relations that have resurfaced because unions are weaker and government agencies have failed to enforce labor laws. A key point of this book is that these re-emerging work regimes have at times changed the legal definition of what it means to be a worker. In the supermarket delivery and for-hire transportation industries, the status of workers was redefined to that of independent contractors or entrepreneurs; though in reality the workers remained employees, albeit employees working like indentured servants.

An essential feature of the globalized economy is the acceleration of the international exchange of capital, technology, and labor. Globalization of labor has taken on new meaning not only because corporations transfer production to new regions, but also because workers today migrate at an unprecedented rate, with no plans to permanently settle. Today, immigrants moving from poor countries of the South to rich countries of the North with a demand for cheap labor are an essential component of the world economy. Although a large proportion of such workers migrate illegally and are often treated inhospitably in their destination countries, they remain crucial to many industries (Castles and Miller 2003; Stalker 2001).

New immigrant workers typically work in situations with substandard wages and working conditions that undercut labor standards in national and regional labor markets. The precarious legal status of these workers further complicates organizing efforts. Even highly skilled workers in the high-tech economy with formal guest-worker status—a government non-immigrant visa that provides legal work permits—can be deported once their employment is terminated. From 2000 to 2002, as the U.S. economy slowed, wages for more highly skilled immigrant workers have declined. Now that much high-tech work can be outsourced by U.S. corporations to professional workers abroad, the necessity for immigrant H-1B workers may begin to decline.

Conditions are even more precarious for the vast majority of undocumented immigrants employed in unskilled and semi-skilled jobs in New York City. Undocumented immigrants are estimated

to comprise 40 percent of the estimated one-million foreign migrants counted by the U.S. Census Bureau that moved to New York
City during the 1990s (Ciurea 2002; Department of City Planning
1999). Employers frequently call in BCIS when undocumented
workers complain about their conditions or attempt to organize
into unions. Further, immigrants themselves often seek to return to
their home countries. Many transnational workers in the three labor
markets examined here report that they migrated only because they
could not earn enough in their home countries and plan to return
once they amass a small nest egg. This makes for a transient labor
force that some consider resistant to organizing efforts.

The very concept of transnational labor implies rebound migration to and from the developing and developed worlds. Transnational migration is particularly common among workers from
nearby countries in the Americas, but demand for cheap labor in
New York City has also been a magnet for immigrants from Asia,
Africa, and Eastern Europe. However, in the post–September 11
environment, stricter border controls, registration requirements,
and policies of detention and deportation for workers overstaying
their visas have made such migration more arduous.

Immigrant Worker Solidarity: Thick and Thin

The worn-out assertion by local and national labor officials that
immigrants in New York City are especially hard to organize is dis-
pelled by the three case studies, which reveal the development of
autonomous forms of solidarity among workers facing conditions
in similar labor markets. The distinct industrial zones that have
buoyed class solidarity in the past may have vanished, but workers
continue to organize at their postindustrial jobs and in the communities where they live. Mexicans communicate on the job and
in barrios throughout the city. Francophone West African delivery
workers form bonds on the job and in the segregated communities
of Harlem and the South Bronx. Black-car drivers, primarily from
South Asia, converse while waiting for customers in commercial
districts, airports, and specific rest areas, and at home in Brooklyn
and Queens.

Immigrant worker organizations based on workplace solidarity persist and grow on their own, even if unnoticed by unions. Many union leaders disparage the formation of these independent organizations as too weak and inadequate to defend labor rights. The small victories of workers organizing autonomously may indeed be transitory and limited in scope, but they mean much to immigrants whose wages, work conditions, and respect on the job have improved as a result.

A theme common to all three organizing drives examined in this book is the self-organization of workers well before the formal inception of union campaigns, a process that occurs among all exploited workers to a greater or lesser extent, depending on working conditions and commonalities that encourage workplace solidarity. In each case study, immigrant workers largely isolated from established unions approached outsiders for help in addressing unresolved labor problems—community groups, legal rights organizations, and unions outside the workplace jurisdiction.

The development of formal and informal organizations reflects workers' wishes to address super-exploitative conditions in each of the respective industries—greengroceries, black-car services, and supermarkets. In each, class solidarity developed out of the enduring identities the workers brought from their home countries, their shared experience of workplace oppression, and the racialized identities imposed on them by their employers, the government, and the rest of the segregated city and region. In all three cases, unions entered the struggle only after the workers had made initial contact. Because the immigrant communities were embryonic and had not developed economically and politically, there were few established groups—sometimes none—that workers could turn to for support.

Initially, Mexican greengrocery workers created an informal organization to collect back wages from employers by staging protests outside their stores. Only after repeating the protests did the workers forge a permanent organization and win support from community groups; eventually a union outside the traditional jurisdiction took notice. Francophone West African supermarket delivery workers organized autonomously and carried out a two-day strike to seek redress for unacceptable conditions. Their new organization—the African Workers Association—approached labor lawyers and state authorities for help. A union outside the traditional jurisdiction wooed the workers, but a union from the traditional jurisdiction reasserted its authority and signed contracts with management. In the black-car industry, immigrant drivers met informally at garages and at common pick-up and drop-off sites. They soon formed an organization, which then approached outside advisers. Their organization, unlike the greengrocery and delivery workers, carried on as an independent union chartered with the International Association of Machinists and Aerospace Workers (IAM).

Isolation as a Source of Transnational Worker Solidarity

This book does not accept that class identities are fixed or that they transcend ethnic, racial, religious, or other ties among workers in the context of immigrant life in New York City. Identity is an elastic formulation that sometimes strengthens and sometimes weakens the power of immigrant workers. As circumstances change, people gravitate to the identities that most advance their interests. When unemployment is high in industries with racial and ethnic divisions, class solidarity may be eviscerated if one group appears to be getting a disproportionately high share of the jobs, as is the case in the construction industry, with a large concentration of white male workers.

Class solidarity among transnational immigrants emerges from home country cultural identities that are called on when workers face exploitation as a specific group. Workers thus project a distinct outlook that demonstrates their cultural awareness and their detachment both from their employer and from civil society. The workplace becomes a site of struggle that redefines the cultural relationships among sometimes-disparate immigrant workers as class relationships. In the case of Africans, an imposed racial identity helps develop a practical class solidarity. Thus, Senegalese and Malian Muslims from Francophone West Africa see themselves in New York City as exploited Africans, because their employers and customers do not make distinctions on the basis of their distinctive religious, ethnic, or national origins, but on the basis of race.

Despite the obstacles to dissent created by their "illegal" status and their unfamiliarity with the new social environment, isolated immigrant workers have a greater propensity to organize and resist oppression on the job than do native-born workers. Seclusion creates a concentrated set of ties among workers on a job, since they have few opportunities to build relationships with other workers. The unforeseen militancy among new immigrant workers cannot be explained by the mere fact of low wages. If low wages alone were a sufficient cause of collective action, many native-born workers would be equally militant. Resistance begins at the workplace through the crystallization of close-knit social networks and isolation from the outside world. In a manner akin to prison labor, isolation is imposed by the requirement to work day and night for employers and labor contractors, severely restricting any life outside the workplace. Immigrant workers' participation in a range of social networks would diminish the importance of their workplace connections based on class, race, gender, ethnicity, and religion.

This argument runs counter to Robert Putnam's view that the more social networks people enter, the better off they are. These networks, termed social capital, are the basis for the revival of American community (Putnam 2000). Rather, the lonely workplace is seen as the primary site of solidarity and the foundation for shaping lasting class bonds that are the basis for challenging the corporate domination that erodes community. In the three cases studied here, it is clear that the relative absence of such networks reaching beyond the workplace has in fact been a source of strength and solidarity among fellow workers, who must rely on themselves to defend and advance their rights. Unlike low-wage native workers who move from one job to another and work sometimes two, three or more jobs, immigrants do not have similar options.

Unions and Immigrants: Preserving the Past, Organizing the Future

We often think of unions as militant or even radical organizations, but in fact most are conservative institutions wedded to preserving the past. By their very nature, unions will oppose any change in a labor market that may weaken the bargaining power of their members. Unions are relatively inflexible institutions that have difficulty reacting to changes in capital formation that alter the predictable composition of work and thereby threaten standards established in the past. This characterization of union conservatism is not meant as an ideological indictment; it is intended simply to describe unions' historical institutional inflexibility in the American state.

Ironically, as Joseph Schumpeter (1942) implies in *Capitalism, Socialism, and Democracy*, capitalist employers must radically and continually transform the conditions of work in order to stay competitive, while it is the workers and their representatives who fight to maintain the status quo. Along with this tendency, however, there is also a dialectic of union institutional conservatism and rank-and-file radicalism that has resonated throughout the history of U.S. labor. In the late nineteenth and early twentieth centuries, facing industrial change, unions struggled mightily to hang on to the regime of craft production and the working traditions that governed their members' lives, even at the cost of disregarding the majority of workers employed in the emerging mass production industries. Similarly, unions today are fighting to preserve mature production and service industries under threat from global competition and corporate restructuring.

It is therefore not surprising that industrial unions today, organized by immigrants in the 1930s and 1940s, are conservative when it comes to recognizing and responding to the changing terrain of capitalism. We can thereby explain the lack of union interest in organizing new members with few associations to past struggles. For example, the United Steelworkers of America better understands the importance of expanding tariffs and quotas—and thus is more keenly interested in lobbying government officials to defend the industry from foreign interlopers—than it does the need to organize new workers in the minimills that are replacing integrated steel plants in the United States. This conservatism places unions at a disadvantage against capital, and also has the potential to alienate prospective new recruits, who frequently find themselves neglected by unions.

If in the early twentieth century the most pressing need in the labor movement was to bridge the antagonistic positions of craft unionism and industrial unionism, today it is to integrate new communities of workers into the labor movement without undermining wage and workplace norms established over decades of collective bargaining. As unskilled and semiskilled unionized workers grow old and leave the labor force, minority and immigrant workers entering the labor market for the first time frequently replace them. In this climate, energetic unions that emphasize the importance of workers' wage and workplace demands, and that have strong connections to new demographic constituencies, are often in a better position to organize immigrant workers in an industry than are more settled unions that may have jurisdiction.

Today, the exponential growth of low-wage jobs in the service sector presents a particular challenge to unions accustomed to representing older workers employed in jobs quickly becoming anachronistic. Thus, as membership and density declines, unions are slow to respond to worker demands for control over their places of work and for a leadership that reflects the membership, as is the case with women and immigrant health care workers who joined SEIU in California (Del Olmo 1995). In New York City and elsewhere, where unions try to retain old industrial jurisdictions, workers organizing in new industries may find it almost impossible to create their own organizations, or to affiliate with national unions that allow autonomous control.

National Labor Organizing

Native-born and immigrant workers are always organizing in some way to improve conditions on the job. The revitalization of the labor movement is not going to happen by happenstance or by waiting for a fusion of nebulous and sometimes contradictory social movements, as argued by Dan Clawson in *The Next Upsurge* (2003).[1] Indeed, social movements do not neatly cohere, so it is fantasy to think they can join together as one force (Clawson 2003). Everyday conflicts that develop from social relations and conditions at the workplace in the neoliberal era of globalization may not lead to traditional forms of unionized labor–management relations. The labor movement does not have to wait but can challenge capital right now if it consciously activates members and nurtures the organization of rank-and-file movements in all communities. If a broader movement is to be built, immigrant organizing must be buoyed by the unions' commitment of support and resources to labor conflicts at workplaces, while giving workers the autonomy to resolve conflicts over conditions. Rank-and-file militancy on the ground is the foundation for building a labor movement capable of championing the cause of workers on a national scale.

The problem is that national and local unions are not willing to commit the resources to organize workers employed in small businesses, which now employ two-thirds of the national labor force. Thus, while the new union position on immigrants is a welcome reversal of policy, no tangible strategy has been developed to organize the majority who work in the unregulated economy in nonstandard jobs. Many immigrants in this sector work for labor contractors and employers who truthfully cannot afford union contracts that include health benefits and pensions; they therefore use immigrant labor as a means to survive.

If a more politically powerful labor movement is to emerge in the United States, unions must facilitate mass rank-and-file organizing capable of changing the body of labor law in a way that gives workers—both native and immigrant—greater institutional power. Nearly a decade after John Sweeney and New Voice took over the AFL-CIO with a bold agenda for advancing the power of working men and women, only a handful of national unions have allocated the resources necessary to support effective organizing with some positive results. Before Sweeney's election as president in October 1995, the AFL-CIO fostered few organizing efforts. Indeed, as president of SEIU, Sweeney had set an important precedent for encouraging new organizing. On average, AFL-CIO unions have spent about 5 percent of their budgets on organizing, compared to the 30 percent spent by SEIU. As AFL-CIO president, Sweeney's goal was to increase organizing budgets fivefold, to approximate the level maintained by SEIU. The Bush administration backlash against labor unions and the unabated outflow of jobs to offshore destinations has hampered worker organizing efforts. In the service industry, where job loss has been the least, several unions have increased budgets for organizing new workers (AFL-CIO 2002).

Since labor has not allocated adequate resources and attention to organizing in the past decade, why should we expect them now to take up the banner of immigrant workers? A hopeful sign is the growing recognition that immigrants make up a growing share of workers in labor markets they seek to organize: custodial and home care workers, hotel employees and restaurant employees, and workers in other service industries. Perhaps a new social movement could emerge from a common struggle uniting organized labor, immigrant workers, and community activists.

Inter-union Conflict in New York

How can inter-union conflict over organizing boundaries be diminished to support the common goal of immigrant worker self organization? Union competition has always been a feature of the New York economy. In the economically restructured labor markets of today, some unions are reaching beyond their traditional jurisdictions to recruit new members. The transformation of the New York City economy has thus increased interunion competition as unions fight to survive. One result of this has been a blurring of jurisdictional lines. Who decides which union should organize workers in new labor markets (e.g., information services, advertising, communications) or restructured industries (e.g., the ubiquitous drugstore chains now also serving as all-purpose markets; gardeners and cleaners employed by nonprofit parks conservatories; street cleaners working for business improvement districts)? Some national unions are carving out expanding segments of the labor market where immigrants tend to work in large numbers both in New York City and throughout the country (e.g., industrial laundries, building maintenance, and institutional cafeterias). But, again it must be asked, how can unions be persuaded to organize immigrants employed in small, decentralized businesses with low profit margins such as smaller laundries, domestic cleaning agencies, and independent fast-food restaurants?

Because of their conservatism, many unions may not wish to respond at all to changes in the labor markets in which they operate; or if they do, their responses may be slow and lumbering. As the three case studies here demonstrate, rival unions often attempt to reclaim these altered labor markets as their own, asserting the right by fiat or calling attention to continuity they have with unions that traditionally have claimed jurisdiction. In certain labor markets—in particular, the service industries—the nebulous nature of representation aggravates inter-union rivalries.

Immigrant Worker Organizing: Success and Failure

The case studies of greengrocery, delivery, and black-car workers reveal commonalities and dissimilarities among immigrants across the service economy. Each labor market is a product of corporate restructuring whereby workers' power, workplace standards, and wages have dramatically been reduced.

The case studies reveal clearly that most national and local unions are unwilling to commit the resources necessary to organize the majority of immigrant workers employed in small businesses. Evidence of this unwillingness in the case studies is most apparent in the greengrocery industry. Even if viewed as a success because wages increased in the industry, the greengrocery organizing campaign must be regarded as a Pyrrhic victory. How might things have turned out differently? The death of Ernesto Jofre at a time when the Mexican worker insurgency was growing was a decisive turning point in the campaign. The union provided resources and protected the autonomous worker organizing from threats stemming from inter-union competition. However, UNITE's national leadership viewed the campaign as little more than good public relations and saw it as out of sync with the union's overall organizing strategy. For them, winning struggles on a shop-by-shop basis—especially in these very small shops—was too slow and expensive to justify the campaign.

Had Jofre lived, the union's long-term strategy of building a strong rank-and-file presence in the shops might have resulted in both greater immigrant participation and new members for the union. Until March 2001, the campaign helped solidify worker confidence in the power of the union and the community, a process that took three years. In the end, however, it was not a "public relations victory," as Mexican workers lost confidence in the ability or willingness of unions to deliver the resources needed to challenge employers.

Economic restructuring in New York's supermarket industry, we saw in Chapter 5, had eroded the power of previous waves of unionized workers, a situation that led the union, wittingly or not, to permit employers to deunionize segments of the industry. The entry of Francophone West African workers in the early 1990s augured a new era of workplace militancy, as isolated immigrant workers engaged in autonomous organizing without the support of a union. The militancy of workers on the job was shaped by workplace conditions that muted public expression of frustration over poor wages and oppressive conditions. Their lack of a voice prompted workers in the industry to unify against the labor contractors and supermarkets. At that point, the union returned and reluctantly recruited the workers into the union. Though conditions improved, the grassroots leadership was removed, stunting a budding immigrant workers' organization.

Of the three groups that initiated organizing drives, the black-car drivers are the only ones to emerge successfully with an autonomous union. Their success indicates that it is possible for unions to sustain and defend immigrant worker organizing. In this instance, both the union and workers benefited from the absence of a rival union staking claim to represent the drivers. Had a national union other than the Machinists sought to compete for members, it is likely that the voice of the workers would have been diminished as higher-ranking leaders decided how to divide the spoils. Had there been interunion competition, leaders might also have pushed workers into existing locals, since divided, the workers may not have had enough members to create a viable organization of their own. The success of the black-car driver campaign demonstrates that national unions must sort out organizing workers on the basis of industry and region and should at all cost avoid competition for members, which may also divide emergent workers' associations themselves, as had happened in the greengrocery industry.

Following the terrorist attacks of September 11, 2001, the black car organizing drive suffered a setback, as most economic activity in the industry came to an abrupt halt. Worse still, the USA PATRIOT Act program of surveillance, detention, and deportation singled out the South Asians, Arabs, and other Muslims who predominate in the industry. The number of violent bias crimes against drivers also increased dramatically. Even in these hard times, however, the union came to the defense of workers who were arrested, beaten, or lost their jobs for no other reason but their identity. Despite the workers' isolation from the larger society, the organizing drives continued.

The three case studies raise a fundamental question pertaining to rank-and-file organizing and worker power: Can small autonomous workers' organizations be built locally without expanding the struggle on a regional or national basis? Production and service industries in the neoliberal economy do not neatly fit into a pattern of uniform labor markets that can be organized nationally. Different localities have industries with immigrant working conditions far removed from those of New York City. To survive and grow, unions must recognize the importance of establishing the institutional power of immigrant and native-born workers ever more dispersed in small, decentralized workplaces.

While formal and informal immigrant organizations may flourish, they need unions to provide the institutional muscle required to take on employers and the state. National and local unions provide workers the resources and confidence to take on employers. Now, more than ever, workers and unions must act locally and think globally. Strong immigrant worker organizations are built through rank-and-file organizing nurtured and backed up by the power of unions. In each of the organizing drives studied here, transnational workers succeeded in improving wages and conditions but found it more difficult to build a lasting organization. These small victories reinforce confidence in the power of class solidarity, but these victories can translate into a more powerful labor movement only if the union movement recognizes their importance and commits to defend and extend them indefinitely.

The research suggests that immigrant workers must have autonomy and control over their organizations, which will otherwise come to be viewed by their members with distrust and cynicism and will eventually die. The organizational power of immigrant workers is achieved through solidarity that is found on the job—a lesson that unions must learn if they are to grow stronger. The lack of uniformity and the dispersal of work in the neoliberal postindustrial economy require unions to welcome diverse forms of worker organizations, forms that do not always fit into the conventional mold of organizing or necessarily end in employer recognition and a collective bargaining agreement.

The Risk and Reward of Immigrant Organizing

The mixed outcomes of the three immigrant organizing campaigns examined here provide important lessons for unions striving to organize low-wage workers in the burgeoning service sector. What can unions learn from the surprising camaraderie new immigrants share when they battle management?

First, the meaning and implications of winning or losing diverges widely for labor unions and immigrant workers. For most unions, winning an organizing campaign almost always requires securing employer recognition, a collective bargaining agreement, and new dues-paying members. More members in discrete labor markets both strengthen unions and increase workers' abilities to better their wages and working conditions. New immigrant workers without doubt have much to gain from a union and a contract that protects them from employer discrimination and provides higher wages and better conditions. For immigrant workers, though, success is less definitive and may not start or end with a union contract. Perhaps the most serious complaint among greengrocery, delivery, and car transportation workers is the lack of respect from employers and customers, demonstrated by racist stereotyping and sweatshop conditions. Unions must comprehend these meanings immigrants ascribe to organizing, though they are different from traditional approaches. Unions may shun industries where they must organize shop by shop, even when workers are already mobilized, simply because mounting standard campaigns through the NLRB is a monumentally difficult task that requires them to deal individually with a range of employers (Lerner 2003). But despite these difficulties, unions will need to respond to the needs of low-wage workers dispersed in small businesses and the underground economy (See Freeman and Rogers 2002).

For more than thirty years, the official position of the AFL-CIO and the majority of national unions was that immigrants erode living standards for native-born workers. In the meantime, labor has not responded to a restructuring of the U.S. economy that has increased employer demand for low-wage immigrant workers. Although unions outwardly express interest in immigrants, only a few have provided the resources or fashioned coherent strategies to organize them. The case studies of greengrocery, delivery, and black-car workers provide concrete evidence that immigrant workers organize themselves in the workplace even before unions come on the scene and that they are eager to improve wages and working conditions through organizing and collective action.

Such widespread risk-taking is not based solely on ethnic, religious, racial, and other forms of ascription or on a radical ideology brought from home, as was the case among German and Russian immigrants in the nineteenth century and Latino and Asian migration in the twentieth century and today (Akamine 1993; Dubofsky 1969; Guerin-Gonzales 1993; Schneider 1993). Immigrant worker militancy is also shaped by the camaraderie that emerges from the workplace, social isolation, and the absence of options.

Poor working conditions reinforce the solidarity that emerges among immigrants on the job. Transnational immigrants tend to work in the unregulated informal economy, but over the last generation wages and conditions have also declined for low-wage native-born workers. Immigrant workers are more militant than are native-born and are more amenable to joining unions, despite labors' past opposition to them. Organized labor has a new opportunity to build power by sustaining self-organization through providing resources and support and allowing immigrants to develop independent organizations that have a voice in their workplaces and in existing unions.

How can we understand why new immigrants, aside from low wages, are more likely to organize unions than native-born workers? Beyond poor conditions, immigrant workers benefit from close social networks growing out of identity-based employer hiring patterns and societal isolation and class struggle on the job. Come what may, formal and informal immigrant workers' organizations take shape on the basis of solidarity that emerges on the job. Manifestations of this solidarity range in intensity from less obvious work disruptions to strikes and protests. The stronger the workers' leverage, the more resolute the challenge.

Notes

Chapter 1

1. Under neoliberal global capitalism the state withdraws business activity regulations that had been instituted to protect the rights of working people. The ideology of neoliberalism holds private property sacrosanct and trusts the market over the state to solve social problems. The term has been used in the last fifteen years to define policies of government deregulation, declining restraints on trade, and policies harmful to the poor and working class throughout the world. The term is used to evoke the *liberalism* of the nineteenth century under mid-Victorian England, when government protection of workers was eliminated as markets were deregulated.

2. In the *Hoffman Plastics* case, the Supreme Court essentially ruled that U.S. immigration law trumps U.S. labor law. The decision allows employers to recruit and hire undocumented workers with minimal penalty. Technically, immigration law prohibits employers from hiring undocumented workers, a law that is unevenly enforced. But transnational workers have availed themselves of National Labor Relations Board protections against employer retaliation for trying to organize into a union. The *Hoffman* decision thus undercuts legal safeguards for union activity, a sacrosanct component of the National Labor Relations Act, and exemplifies the significant obstacles immigrants face not just in organizing unions, but also in complaining to their employers and government authorities about substandard wages and poor working conditions.

3. The workers are male and are referred to as deliverymen throughout.

Chapter 2

1. Guerin-Gonzalez and Strikwerda (1993) argue that "A vital and an often overlooked characteristic of labor migration is that in-migration of workers is actively encouraged and even initiated by employers in advanced industrial countries despite the presence of unemployed native-born workers who could be recruited for these jobs (16).

2. Hondagneu-Sotelo (2001) notes that women have assumed work in domestic services; adult male immigrants have largely replaced the native-born low-wage men in providing private transportation and making deliveries and adolescent boys in delivering newspapers and groceries, mowing lawns, and running errands.

3. One anonymous driver, interviewed after a gathering in defense of immigrant rights, spoke for many others at a meeting held in September 2003: "When we look for a job driving a car, we are asked two questions. The first is 'What country are you from?' This answers the second question, because usually people know your religion if they know where you are from. If people say they are from countries with large Muslim populations, they are then asked: 'Are you a Muslim?' Once they know that you are Muslim, they shake your hand and say 'Salaam Ale Ichim' (peace be unto you)."

4. In the case of Wal-Mart and a growing number of large retailers, the term "employee" is not even used. At Wal-Mart, employees are referred to as "associates." At Target, another big box store, employees are known as "team members." Thus, low-wage American workers do not see themselves as employees of businesses but in business for themselves, leading to a decline in class consciousness. The fact that workers in these establishments have limited job stability further erodes class solidarity.

5. Dubofsky (1969) makes clear that the abundance of low-wage labor did not deter immigrants from organizing to improve their conditions: "The metropolitan economy . . . attracted a large proportion of less skilled immigrant workers who satisfied the needs of small trades with minutely subdivided operations. Lacking scarce skills and trade unions, the great majority of the city's workers suffered the anxieties wrought by low wages and economic insecurity. Realizing that conditions were far from ideal, that they were in fact often intolerable, the unorganized refused to accept poor conditions and unsatisfactory remuneration as either inevitable or permanent (13)."

6. The notion of a "working class New York" put forward by Joshua Freeman (2000) is rooted in the mid-twentieth century, when working-class conflict and power erupted throughout the United States. The absence of union strength today is reflected in greater business hostility toward labor, the erosion of labor standards, weaker labor laws, and a decline in government enforcement of worker safeguards. Still, Freeman asserts that New York remains a "working class" city due to its long legacy of mass labor militancy that created an abundance of unions.

Chapter 3

1. In the 1990s, unions in industries with large immigrant workforces began a drive to rescind the I-9 sanctions. SEIU and UNITE have been at the forefront of this effort. Both unions issued resolutions and lobbied the AFL-CIO's Executive Council to change its position on immigrant workers. The SEIU's Justice for Janitors campaign in California organized large numbers of undocumented workers who faced dismissal and deportation under the IRCA.

2. John Wilhelm, president of HERE and himself a 1960s student freedom rider, was the primary proponent of the 2003 Immigrant Workers Freedom Ride among national union leaders (see JoAnn Wypijewski, *Counterpunch*, October 2003).

3. As noted in Chapter 1, immigrants also receive less protection under labor law than do native-born workers, obstacles magnified by *Hoffman Plastic Compounds v. NLRB*, the 2002 U.S. Supreme Court ruling that encourages employers to dismiss undocumented workers who try to organize a union under the National Labor Relations Act (NLRA), holding that all employees must present at the time they are hired documents establishing their identity and authorization to work. The Supreme Court's legal decision effectively undermines union efforts to organize under the NLRA and leaves undocumented workers with few groups to turn to for help.

4. In 2004, the public-sector union density rate in the United States was 35 percent while the private-sector density rate was under 9 percent and falling, due to the continued decline in the manufacturing sector.

Chapter 4

1. From 1991 through 1996, Local 169's membership in the garment sector declined among unionized shops in the formal economy, but grew in the non-union informal economy, in which new immigrant workers from China and Latin America labored under substandard conditions. The informal segment of the industry was dominated by sweatshops that paid workers much less than the minimum wage, depressing pay scales throughout the unionized sector as well (Bender and Greenwald 2003; Kwong 1997; Ness 1998, 2003). By 2002, about half of the 120,000 garment production workers in New York City were employed in sweatshops (interview, May Chen, UNITE Local 23–25, April 30, 2002). Union shops were compelled to compete with sweatshops that had emerged almost without warning in the previous decade as large retailers and contractors frequently shifted production from union shops to lower-cost nonunion subcontractors operating under even worse conditions. A 1997 Labor Department study found that more than 63 percent of New York garment firms (59 of the 94 investigated) paid workers below the federal minimum wage of $5.15 an hour, without overtime pay, in violation of the U.S. Fair Labor Standards Act (Haq 1998).

2. Although eager to try out the community–labor strategy on their home turf, Mexican organizers and Lower East Side community suppporters made the trek to Brighton Beach, an immigrant neighborhood in Brooklyn to lend a hand. Soon, Local 169 joined the effort, and in August, Mexican Gerardo Dominguez was hired as a full-time organizer. AMAT remained an autonomous

organization, although in time the campaign expanded to other areas of the city and Local 169 hired additional Mexican activists as labor organizers.

3. Two greengroceries that replaced Mexican workers with Koreans were located on Avenue B and 10th Street (where an exclusively Korean workforce was established) and on 9th Street and First Avenue (where a majority of Koreans were hired). A market on Avenue A between 6th and 7th Street also reduced the number of Mexican workers to avoid unionization.

4. UFCW Local 1500 is one of two major food worker unions in the New York metropolitan region, representing 20,000 supermarket workers from Long Island to Albany. RWDSU (Retail Wholesale and Department Store Union) Local 338 is the other food union representing retail food workers (see Chapter 5 for more on Local 338).

5. According to Guerrerro, the Code of Conduct is little more than a fig leaf that gives employers the imprimatur of legitimacy while they violate the law. In March 2003, the owner of Alpine Deli, a signatory to the Code of Conduct, summarily fired all its Mexican workers when they demanded that management negotiate a contract after a year of stalling. But Alpine Deli is more the exception than the rule. The Unpaid Wages Act is still in effect, so any employer violating the law can be forced to pay back-wage claims.

6. The efforts of ILA Local 1964 to diffuse the organizing campaign continued despite the efforts first of UNITE Local 169 and then of UFCW Local 1500, and despite legal setbacks before the AFL-CIO and the New York State Supreme Court. In May 2001, State Supreme Court Justice Sheila Abdus-Salaam ruled that boycott lines organized by Local 1964, KADA, and the Han Family were illegal, and ordered that they be stopped (*New York Times*, May 12, 2001). Yet by the end of 2003, while UFCW Local 1500 continued to pursue large greengroceries, among the three unions, Local 1964 still had the most agreements signed with owners (interview, Anonymous, January 7, 2004).

Chapter 5

1. For example, inter-ethnic rivalries and civil wars set off massive migration from Sierra Leone and the Ivory Coast to Ghana; Liberia to Nigeria; Rwanda and Burundi to the Democratic Republic of Congo, Uganda, and Tanzania; and Sudan to Uganda.

2. Interviews with four Francophone West African immigrants to New York City revealed a general impression among the population that the United States was more welcoming to newcomers than was France.

3. Between the 1960s and the 1990s, Africa's share of migration to the United States tripled from 1 percent to 3 percent of all legal immigrants living in the United States, with a majority arriving in New York City, Washington,

DC, Houston, Los Angeles, and other major population centers. The Horn of Africa and West Africa, regions in which the United States had been economically, militarily, and politically engaged during the last quarter of the twentieth century, are the two leading sources of sub-Saharan African immigration (Arthur 2000, 1–10).

4. The growth in the number of new African immigrants in New York City mirrors similar transnational migration patterns across the United States that began in the late 1980s, when the number of Africans increased at an annual rate of 6 percent (Djamba 1999).

5. In *Money Has No Smell*, Paul Stoller (2003) demonstrates that the significant increase in the number of West African immigrants and the expansion of the informal economy of African traders in New York City is an outcome of the effects of globalization on major urban communities in the United States.

6. For a comprehensive treatment of the development and expansion of brand loyalties, see Naomi Klein's *No Logo: Taking Aim at the Brand Bullies* (2000), which examines how global corporations have left the business of production and servicing to subcontractors in an effort to cut labor and overhead costs and streamline operations.

7. To avoid recognition by unions and government authorities, the two leading labor subcontractors in New York City do not maintain permanent business addresses. The companies' business cards list only a residential address or a post office box. Most workers suspected that businesses were operated out of labor contractors' residences.

8. Although many supermarkets began to contract out work as a cost-cutting measure in the mid-1980s, not every major chain in the city resorted to this procedure. For example, D'Agostino's, a leading New York supermarket chain, continued to maintain in-house delivery.

9. The Allied Trades Council (now affiliated with Local 338), the union for Duane Reade retail drug stores, has only represented supervisory personnel (see end of Chapter 4).

10. The death of the sixteen-year-old Mexican immigrant was reported in the *Daily News* and local Spanish-language papers. Interviews with workers by union organizers for UNITE Local 169 demonstrated that workers were unaware of union representation at West Side Market.

11. The Senegalese deliveryman's name is withheld for legal reasons related to the ongoing lawsuit to regain lost wages.

12. The three supermarkets were Gristede's Operating Corporation, Great Atlantic & Pacific Inc., which operates Food Emporium, and Shopwell, a supermarket chain based in Montvale, New Jersey; the drugstore chain was Duane Reade.

Chapter 6

1. According to an interview with Henry Zeiger in June 2002, the Lease Drivers' Benefit Fund "depended solely on forced contributions from drivers; the owners never chipped in a nickel." Although workers paid $3 per day in dues, few drivers received any health benefits from the depleted fund, and no drivers received pensions or vacations. Many workers were delighted when the union failed to reach an agreement with the fleet owners and the dues and benefit fund check-off was eliminated.

2. In 1991, New York City had an average of 4.3 taxicabs per one thousand persons. Other leading cities with large concentrations of taxicabs include Atlanta, New Orleans, Boston, and Dallas, which all had more than two taxicabs per one thousand persons. Cities with fewer than two taxicabs per one thousand persons include Los Angeles (0.4), Philadelphia (0.9), Houston, San Francisco, Baltimore, and Chicago (International Taxicab and Livery Association 1991). New York City's taxicabs are concentrated in the central business district of Manhattan, where there are an average of 8.2 taxicabs and other for-hire vehicles per one thousand persons during the daytime hours.

Chapter 7

1. Waldinger and Lichter (2003) argue that unskilled low-wage immigrant labor is in high demand to work in jobs that are "are the least attractive" and to fill "vacancies at the bottom of the totem pole" that are essential to the organization of the U.S. capitalist economy.

2. In the weeks after September 11, some franchise owners waved drivers' $75-a-month dues (McCarthy 2001).

3. Registration requirements began on January 16, 2003 with the calling in of citizens or nationals of Iran, Iraq, Libya, Sudan, and Syria. Later, the registration requirement expanded to include citizens and nationals of Afghanistan, Algeria, Bahrain, Eritrea, Lebanon, Morocco, North Korea, Oman, Qatar, Somalia, Tunisia, United Arab Emirates, and Yemen and, still later, citizens or nationals of Bangladesh, Egypt, Indonesia, Jordan, and Kuwait.

Chapter 8

1. Clawson argues that unions must do away with the boundaries created between work and community to build a stronger labor movement. This argument is couched in the language of new social movements that have not developed broad popular support or even recognition, such as student activism against sweatshops and even the fight for immigrant rights. Indeed, the predominant sentiment among most Americans tends to be based on nativist

attitudes, particularly in the post–September 11 era and the erosion of middle-wage jobs. Certainly, Clawson is correct in noting that the labor movement is likely to grow through a massive burst of energy inside and outside the labor movement, but it is likely to emerge through traditional struggles for broader social rights rather than the culturally based new social movements. Without repudiating the importance of cultural-based movements of the last thirty years, in *After Theory*, Terry Eagleton (2003) asserts that global movements that form on the basis of poverty and class are the wave of the future rather than idiosyncratic cultural currents that are now losing relevance to the broad masses.

References

Books, Chapters, Articles, Reports, and Press Releases

Abelman, Nancy, and John Lie. 1997. *Blue Dreams: Korean Americans and the Los Angeles Riots*. Cambridge: Harvard University Press.

AFL-CIO. 2001. Article XXI Decision. Letter, January 13.

AFL-CIO Executive Council Actions. 2000. "Immigration." New Orleans, LA, Press Release, February 16, 1–4.

Akamine, Ruth. 1993. "Class, Ethnicity, and the Transformation of Hawaii's Sugar Workers, 1920–1940." In *The Politics of Immigrant Workers: Labor Activism and Migration in the World Economy since 1830*, ed. Camile Guerin-Gonzales and Carl Strikwerda, 175–195. New York: Holmes & Meier.

Arthur, John A. 2000. *Invisible Sojourners: African Immigrant Diaspora in the U.S.* Westport, CT: Praeger Publishers.

Bacon, David. 2000a. "Immigrant Workers Ask Labor 'Which Side Are You On?'" *Working USA: The Journal of Labor and Society* 3 (5): 7–18.

———. 1998. "U.S. Immigration Law Tool for Bringing Back the Sweatshop," labornet, e-mail communication, October 11.

Bailey, Thomas, and Roger Waldinger. 1991. "The Changing Ethnic/Racial Division of Labor." In *Dual City: Restructuring New York*, ed. Mollenkopf, John and Manuel Castels. 73–78. New York: Russell Sage Foundation.

Basch, Linda, Nina Glick Schiller, and Cristina Szanton Blanc. 1993. *Nations Unbound: Transnational Projects, Postcolonial Predicaments and Deterritorialized Nation States*. Langhorne, PA: Gordon and Breach.

Bender, Daniel E., and Richard A. Greenwald. 2003. *Sweatshop USA: The American Sweatshop in Historical Perspective*. New York: Routledge.

Berkey-Gerard, Mark, Gail Robinson, and Alex Viado. 2001. "Immigrants Under Attack." *The Gotham Gazette*, October 1. http://www.gothamgazette.com/article/20011001/200/180

Bernhardt, Annette. 1999. *Performance Without the High: Firms and Technology in Low-End Services*. Madison, WI: Center on Wisconsin Strategy.

Bernhardt, Annette, and Kate Rubin. 2003. *Recession and 9/11: Economic Hardship and the Failure of the Safety Net for Unemployed Workers in New York City*. New York: Brennan Center for Justice.

Bernstein, James. 2003. "Duane Reade Dispute: Drugstore Chain, Workers Battle Over Union Affiliation, Contract," *Newsday, Queens Edition*, June 6, A58.

Briggs, Vernon M., Jr. 2001. *Immigration and American Unionism.* Ithaca: Cornell University Press.

Bronfenbrenner, Kate. 2000. "Uneasy Terrain: The Impact of Capital Mobility on Workers, Wages, and Union Organizing." Paper presented to U.S. Trade Deficit Review Commission, Washington, DC.

Bronfenbrenner, Kate, Sheldon Friedman, Richard W. Hurd, Rudolph A. Oswald, and Ronald L. Seeber. 1998. *Organizing to Win: New Research on Union Strategies.* Ithaca: Cornell University Press.

Buchanan, Patrick. 2001. *The Death of the West: How Mass Immigration, Depopulation and a Dying Faith Are Killing Our Culture and Country.* New York: St. Martin's Press.

Bureau of Labor Statistics. 2002. *Metropolitan Area at a Glance.* New York: U.S. Department of Labor, Northeast Regional Office.

Business Week. 1982. "Local Unions May Give A&P Its Best Bargains." May 3.

Camarota, Steven A., and Nora McArdle. 2003. *Where Immigrants Live: An Examination of State Residency of the Foreign Born by Country of Origin in 1990 and 2000.* Washington, DC: Center for Immigration Studies, September.

Cason, Jim, and David Brooks. 2001. "Indocumentados, las victimas invisibles del atentedo WTC," September 25. http://www.jornada.unam.mx/

Castles, Stephen. 2002. "The International Politics of Forced Migration." In *Fighting Identities: Race, Religion and Ethno-Nationalism,* ed. Leo Panitch and Colin Leys. 172–192. London: Merlin Press.

Castles, Stephen, and Godula Kosack. 1973. *Immigrant Workers and Class Structure in Western Europe.* London: Oxford University Press.

Castles, Stephen, and Mark J. Miller. 2003. *The Age of Migration: International Population Movements in the Modern World.* New York: Guilford Publications.

Cheng, Mae M. 2003. "Lining Up, Signing Up: Immigrants Pour in to Meet Feds' Deadline for Reporting." *New York Newsday,* January 11. http://www.newsday.com/mynews/ny-nyins113083153jan11,0,4386315,print.story

Ching Louie, Miriam. 2001. "September 11's 'Invisible' Victims: Migrant Workers." *The Nation,* December 3, p. 7.

Chishti, Muzaffar. 2000. "Employer Sanctions Against Immigrant Workers." 71–76. *Working USA: Journal of Labor and Society* 3 (6).

Ciurea, Michelle. 2002. *Slicing the Apple: Need Amidst Affluence in New York City, 2002.* New York: United Way of New York City.

Clawson, Dan. 2003. *The Next Upsurge: Labor and the New Social Movements.* Ithaca: Cornell University Press.

Cole, David. "Taking Liberties: Ashcroft: 0 for 5,000." *The Nation.* September 16, 2004. http://www.thenation.com/doc.mhtml?i=20041004&s=cole.

Cordero-Guzmán, Héctor, Robert C. Smith, and Ramón Grosfoguel, eds.

2001. *Migration, Transnationalization, and Race in a Changing New York.* Philadelphia: Temple University Press.

Del Olmo, Frank. 1995. "Perspective on Labor: Empowerment Has its Problems: The Sudden Prominence of the Service Workers' Union Belies the Trouble the Old Guard Has With its Base of Minorities and Women." *Los Angeles Times,* October 29, M-5.

Delgado, Hector. 1993. *New Immigrants, Old Unions: Organizing Undocumented Workers in Los Angeles.* Philadelphia: Temple University Press.

Department of City Planning, City of New York. 1992. *The Newest New Yorkers: An Analysis of Immigration into New York City during the 1980s.* New York: New York Department of Planning.

———. 1999. *The Newest New Yorkers: 1995–1996: An Update of Immigration to New York City in the Mid-1990s.* New York: New York City Government.

Dewan, Shaila K. 2001. "Spitzer Sues Owners of Three Delis As a Labor Battle Escalates." *New York Times,* May 3.

Djamba, Yanki K. 1999. "African Immigrants in the U.S.: A Socio-Demographic Profile in Comparison to Native Blacks." *Journal of Asian and African Studies* 34 (2): 210–216.

Duane Reade, Inc. and Allied Trades Council and Local 340-A, UNITE, AFL–CIO. 2003. Cases 2–CA–32871–1, 2–CA–33148–1, 2–CA–33177–1, 2–CA–33424–1, 2–CB–17982–1, 2–CB–18005–1, and 2–CB–18146–1, April 14. United States National Labor Relations Board. New York Branch Office. http://www.nlrb.gov/nlrb/shared_files/decisions/ALJ/JD(NY)-41-04.htm

Dubofsky, Melvyn. 1968. *When Workers Organize New: York City in the Progressive Era.* Amherst: University of Massachusetts Press.

Dubofsky, Melvyn. 1969. *We Shall Be All: A History of the Industrial Workers of the World.* Chicago Quadrangle Books.

Dworkin, Ronald. 2003. "Terror & the Attack on Civil Liberties." *New York Review of Books,* November 6. 50 (17) http://www.nybooks.com/contents/20031106.

Eagleton, Terry. 2003. *After Theory.* New York: Basic Books.

Ebaugh, Helen R.F., and Janet S. Chafetz, eds. 2000. *Religion and the New Immigrants: Continuities and Adaptations in Immigrant Congregations.* Lanham, MD: Rowman and Littlefield.

Elite Limousine Plus. 2000. Letter, "To All Our Valued Customers Re: Rate Increase Effective April 5, 2000."

Ellwood, Mark E. *Cornering the Corner Market: Grace Dancyger Introduced Branding to the Korean Deli—and Ended Up with an East Village Empire.* New York Metro, October 4, 2004, http://newyorkmetro.com/nymetro/food/features/9949/,

Feránandez-Kelly, M.P., and Saskia Sassen. 1991. *A Collaborative Study of Hispanic Women in Garment and Electronics Industries.* New York: Monograph.

Fink, Leon. 2003. *The Maya of Morganton: Work and Community in the Nuevo South*. Chapel Hill: University of North Carolina Press.

Fiscal Policy Institute analysis of Current Population Survey Outgoing Rotation Group files provided by Economic Policy Institute; U.S. Census 2000.

Foner, Nancy. 2001. *From Ellis Island to JFK: New York's Two Great Waves of Immigration*. New Haven: Yale University Press.

Foner, Nancy, Rubén G. Rumbaut, and Steven J. Gold, eds. 2000. *Immigrant Research for a New Century. Multidisciplinary Perspectives*. New York: Russell Sage Foundation.

Freeman, Joshua. 2000. *Working Class New York: Life and Labor since World War II*. New York: The New Press.

Freeman, Richard B., and Joel Rogers. 2002. "A Proposal to American Labor." *The Nation*, June 24, 18–24.

Giuliani, Rudolph W. archives. 1997. "Announcement of Immigration Coalition." March. http://www.nyc.gov/html/rwg/html/97a/immcoal.html

Gordon, April. 1998. "The New Diaspora: African Immigration to the U.S." *Journal of Third World Studies* 15 (1): 79–103.

Gordon, Jennifer. 1999. *"The Campaign for the Unpaid Wages Prohibition Act: Latino Immigrants Change New York Wage Law*. Working Paper 4, International Migration Policy Program, Carnegie Endowment for International Peace.

Grava, Sigurd, Elliott Sclar, and Charles Downs. 1987. *The Potentials and Pitfalls of Private Sector Transportation Services: Activities in the New York Region*. New York: Division of Urban Planning, Columbia University.

Great Atlantic & Pacific Tea Company, Inc. 1984. Washington, DC: Securities and Exchange Commission Form 10-K. Original A 31-895. May 25.

Greenhouse, Steven. 2000. "Labor, in Switch, Urges Amnesty for All Illegal Immigrants." *New York Times* (national edition), February 17, A23.

Greenhouse, Steven. 2002. "Korean Grocers Agree to Double Pay and Improve Workplace Conditions." *New York Times*, September 18, B-1, B-6.

Greenhouse, Steven. 2003. "Immigrants Rally in City, Seeking Rights. *New York Times*, October 5.

Greer, Richard. 2000. "AFL-CIO Calls for New Direction in U.S. Immigration Policy to Protect Workers, Hold Employers Accountable for Exploitative Working Conditions: The Current System of Immigration Enforcement is Broken," news release, New Orleans: AFL-CIO, February 16.

Guerin-Gonzales, Camille. 1993. "The International Migration of Workers and Segmented Labor: Mexican Immigrant Workers in California Industrial Agriculture, 1900–1940." In *The Politics of Immigrant Workers: Labor Activism in the World Economy since 1830*, ed. Camille Guerin-Gonzales and Carl Strikwerda. 155–174. New York: Holmes & Meier.

Guerin-Gonzalez, Camille, and Carl Strikwerda. 1993. *The Politics of Immigrant Workers: Labor Activism and Migration in the World Economy since 1830*. New York: Holmes & Meier.

Guest, Kenneth J. 2003. *God in Chinatown*. New York: New York University Press.

Haq, Farhan. 1998. "Labour–US: Garment Union Under Attack from All Sides." *Institute for Policy Studies*, Occasional Paper. June 2.

Harris, Nigel. 1995. *The New Untouchables: Immigration and the New World Worker*. London: I.B. Tauris Publishers.

Haus, Leah. 2002. *Unions, Immigration, and Internationalization: New Challenges and Changing Coalitions in the United States*. London: Palgrave Macmillan.

Hetter, Katia. 2001. "Union Keeps Up Fight for Grocery Presence: Files Petition for Vote at Fourth Location." *Newsday*, August 20.

Hirsch, Barry, and David, Macpherson. 2004. "Union Membership and Coverage Database from the Current Population Survey." Unionstats.com.

———. 2003. "Union Membership and Coverage Database from the Current Population Survey: Note." *Industrial and Labor Relations Review*, 56 (2): 349–354.

Hirschman, Albert O. 1990. *Exit, Voice, and Loyalty: Responses to Decline in Firms, Organizations, and States*. Cambridge: Harvard University Press.

Hondagneu-Sotelo, Pierrette. 2001. *Doméstica: Immigrant Workers Cleaning and Caring in the Shadows of Affluence*. Berkeley: University of California Press.

Hughes, Katherine L. 1999. *Supermarket Employment: Good Jobs at Good Wages?* Working Paper 11, Institute on Education and the Economy, Teachers College, Columbia University, New York.

Immigration and Naturalization Service. 1998. *1998 Statistical Yearbook of the Immigration and Naturalization Service*. Washington, DC: U.S. Department of Justice, INS.

International Association of Machinists. 2000. "Legal Department Officer's Report." Washington, DC: IAM. November 7.

International Taxicab and Livery Association. 1991. *Taxicab Fact Book*. Kensington, MD.

Jacobs, Andrew. 1999. "Walkers Make a Tentative Stand; African Deliverymen Complain, Gently, of a Tough Job." *New York Times*, November 10.

Jayaraman, Saru, 2003. "In the Wake of September 11: New York Restaurant Workers Explore New Strategies," *Labor Notes*, August, p. 6.

Jones, Gawin W., ed. 1997. *The Continuing Demographic Transition*. New York: Oxford University Press.

Katznelson, Ira. 1991. *City Trenches: Urban Politics and the Patterning of Class in the United States*. Chicago: University of Chicago Press.

Kershaw, Sarah. 2001. "Union Drive Collides with Korean Grocers." *New York Times*, February 15.

Kieffer, David, and Immanuel Ness. 1999. "Organizing Immigrant Workers in New York City: The LIUNA Asbestos Removal Workers Campaign." *Labor Studies Journal* 24 (1): 12–26.

Kim, C laire Jean. 2000. *Bitter Fruit: The Politics of Black–Korean Conflict in New York City*. New Haven: Yale University Press.

Kim, Dae Young. 1999. "Beyond Co-ethnic Solidarity: Mexican and Ecuadoréan Employment in Korean-owned Businesses in New York City." *Ethnic and Racial Studies*, 22 (3): 581–605.

Kim, Ilsoo. 1981. *New Urban Immigrants; The Korean Community in New York*. Princeton: Princeton University Press.

Korea Central Daily. "Fight against the Union Continues," January 20, 2000. [New York newspaper in Korean language]

Kwong, Peter. 1997. *Forbidden Workers: Illegal Chinese Immigrants and American Labor*. New York: The New Press.

Laub, Emanuel. 1985. "The Way I See It." *Local 338 News: Labor Voice of the Food Industry*, March–April: 2.

Lerner, Steven. 2003. "Immodest Proposal: A New Architecture for the House of Labor." *New Labor Forum*, vol. 12, no. 2, Summer 2003. 9–30.

Lessinger, Joanna. 1995. From the Ganges to the Hudson: Indian Immigrants in New York City. Boston: Allyn and Bacon.

Levitan, Mark. 2000. *Building a Ladder to Jobs and Higher Wages: A Report by the Working Group on New York City's Low-Wages Labor Market*. New York: Community Services Society.

Levy, Frank, and Richard J. Murnane. 2004. *The New Division of Labor: How Computers Are Creating the Next Job Market*. Princeton: Princeton University Press.

Lynd, Staughton and Alice Lynd. 2000. The New Rank and File. Ithaca, NY: Cornell University Press.

Marcelli, E., M. Pastor, and P. Joassart. 1999. "Estimating the Effects of Informal Economic Activity: Evidence from Los Angeles." *Journal of Economic Issues* 33 (3): 579–607.

Massey, Douglas, Rafael Alarcón, Jorge Durand, and Humberto Gonzalez. 1990. *Return to Aztlan: The Social Process of International Migration from Western Mexico*. Berkeley: University of California Press.

Massey, Douglas S., Jorge Durand, and Noland J. Malone. 2003. *Beyond Smoke and Mirrors: Mexican Immigration in an Era of Economic Integration*. New York: Russell Sage Foundation.

Mayor John Lindsay's Taxi Study Panel. 1966. *Regulation of the Taxi Industry*.

McCarthy, Nora. 2001. "Driven Out." citylimits.org. November. www.citylimits.org/content/ articles/articleView.cfm?articlenumber=270

Merriam-Webster's Eleventh New Collegiate Dictionary. 2003. Springfield, MA: Merriam-Webster.

Milkman, Ruth, ed. 2000. *Organizing Immigrants: The Challenge for Unions in Contemporary California.* Ithaca: Cornell University Press.

Milkman, Ruth, and Kent Wong. 2000. *Voices from the Front Lines: Organizing Immigrant Workers in Los Angeles.* Los Angeles: Center for Labor Research and Education, UCLA.

Min, Pyong Gap. 1996. *Caught in the Middle: Korean Merchants in America's Multiethnic Cities.* Berkeley: University of California Press.

Minnite, Lorraine. 2004. "Legally Admitted Immigrants: Top 20 Source Countries to New York City Primary Metropolitan Statistical Areas, Fiscal Years 1992–2002." Tabulation. New York.

Morris, A. 1985. "Taxi School: A First Step in Professionalizing Taxi Driving." *Transportation Research Record* 1103:40–48.

National Employment Law Project. 2000. Lawsuit, *Ansoumana et al. v. Gristedes et al.*: Grocery Worker Complaint." November.

———. 2002. *From Orchards to the Internet: Confronting Contingent Worker Abuse.* New York: NELP. March.

———. 2003. "Delivery Workers Win Ruling against Duane Reade," news release, February 4.

National Immigrant Law Center. 2003 "Ansoumana et al. v. Gristedes Operating Corp. et al.: Immigrant Delivery Workers Found to be Employees Covered by Federal Minimum Wage Law." *Immigrants' Rights Update* 17 (2). http://www.nilc.org/immsemplymnt/emprights/emprights061.htm

Ness, Immanuel. 1998. "Organizing Immigrant Communities: UNITE's Workers Center Strategy." In *Organizing to Win: New Research on Union Strategies,* ed. Kate Bronfenbrenner, Sheldon Friedman, Richard W. Hurd, Rudolph A. Oswald, and Ronald L. Seeber. 87–101. Ithaca: Cornell University Press.

———. 2003. "Globalization and Worker Organization in New York City's Garment Industry." In *Sweatshop USA:. The American Sweatshop in Historical and Global Perspective,* ed. Daniel E. Bender and Richard A. Greenwald. 169–184. New York: Routledge.

New York City Taxi and Limousine Commission. 2000a. "TLC Rules Amended to Require Compliance with State Workers' Compensation Laws." Industry Notice #00-16. April.

———. 2000b. "Modification of TLC Industry Notice #00-16 Regarding Workers' Compensation Coverage." Industry Notice #00-22. July.

New York Immigration Coalition. 2003. news release, "Protesters Tell Feds to REGISTER THIS! Community and Religious Leaders Condemn Arab and Muslim Registration Program as Discriminatory, Ineffective, and a Cause of Increasing Immigration Backlogs for All." November 17.

New York Times. 2000. "Mamadou Camara: Public Lives—Standing Up for Deliverymen's Liberation." January 20, B-2.

New York Times. 2001. "Injunction Granted Over Picketing at Deli." May 12.

Office of New York State Attorney General Eliot Spitzer. 2003. "Laundry to Reinstate Workers Illegally Fired for Cooperating With Investigation of Labor Exploitation," news release, July 21.

Outten & Golden LLP. 2001. "Wage and Hour Immigrant Delivery Workers in New York Can Proceed with Class Minimum Wage Suit." *Daily Labor Reporter*, June 1.

Piore, Michael. 1979. *Birds of Passage*. New York: Cambridge University Press.

Polakow-Suransky, Sasha. 2001. "The Invisible Victims." *The American Prospect* 12 (21): 11–12.

Portes, Alejandro, ed. 1995. *The Economic Sociology of Immigration*. New York: Russell Sage Foundation.

Portes, Alejandro, and Manuel Castels. 1991 "World Underneath: The Origins, Dynamics, and Effects of the Informal Economy." In *The Informal Economy: Studies in Advanced and Less Developed Countries*, ed. Alejandro Portes, Manuel Castels, and Lauren Benton. 11–37. Baltimore: Johns Hopkins University Press.

Prashad, Vijay. 1998. "Taxi Workers Strike Back." *Frontline: India's National Magazine* 15 (12). http://www.frontlineonnet.com/fl1512/15120550.htm.

Putnam, Robert D. 2000. *Bowling Alone: The Collapse and Revival of American*. New York: Simon & Schuster.

Reimers, David M. 1994. *Still the Golden Door: The Third World Comes to America*. New York: Columbia University Press.

Rivera-Batiz, Francisco. 2003. *The State of Newyorktitlan: A Socioeconomic Profile of Mexican New Yorkers*. New York: Teachers College, October.

Robbins, Tom. 2001. "The Sweetheart Union: As Sugar Strike Fails, Longshoremen's Union Butts into Greengrocer Campaign." *Village Voice*, March 21–27.

Rogoff, Edward G. 1980. "Regulation of the New York City Taxicab Industry." *City Almanac*, August.

Ruffini, Gene. 2002. *Harry Van Arsdale: Labor's Champion*. Armonk: New York: M.E. Sharpe Publisher.

Sassen, Saskia. 1991. *The Global City: New York, London, Tokyo*. Princeton: Princeton University Press.

———. 1999. *Globalization and Its Discontents: Essays on the New Mobility of People and Money*. New York: New Press.

Savas, E. S. Sigurd Grava, and Roy Sparrow. 1991. *The Private Sector in Public Transportation in New York City: A Policy Perspective*. New York: Institute for Transportation Systems, City University of New York.

Schaller, Bruce. 1993. *The New York City For-Hire Vehicle Fact Book*. New York: New York City Taxi and Limousine Commission.

————. 2001. *Taxi and Livery Fact Book*. New York: Schaller Consulting.

Schlosser, Eric. 2003. *Reefer Madness: Sex, Drugs, and Cheap Labor in the American Black Market*. Boston: Houghton Mifflin Company.

Schneider, Dorothee, 1993. "The German Bakers of New York City: Between Ethnic Particularism and Working Class Consciousness." In *The Politics of Immigrant Workers: Labor Activism in the World Economy since 1830*, ed. Camille Guerin-Gonzales and Carl Strikwerda. 49–69. New York: Holmes & Meier.

Schumpeter, Joseph Alois A. 1942. *Capitalism, Socialism, and Democracy*. New York: Harper & Brothers.

Smith, Michael Peter. 2001. *Transnational Urbanism: Locating Globalization*. Malden, MA: Blackwell.

Smith, Richard B. 1982. *Recommendations*. Mayor's Committee on Taxi Regulatory Issues, March 29.

Smith, Robert C. 1996. "Mexicans in New York: Membership and Incorporation in a New Immigrant Community." In *Latinos in New York: Communities in Transition*, ed. Gabriel Haslip-Viera and Sherrie L. Baver. 57–103. Notre Dame, IN: University of Notre Dame Press.

Spitzer, Eliot. 2001. "Spitzer and Consulate General Announce Settlement of Labor Abuse Cases Against Greengroceries: Agreement Reached to Redress Exploited Immigrant Workers." News from Attorney General Eliot Spitzer, November 20.

————. 2002. "Landmark Code of Conduct to Improve Working Conditions in the Greengrocery Industry," news release, September 17.

Stafford, Walter. 1985. *Closed Labor Markets: Underrepresentation of Blacks, Hispanics and Women in New York City's Core Industries and Jobs*. New York: Community Service Society.

Stalker, Peter. 2001. *The No-Nonsense Guide to International Migration*. New York: Verso.

Stalnaker, Tim. 1993. *Employer's Guide to Using Independent Contractors*. Rockville, MD: Bureau of National Affairs.

Stoller, Paul. 2003. *Money Has No Smell: The Africanization of New York City*. Chicago: University of Chicago Press.

Stoller, Paul. 2001. "West Africans: Trading Places in New York." In Foner, Nancy, ed. *New Immigrants in New York*. New York: Columbia University Press.

Strozier, Matthew. 1999. "Organizing Drive." *City Limits*, June. http://www.citylimits.org/content/articles/articleView.cfm?articlenumber=77

Strunsky, Richard. 1983a. "Supermarkets' Bottom Lines Way Up for '83." *Local 338 News: Labor Voice of the Food Industry* (March–April): 1, 3.

————. 1983b. "See Compromise between Productivity and Technology for Future of Food Industry." *Local 338 News: Labor Voice of the Food Industry* (March–April): 1.

————. 1983c. "Union Negotiates Best-Ever Contract." *Local 338 News: Labor Voice of the Food Industry* (March–April): 1.

Swarns, Rachel L. 2003. "Special Registration for Arab Immigrants Will Reportedly Stop." *New York Times*, November 22, A16.

Swobada, Frank. 2000. "Unions Reverse on Illegal Aliens." *Washington Post*, February 17, A1.

Tannock, Stuart. 2001. *Youth at Work: The Unionized Fast-Food and Grocery Workplace*. Philadelphia: Temple University Press.

Thompson, Ginger, 2003. "A Surge in Money Sent Home by Mexicans." *New York Times*, October 28, A-14.

Tichenor, Daniel J. 2002. *Dividing Lines: The Politics of Immigration Control in America*. Princeton: Princeton University Press.

Tomlins, Christopher L. 1979. "AFL Unions in the 1930s: Their Performance in Historical Perspective." *The Journal of American History* 65 (4): 1021–1042.

Uchitelle, Louis. 2000. "INS is Looking the Other Way as Illegal Immigrants Fill Jobs: Enforcement Changes in Face of Labor Shortage." *New York Times*, March 9.

United Nations. 1995. *The World's Women: 1995 Trends and Statistics*. New York: United Nations.

————. 1996. Department of Economic and Social Information and Policy Analysis, Population Division. *Levels and Trends of Contraceptive Use as Assessed in 1994*. New York: United Nations.

United States Department of Justice. 1998. *Statistical Yearbook of the Immigration and Naturalization Service*. Publication M-367.

United States Supreme Court. 2002. *Hoffman Plastic Compounds, Inc. v. NLRB*. No. 00-1595 (S. Ct.). The National Labor Relations Board, March 27.

Vargas, Theresa. 2001. "Pedaling Uphill to Survive: Mexican Youths Eke Out a Living with Deliveries on Bikes." http://www.jrn.columbia.edu/studentwork/children/downlow/biker.shtml

Vidich, Charles. 1976. *The New York Cab Driver and His Fare*. Cambridge, MA: Schenkman Publishers.

Voice@Work. 2003. "Employee Free Choice Act: Restoring Workers' Freedom to Form Unions." AFL-CIO, November 13. www.aflcio/aboutunions/voiceatwork/ns11132003.cfm

Wadler, Joyce. 1999. "An Unlikely Organizer as Cabdrivers Unite." *The New York Times*, December 8.

Waldinger, Roger. 1996. *Still the Promised City? African-Americans and New Immigrants in Postindustrial New York*. Cambridge: Harvard University Press.

————. ed. 2001. *Strangers at the Gates: New Immigrants in Urban America.* Berkeley: University of California Press.

Waldinger, Roger, and Michael Ira Lichter. 2003. *How the Other Half Works: Immigration and the Social Organization of Labor.* Berkeley: University of California Press.

Walsh, John P. 1993. *Supermarkets Transformed: Understanding Organizational and Technological Innovations.* New Brunswick, NJ: Rutgers University Press.

Watts, Julie R. 2002. *Immigration Policy and the Challenge of Globalization: Unions and Employers in Unlikely Alliance.* Ithaca: Cornell University Press.

Wyatt, Edward, and Joseph P. Fried. 2003. "Two Years Later: The Money; Downtown Grants Found to Favor Investment Field." *New York Times,* September 8, A-1.

Wypiejewski, Joanne. 2003. "The New Unity Partnership: A Manifest Destiny for Labor." *Counterpunch,* October 6. www.counterpunch.org/jw10062003.html.

Zeiger, Henry. 1998. "Hailing Cab Drivers: Labor's Lost Opportunity." *Association for Union Democracy* Newsletter. 120 (September).

Web Sites

www.afl-cio.org (for details on AFL-CIO policy positions on immigration and organizing)

www.behindthelabel.org (multimedia news Web site initiated by UNITE HERE; information on labor rights in the global clothing industry)

http://dwaynegreed.com (sponsored by the Allied Trades Council/Local 338; information on the labor conflict between organizers and Duane Reade drugstores)

www.unionstats.com (for private and public sector union membership)

Interviews

Workers

A total of seventy-nine interviews were conducted among workers in each of the industries. Most of the interviews were held anonymously to protect the identity of the workers. Some interviews were tape recorded and others were recorded by hand. Some more prominent workers and organizers are named in each of the three case studies and listed below. The interviews are broken down as follows:

- Forty-eight workers in the greengrocery industry from April 1998 to March 2001

- 10 Korean owners of greengroceries, March 1998 to June 2003.
- Seventeen supermarket and drugstore deliverymen from March 1999 to October 2003
- Twenty four black-car drivers from July 2001, August, 2001, October 2001, November 2003

Other Interviews

Anonymous Interviews with individuals, workers, union officials, and staff, November 1997–June 2004.

Beltran del Rio, Salvador. Mexican Consul General. New York. April 4, 2001

Bah, Mamadou, Malian deliveryman at supermarket, who became one of the strike leaders, June 15, 2000.

Camara, Mamadou. Founder and lead organizer, African American Workers Association, and food dispatcher, Food Emporium, Broadway and 68th Street, New York. 1999, 2000, 2001.

Chen, May. Manager, UNITE Local 23–25. April 30, 2002.

Cho, John (pseudonym). Korean greengrocery business owner. October 2001.

Chun, Hong K. President, Korean Produce Association. August 20, 1998.

Desai, Bhairavi. Co-founder and Director of Taxi Workers Alliance-New York (TWA-NY), September 23, 2003

Diakite, Siaka, New York City supermarket deliveryman and labor organizer, April 1, 2000.

Dominguez, Geraldo. President, AMAT (Mexican American Workers Association), former organizer with UNITE Local 169. 1998, 2000, 2001, and 2002.

Donovan, Michael. Research Director, UNITE Local 169. August 12, 1999; August 22, 2001.

Eichler, Jeffrey. Organizing Director, UNITE Local 169. August 1, 2001.

Gonzalez y Gonzalez, restaurant and bar on Broadway north of Houston Street, Manager, April 4, 2002

Gordon, Jennifer. Former director of Workplace Project. May 13, 2002.

Gerstein, Teri. Assistant New York State Attorney General. March 15, 2002.

Guerrrero, Manuel. Union organizer, UNITE Local 169. August 23, 2001.

Haro, Juan. Labor organizer, Restaurant Opportunity Center-New York (ROC-NY), March 11, 2003.

Jayaraman, Saru. Executive Director, Restaurant Opportunity Center-New York (ROC-NY), October 4, 2003.

Jofre, Ernesto. Manager, UNITE Local 169 and Northeast Regional Joint Board. November 10, 1997, August 5, 1998, October 3, 1999.

Lucas, Daniel. Greengrocery worker and organizing committee member at Adinah's Farms. December 31, 1999.

Lynch, Kevin. Organizing Director, International Association of Machinists District 15. August 21, 2001.

Macote [no first name given]. Greengrocery worker, November 12, 1998.

Ngouvi, Jaques Legrand, West African delivery worker (no country given), September 23, 2001.

Obiang, Justin, West African delivery worker, September 26, 2001.

Ott, Ed. Public Policy and Worker Education Director, New York City Central Labor Council, November 12, 2003.

Pezenik, Steve. Public Relations Director United Food and Commercial Workers—Retail Wholesale, Department Store Union Local 338. September 14, 2001.

Purcell, Pat. Organizing Director, United Food and Commercial Workers Local 1500. 2001 2002, 2003, 2004.

Resto, Nelson. Business Agent, United Food and Commercial Workers—Retail Wholesale, Department Store Workers Union Local 338. September 14, 2001.

Ruckelshaus, Catherine K. Litigation Director, National Employment Law Project, New York. October 2, 2001.

Terrazas, Noberto. Mexican Consulate Officer, New York. April 4, 2002.

Smith, M. Patricia. Head of Labor Bureau, Office of New York State Attorney General Eliot Spitzer, May 6, 2003.

ul-Asar, Syed Armughan. Manager, IAM Local Lodge 340. October 26, 2001; September 27, 2003; December 14, 2003.

Unger, Nick. Former Mobilization Director, New York Central Labor Council. August 1, 2001; August 14, 2002.

Van Arsdale, Thomas. Former President, New York City Central Labor Council. May 22, 2002.

Vargas, Edgar. Political Director, UNITE International Union. August 24, 2000.

Zeiger, Henry. Former rank-and-file organizer in the taxi industry. June 27, 2002.

Index

Note: Page numbers followed by letter *t* indicate tables.